Advance Praise for
Becoming a Chef
With Recipes and Reflections from America's Leading Chefs

"Approach *Becoming a Chef* as you would a fine meal: Come to it with hunger, curiosity and an open mind. You are certain to come away satisfied, enlightened, renewed."
Patricia Wells, Author, *Simply French* and *Bistro Cooking*

"Fascinating...An excellent overview of culinary history, together with some of the chefs, and their restaurants, who have helped guide America into culinary prominence during the last quarter of this century."
Chuck Williams, Founder, Williams-Sonoma, Inc.

"An extraordinary book—*Becoming a Chef* is far and away one of the most insightful and practical introductions to a profession that I have ever seen. Anybody who loves food will love the book; anybody who loves to cook will love the recipes; anybody who harbors the slightest desire to experience life as a chef does will use the book as a bible!"
Leonard Schlesinger, Professor, Harvard Business School; former Chief Operating Officer, Au Bon Pain, and Co-Author of *The Real Heroes of Business*

"*Becoming a Chef* is as requisite for anyone considering a career in the culinary arts as are *Larousse Gastronomique* and a good set of knives. And for anyone simply interested in restaurants and American gastronomy, this is a fascinating trove of information and fine, modern recipes."
John Mariani, Author, *The Dictionary of American Food & Drink*

"A unique perspective offering valuable insights into all aspects of the culinary arts..."
Ferdinand E. Metz, President, The Culinary Institute of America

"For anybody who has ever envisioned becoming a professional cook, this book is an absolute must-read and it's a fascinating one as well. In my opinion, it's the most important first step you can take..."
Peter Kump, President, The James Beard Foundation and President, Peter Kump's New York Cooking School

(Continued on next page)

"*Becoming a Chef* is as thoughtful, eclectic and enjoyable as Andrew
Dornenburg's cooking. Which is to say, very."
Robert B. Parker, Gourmet and Best-selling author of the Spenser series of thrillers

"While this book is most practical and inspirational for budding professional
chefs, it makes lively and insightful reading for all food and restaurant buffs."
Mimi Sheraton, Food Critic and Author, *The Whole World Loves Chicken Soup*

"An unusual combination of lovely photographs, engaging and personal text,
and wonderful recipes. A really fresh way to do a book on the subject."
Milton Glaser, Restaurant Designer

"Fine food is one of the great passions of my life. Memories filled my senses as
I read this delectable book. I am not a chef, nor will I ever become one. Yet
this book is just as grand an experience for me to read about some of my
favorites in New York, Boston, Chicago, Los Angeles and San Francisco. How
lucky I feel to learn more from them here. Consume this book—it's delicious."
Rikki J. Klieman, Anchor, Court T.V.

"Are chefs born or made? *Becoming a Chef* unveils formative experiences that
elevated food to a central place in the lives of well-known American chefs.
I was fascinated how seeds planted long ago ripen into a career, and how
the palate is trained into an instrument of discernment. Food memory
of meals eaten years ago is photographic in detail, complete with emotion,
ambience, sights, sounds, and textures—a tasting in the mind. The authors
show that the best chefs are alchemists, able to turn ordinary food into
gold that transforms the spirit."
Richard E. Cytowic, M.D. and Author, *The Man Who Tasted Shapes*

BECOMING a Chef

BECOMING a Chef

WITH RECIPES AND REFLECTIONS FROM AMERICA'S LEADING CHEFS

Andrew Dornenburg and Karen Page

Foreword by Madeleine Kamman

Photographs by Jamie Columbus

Endicott College
Beverly, Mass. 01915

VAN NOSTRAND REINHOLD

I⊤P™ A Division of International Thomson Publishing Inc.

New York • Albany • Bonn • Boston • Detroit • London • Madrid • Melbourne
Mexico City • Paris • San Francisco • Singapore • Tokyo • Toronto

Authors' Note

Although this book is the result of a complete collaboration between the two authors, it is written in the first person singular voice of Andrew Dornenburg, so as to spare the reader confusion of identities.
—A.D. & K.P.

Van Nostrand Reinhold Staff

Senior Editor: Melissa A. Rosati
Editorial Assistant: Amy Beth Shipper
Marketing Manager: Linda L. Wetmore
Marketing Assistant: Craig Wolynez

Production Director: Jacqueline A. Martin
Production Manager: Louise Kurtz
Art Director: Mike Suh
Designer: Paul Costello

IP™

A division of International Thomson Publishing, Inc.
The ITP logo is a trademark under license

Printed in the United States of America

For more information, contact:

Van Nostrand Reinhold
115 Fifth Avenue
New York, NY 10003

International Thomson Publishing GmbH
Königswinterer Strasse 418
53227 Bonn
Germany

International Thomson Publishing Europe
Berkshire House 168-173
High Holborn
London WCIV 7AA
England

International Thomson Publishing Asia
221 Henderson Road #05-10
Henderson Building
Singapore 0315

Thomas Nelson Australia
102 Dodds Street
South Melbourne, 3205
Victoria, Australia

International Thomson Publishing Japan
Hirakawacho Kyowa Building, 3F
2-2-1 Hirakawacho
Chiyoda-ku, 102 Tokyo
Japan

Nelson Canada
1120 Birchmount Road
Scarborough, Ontario
Canada M1K 5G4

International Thomson Editores
Campos Eliseos 385, Piso 7
Col. Polanco
11560 Mexico D.F. Mexico

5 6 7 8 9 10 QEB-FF 01 00 99 98 97 96

Library of Congress Cataloging-in-Publication Data

Dornenburg, Andrew.
Becoming a chef: with recipes and reflections from America's leading chefs / by Andrew Dornenburg and Karen Page : foreword by Madeleine Kamman.
p.   cm.
Includes index.
ISBN 0-442-01513-5
1. Food service—Vocational guidance—United States.   2. Cookery—Vocational guidance—United States.   3. Cooks—Training of —United States.   I. Page, Karen.   II. Title.
TX911.3.V62D67   1995   94-47316
647.95'023'73—dc20   CIP

*To all those who make their living working with food
who do so with a spirit of professionalism, pride, and passion
K.P.*

*and especially
To Chris Schlesinger, who has been both a role model and a mentor to me
and whose spirit of cooking continues to inspire me,
and to Cary Wheaton, who originally hired me into the East Coast Grill;*

*To Lydia Shire and Susan Regis, who managed to convince me
that putting my arm in a 600-degree tandoori oven was a good idea,
for their liveliness and generosity;*

*To Anne Rosenzweig, who was a tireless teacher, whether at the restaurant
or at special events where I had the privilege of assisting her;*

*To Madeleine Kamman, for being the guiding light and inspiration that she is to me
and to countless other American cooks and chefs; and*

*To Bobby Delbove, Paul O'Connell, Paula Danilowicz, Rebecca Charles,
and Tony Bonner—my sous chefs over the years—
who were responsible for a lot of my on-the-job learning
and are surely the leading chefs of tomorrow*
A.D.

CONTENTS

List of Recipes

The authors requested of every chef interviewed for Becoming a Chef a recipe which held special meaning to his or her development as a chef. The recipes contributed range from old family recipes to original creations of which the chefs are most proud, and their special meanings typically underscore some aspect of the subject of the particular chapter. As much as possible, the recipes remain as the chefs intended them, with minimal (if any) editing of abbreviations, terminology, length, or other aspects of style. This provides further illustration of the personality and unique "point of view" of each individual chef.

ACKNOWLEDGMENTS

*W*e never could have written this book without the generous help of many people.

First and foremost, it is impossible to express our deep gratitude to the chefs we interviewed, who were overwhelmingly generous in sharing with us their time—which we know all too well is their most precious commodity—as well as their insights, their advice, their recipes and, quite often, their hospitality, their food and even their homes. The experience of getting to know them is one we will cherish all our lives.

Nor can we thank Madeleine Kamman enough: for making the time to review and critique (ouch!) our manuscript by staying up all night in order to do so, for making suggestions of ways to improve it, for contributing her beautiful Foreword and, most of all, for her friendship. (We love you, Madeleine!) Our sincere thanks, too, to Mark Miller and Jimmy Schmidt for reviewing our manuscript and offering specific comments and encouragement, and to Mark for praising it so loudly to the food press that it made our phone ring!

We'd like to thank those at Van Nostrand Reinhold who shared our passion for seeing this book come to life. *Becoming a Chef* was blessed with three godmothers, each of whom ably adopted this book as her own: from acquiring editor Pam Chirls to Caroline Schleifer to Melissa Rosati. Our thanks to the rest of the VNR team, especially Paul Costello, Louise Kurtz, Jackie Martin, Amy Shipper, Mike Suh, Veronica Welsh, Linda Wetmore, and Craig Wolynez. Thanks, too, to James Peterson and others who took time to read and critique various drafts of our manuscript.

Thanks to Kitchen Arts and Letters for existing, and to Nach Waxman for doing what he does so well—the bookstore was an invaluable resource for gathering information. Our thanks to Chris Hussey, Sumi Luth, and others who shared with us their experiences abroad as *stagiaires,* and to Rori Spinelli, for her comments as a former chef.

Special thanks are due to our very talented and dear friend, photographer Jamie Columbus, whose beautiful photographs adorn these pages; this book would not have been the same without her!

We join her in thanking Lexington Labs and the Union Square Greenmarket, as well as the following establishments in New York City for allowing her to photograph their kitchens and/or dining rooms: Café des Artistes, City Bakery, Daniel, Lola, March, Neuman & Bogdonoff Caterers, Nosmo King, Rosemarie's, The Sea Grill, Symphony Cafe (and especially pastry chef Richard Leach), and Vong.

Other friends were supportive in ways too numerous to detail, but we'd like to give special thanks to Cynthia Penney, an exceptional writer who was an invaluable sounding board, and Cynthia Gushue and Leo Russell, for their loan of a computer at a critical time. Andrew would like to thank chefs Ed Brown and Jamie Bergin for all he's learned from them. Karen would like to thank those people who played an important role in developing her own love for food, including her family, with whom she has enjoyed many wonderful food memories (from Yates apple cider to White Castle hamburgers!); the late Eleanor Van Alstyne, whose enormous backyard garden was a child's paradise; Larry, who introduced her to Chicago's food scene; and Tracy, with whom she first explored Manhattan's. She also thanks her National Endowment for the Humanities research subjects (especially Susan Davis) as well as her former career and admissions advisory clients over the years, from whose candid stories she developed an ear for the rhythm of chronicling others' careers and lives.

We'd like to thank all our friends and family members who offered their encouragement, who never tired of asking, "How's the book coming?" (even after we'd long tired of answering), and who stood by with patience and understanding while we traveled or secluded ourselves, weekend after weekend, in order to research and write it. It's done! We've missed you, and we can't wait to see you again.

And, finally, we'd like to thank each other, for persevering through the many challenging moments of this collaboration. Then again, our nearly 10-year relationship has survived other tough challenges: after eating our way through Québec City and Montréal, we both ran the Montréal International Marathon on the last day of our honeymoon. Here's to crossing yet another finish line together!

Andrew Dornenburg and Karen Page

FOREWORD

On June 9th of 1940, my mother and I took the last train leaving Paris for the Loire Valley before the Germans invaded our native city of Paris. It took us two full days to reach the small market town of Château La Vallière where we were to find refuge in the home of my great aunt Claire. Claire was the owner-chef of her small Michelin-starred hotel and restaurant.

Exhausted as a nine year old would be after 48 hours of travel to cover only 170 miles, I was not too aware of much as I entered the hotel, except that the house was extremely busy, that there were many people in the dining room, and that something smelled so good that my stomach positively started to convulse. Having been recognized as a possible casualty of my own hunger, I received a plate of sweetbreads in Madeira cream sauce; I nearly swooned over it, it was so good. . . . My double career as an inveterate eater and cook had started. We are now in 1995, it is still lasting and probably will last in one way or another until I finally bow out of this world.

In between the many vacations spent working in the kitchen and serving in the dining room of my aunt or washing thousands of plates in her scullery, I acquired the strenuous education given to all French children by the government of their Republic. I relished learning several modern languages and Latin. I delved in to French, English, and German literatures, geography, world history and geology with glee, tolerated mathematics, loved chemistry, biology, and botany. It was hard work, with many nights spent studying long, unreasonable hours, but it was well worth it, for much later, when I finally became a chef and restaurateur, I realized how much I was using all the culture acquired on the school benches.

I met Alan, my Philadelphia-born husband, in Paris while I was directing the reservation office of Swissair and he was conducting a tour of American engineers across Europe. We worked together for a very short time and liked each other so much that, four months later, we married. Marriage between two persons of different nationalities is always interesting and at the same time difficult, for each must get accustomed to very different traditions. After the birth of my first son I had such a strong bout of homesickness that I countered it by immediately looking for something to keep my brain occupied with a challenge. Since America speaks mostly English, there was no question for me to use my knowledge of foreign languages, so I started to cook for fun. Of course, cooking meant my native French cooking and the challenge consisted in making French food taste really French with the American ingredients of the early sixties. There was not a shallot in sight, not a leek. Fresh herbs were not to be found anywhere except in a few gardens well surrounded by high fences; herbs came only dried in small glass jars; the bread was English-style white bread, mushy and pasty to my teeth used to the crunch of French baguettes. Ah . . . what to do? Simply show people that nothing is impossible to the adventurous. Having received a catalogue of the adult education classes offered at the Greater Philadelphia Cheltenham High School, I reached for the telephone and asked the director of the school whether, per chance, she could use a French cooking teacher. I passed her test of proficiency, which consisted in cooking a serious, professional-style meal for her, and I started teaching classes in the basics of French cuisine at night, after enjoying raising my children during the day.

The classes were so popular that besides teaching at the Adult School, I started also giving classes in my own kitchen. My second son, born in between, complied with my timetable by sleeping just long enough for the lessons to be over and then have his little French lunch. He loved it too: Mommy's nice meat mashed with fresh potatoes and a dab of sauce mixed in pleased him much more than the cans of Gerber baby food.

When I started writing my first cookbook, I gave him three percolators of three different sizes all jumbled up, and one hour later, after I had peacefully written a few pages, he had reconstructed all three percolators and we celebrated with Oreos and milk. With time forging ahead, both boys went to full-time school and we moved to Boston, where it all happened.

Boston in 1969 was still a very colonial American city. But there was also wonderful, intellectual Cambridge on the other side of the Charles, with its universities and their wonderful collections of food chemistry books. I decided to start investigating food chemistry after several of my students repeatedly asked me why I chose to execute a dish with one technique rather than another. At first I answered as plainly as I could, thinking the answer out myself, but soon I realized that there was something more behind my explanations.

In 1971 I took the school out of my house to make it a legitimate business. With it came all the worries of legitimate businesses: advertising properly, coping with the ever-increasing number of students, insuring the business, paying taxes, training assistants and teachers, etc. . . . It was the training of the assistants which revealed the crux of the true problem: my school was a drop in the bucket of the enormous amount of education which was needed to bring the United States into a league able to compete with Europe and its wonderful technical schools for cooking and restaurant procedures. Boston at the time had no really modern professional program, so I decided to offer one. It took me three years to have it run as smoothly as I wished and I shall be forever grateful to Dr. Rachel K. Winer of the Massachusetts Board of Education for her guidance through this very important project.

A year after the opening of the professional program some rather interesting circumstances brought on the opening of our restaurant, which I called Chez La Mère Madeleine, but which everyone called Modern Gourmet, which was the name of the school. Two years after the opening of the restaurant, the Mobil guide gave us a four-star rating, and three years after the opening, Anthony Spinazzola, then restaurant reviewer for *The Boston Globe*, gave us a five-star rating. Using all the knowledge I had brought from France, long hours of studying and reading American technical texts, the latest French culinary publications, and cookery books from all over the world, I had become, with Alice Waters (of Chez Panisse) and Leslie Revsin (of Restaurant Leslie and later the Waldorf Astoria), one of the first three "visible" women chefs in the United States.

The dictionary defines the substantive chef as "a cook, especially the chief cook of a large kitchen staff." The word came from the Latin *caput*, meaning the *head* and by derivation, the chief of any social, military, or political body. In old French, the "chef" meant the physical head; the medieval French word for kitchen chef was "queux" which is related to the English *cook*; chef had slowly acquired its meaning of kitchen chef by the end of the 17th century.

Up until the last two decades, the title of chef applied only to the highly visible and widely recognized men whose names you will find in the historical review starting on page 4. But there were also other chefs, called "cuisinières," accomplished and often very distinguished women, whose great talents remained, up to the 1930s, hidden in large upper class, forever entertaining households. One purposefully never spoke of one's cuisinière for fear of losing her to a wealthier house. Claire had started her career as one of those cuisinières. Modern times, with the arrival of the automobile and the development of popular tourism, have changed all that, as the cuisinières slowly acquired small restaurants of their own. Even if the progress is not as fast as one would wish it, chefs now come in the masculine and the feminine, all working under the pressures of producing elegant fare for an ever more-demanding public. It has become so prestigious an occupation to be a chef—a welcome change that is due mostly to the large amount of public relations work done by French Chef Paul Bocuse in the 1960s and 70s—that by now the title tends to be given to untrained home cooks or backyard barbecuers who, although lovely cooks, have not undergone the grueling baptism by fire true chefs receive.

Andrew and Karen have written this interesting book on how to become one of those men or women whose profession it is or has been to prepare and serve large numbers of meals per day to larger numbers of people. Their book is interesting because it brings you into personal contact with many younger women and men who, in our days of stringent labor laws and often less-than-understanding investors, have worked to bring their restaurants to national notoriety, with often nothing more than tiny assets and an inspired and dedicated skeleton crew. Their words will reveal the passion and knowledge that is required to be a chef. More than one of the chefs you will read about will give you the impression that he or she "fell into the work"; indeed quite a few did, but any one of them will tell you that their profession is their passion in spite of the many dilemmas and choices it brings into their lifes.

This book is also about some of these choices. The first choice is usually made between schooling or apprenticeship. Each of them, as you will see, presents advantages and disadvantages. A school puts a seal of approval on a graduate, but so does a good master. After teaching two generations of American chefs, both in the classroom and at the stove, I remain a great advocate of the European system which combines schooling in the daytime and restaurant work at night, for it is a fitting and demanding preparation to practice a profession, which I believe to be the most demanding existing.

Whichever way you choose to become a chef, be sure that it spells enrichment for that sort of "holy trinity" which is the foundation of your future profession: Your mind, your heart, and your hands. Challenges will come to you daily at such speed that, more than once, you will feel like throwing your hands up in the air and your apron in the hamper, and want to yell: "Enough is enough, I quit!" . . . while in the back of your mind, that lovely voice will say, "Oh no, you don't, you know you can do it, don't quit." This will be the moment to stop right then and there for one minute, void your mind altogether, take a deep breath, and simply continue working. This will be the time when you realize that your chef, the woman or man you entrusted with a phase of your professional development, is caught in the same dilemma as you. For your chef there is not only you; there are also your colleagues who make their own mistakes, there is that bottom line at the end of the month and the end-of-the-year statement to greet the New Year and there are growing family responsibilities, so important and to which it feels like one can never devote all the time one would like to.

Aim high in your choices of masters and of restaurants in which to train. Be persistent, until you find the master who can teach you nothing but the best, whether she or he has the reputation of being mean. What will count in the long run is what you will learn. In my many years of helping young people find the right corner in the best possible kitchens, I have had some striking successes and a few disappointments, the latter coming in 99 percent of the cases from a lack of maturity and patience on the part of the student/apprentice. It takes a nice and long number of years to become a full-fledged chef, one who has the vision and the sensitivity not only of an artist but also of a great business person.

Prepare yourself for following orders for a number of years. Oh, I know, you are in a great hurry to acquire your own restaurant and to be your own Master. Well . . . slow down, take your time and think about it for a while. A restaurant, any restaurant, is not to be started on half the amount of knowledge needed, especially in the modern economic climate, and yet another choice is facing you.

Will you start your own very small restaurant, very humbly and gradually building your business and improving your house year after year all the while you are honing your business acumen? Or will you precipitate yourself into a partnership or even end up on "sweat equity," while an entrepreneur puts up financing for you? Reflect and think hard before you take any decision for momentous consequences can result from being over enthusiastic. Whereas sweat equity may work out very well, it may also bring on frustration, lack of creative personal freedom, and resentment between business partners, especially if a reviewer visits your dining room precisely on the night you were sent out to the antipodes to "do an event."

Remember always, it is your choice; you can concentrate on becoming the absolute master of your work, let your plates speak for themselves and display your work at its best, or you can let your sponsor put his publicity agent to work. It depends entirely on what you want most: the inner certitude that your work reflects you fully or a quicker success and better income faster.

Either way, you will know that you have achieved something special when copies of your work will start appearing here and there on colleagues' tables, and when minor food writers will paraphrase and imitate your culinary conceptions. Remain unflapped and peaceful, for what you created can only be brought from concept to reality by yourself; imitations will remain imitations, which brings to mind the concept of competition. I cannot remember the number of times that I was asked by newspaper reporters who my competition was. From the start, set your mind to the fact that success evolves from having only one competition: Yourself and your will to become always better. Unless this principle becomes a religion to you, you will be heading for troubles, for worrying about what the others do is a loss of time, energy, and concentration. Be "an athlete of the plate"; give your best performance at all times. Know yourself, be yourself, and give of yourself: this principle is the only road to total success.

Brace yourself for the day when a review of your work will appear in a newspaper. Think of it this way: since we all have to eat, we are all food experts. That includes, of course, the reviewer who, unlike you, did not necessarily spend years studying the techniques of the Masters, reading Gray's Anatomy at 3 A.M. to understand the structure of meats, nor spent years poring over food history and food chemistry books. A reviewer is just another human being who has to eat, and consequently is a food expert, and will remain forever incapable of perceiving tastes and textures exactly the same way you or any of your sous chefs or cooks ever will. So, forget all about reviewers, taste your food productions carefully, and watch your plates both as they go out to the dining room and when they come back from it, for if they are not "licked clean" and empty, beware . . . something may not be right.

And then, as you work like a Roman (a euphemism for the probably more-accurate "slave"), you will have to try to keep in good physical shape if you want to be able to pursue your passion for food preparation until you reach the pinnacle of your career. It will mean eating and drinking wisely, sleeping enough, exercising a bit each and every day (or at least every second day), and learning to leave all work irritations at the kitchen door so that your time at home with family is a relaxing one.

Also have another passion. Travel as much as you can, ride a bike, run, climb mountains, swim, read mysteries or history, collect old porcelains or whatever, make wine or beer, be a Buddhist or a philosopher, but do something that will replenish your font of creativity, for since you will be giving a lot of yourself to many, it is essential that you never forget to give your soul a little nourishment. If you do not, you will slowly become overtired and put yourself in danger of becoming less efficient and creative.

Go ahead, enjoy your kitchen career and do not ever suffer those prophets of doom who will try to tell you that after all, if you become a chef, you will be practicing "just another craft." If you learn well, practice, and persevere, you will live to become a true culinary artist whose plates will be models of good taste, in both senses of the term, for a new generation of cooks. I can guarantee you that you will acquire the most amazing sense of humor and become a social success, if only for all the stories that you will have to tell at dinner parties. If I ever meet you, just ask me for the story of the gentleman who spread his butter on my tablecloth because he did not like the size of my porcelain plate; we shall have a good giggle together. Good-bye. Meet you in your restaurant.

Madeleine Kamman
Woman, Wife, Mother, Grandmother,
Culinary educator, Chef, Former restaurateur,
Author, and TV personality

Director, School for American Chefs
at Beringer Vineyards

Chez La Mère Madeleine

(Madeleine's menus have a certain timeless quality to them—
this menu sounds as fresh and inviting today as we're sure it did in 1976!)

Menu for Friday and Saturday nights from June 1st to July 15, 1976

Due to the difficulty of finding some ingredients and the irregularity of arrival of quality meats and fish in Boston, we may have to change a few of the items on our menu each week. We apologize for any possible change. We thank our guests for understanding that all changes are made for the sake of always fresh looking and fresh tasting dishes.

First Courses

Cream of red peppers with a garnish of saffron butter
and a fine julienne of zucchini 2.75
Salad of large shrimp with watercress dressing and a small garnish
of red radishes and zucchini salad 6.00
Soft shell crab sauteed in lightly curried butter
with warm slices of avocado and papaya 6.00
Terrine of veal sweetbread with green herbs and carrots served
with a tiny garnish of etuveed yellow squash and dill 5.50
Lukewarm rabbit salad with toasted hazelnuts, bitter greens, carrots,
baby peas and cucumbers in sherry vinegar dressing
with a dash of Armagnac 5.50

Main Courses

Braised squab pigeon with cooked garlic and honey sauce garnished with cooked
garlic cloves, pignoli and chopped parsley 18.00
Saddle of lamb with mustard and gremolata sauce 18.00
Mousse of chicken with a puree of artichokes sauce and a garnish of diced ham and baby peas 18.00
Tenderloin steak with button mushrooms, wild "marasmius oreades"
mushrooms, pancetta and persillade garnish 18.00
Mousse of salmon with a rhubarb and citrus rind sauce 18.00

Vegetables

Spinach, baby tomatoes, Jerusalem artichokes with scallions, jardiniere
of carrots, white radishes and asparagus or fresh pickles when the asparagus is
out of season, small green salad with a very light blue cheese dressing
All vegetables as well as the salad are included in the
cost of the main course

Desserts

French cheeses as available on the market 4.50
Fresh strawberry sherbet and coconut and Kirsch sherbet 4.00
Frozen velvet ice cream flavored with coffee and 2 liquors 4.00
Tartlet with strawberries and raspberry puree 4.00
Galliano succes cake 4.00

PREFACE

*T*hrough six years in the kitchen as a full-time professional cook, the only thing that becomes clearer each day, as I discover a great technique I've never seen used before or a wonderful ingredient I've never tasted before, is that I know absolutely nothing about cooking. Often my realization of how much there is to know is overwhelming, and that's exactly the feeling that drives me into the cookbook sections of bookstores or prompts me to set my alarm clock early to squeeze in time for reading before I leave for work.

It's also the feeling that drove me to undertake a task as daunting as co-authoring this book. In combing through bookstores, I noticed a void: While there were many books *by* chefs, I could find none strictly *about* chefs. In most cookbook introductions, chefs typically give only very brief overviews of their careers and cooking philosophies. While I clearly knew that becoming a good cook had infinitely more to do with cooking than with reading, I was looking for some additional guidance and inspiration on how to get the most out of all the time I did spend in the kitchen. As a cook just starting out in my career, I always wanted to know more.

I wanted to know about their first jobs and whether they started out with a cooking school diploma, or started at the bottom and worked their way up through the ranks. How did they get noticed? Was it a straight and steady path, or did they face setbacks along the way? How did they turn things around? Did they know, through years of low pay and back-breaking work, that they would eventually succeed? What helped them keep pushing?

Part of the reason I wanted to know was to see whether I was on the right track. What I've since learned is that there is no single "right track." Sure, some European-born chefs started in the kitchens of three-star restaurants at the age of 13. But other leading American chefs actually got their start in their later teens at the local Carvel or Friendly's. This was a relief to me, because my first restaurant job—like that of millions of other American teenagers—was at the local McDonald's.

I grew up in a San Francisco Bay Area neighborhood transitioning from farmland to suburb; our backyard had five fruit trees and three walnut trees. My earliest memories were of gathering walnuts and getting to crack them for winter pies. Three days out of high school, my love of the outdoors led me to a job fighting fires for the Northern California Division of Forestry during one of the worst summers for forest fires in the state's history. As an 18-year-old, I found myself spending 12-to-15-hour days for six weeks straight battling a single fire. But once the blaze had been extinguished and the last K-ration eaten, I took on the responsibility of cooking for the guys in the firehouse one day a week. It was the best day. I would read cookbooks and reproduce large-quantity versions of the dishes I knew, from creamed tuna on biscuits to spaghetti with meat sauce.

The next summer, my two best friends and I decided to move to Wyoming, hoping to make our fortunes working on an oil rig. After none of us could find a job on a rig, and we were down to our last $20, I fortunately landed a job as a cook—at the Holiday Inn in Cody. I discovered that cooks can learn something anywhere. Wyoming is cattle country, and I learned the importance of a sharp knife and how to butcher meats. I knew I was making progress when they let me trim the filet mignon.

The following summer I trekked to Alaska, and ended up working in a salmon processing plant. I loved getting to work with fish at its source, instead of out of the freezer. I gorged myself on fresh 100-pound halibut and grilled salmon, and learned how to tell salmon apart by the width of their tails. I processed salmon roe to be consumed in Japan, and I learned a new respect for food from the Japanese technicians. While I found the Japanese to be stern taskmasters when it came to salting and packing the roe, they were all smiles when they made and shared their sushi with the crew.

All the while, I found my on-again-off-again college education less and less fulfilling. After I moved to Boston in 1985, I took a job as a waiter, and soon realized that I loved the restaurant business more than anything I was studying in college. While working at the East Coast Grill in Cambridge, Massachusetts, I asked chef-owner Chris Schlesinger about cooking schools. Instead, Chris handed me a knife and a case of cabbage, along with a chance to work part-time in his kitchen.

My apprenticeship there gave me one successful chef's insights. Chris taught me a lot about how to run a restaurant—ordering, receiving, storing, rotating foods, and other day-to-day tasks that are a core part of running a kitchen—as well as the amount of dedication it takes. There's no such thing as "good enough" when receiving ingredients or plating a dish. I learned to respect my fellow cooks, our equipment, even the floor of the kitchen itself—that a floor deserves as much attention and respect as the edge of your knife blade, because it's a part of the machinery that makes up a well-functioning kitchen. I also learned a respect for the history of cuisine and the sense of community among chefs through two gifts from Chris: a copy of Escoffier's *Guide Culinaire* and a membership in the American Institute of Wine and Food.

I left the East Coast Grill in 1989, with Chris's blessing, to cook at Lydia Shire's brand-new restaurant, Biba, in Boston. Every day in Biba's kitchen reminded me that there do not have to be culinary boundaries in a restaurant—the world is Lydia's pantry. Seeing her love for various foods, even for the simplest dishes like spaghetti with breadcrumbs, was an inspiration to expand my own food horizons.

Along the way, I always asked my chefs and sous chefs for advice on books to read or classes to take, particularly since I never attended a full-time cooking school program. I made an effort to attend the demonstration or presentation of any leading food authority passing through Boston to promote a restaurant or book, and I was lucky enough to see Julia Child, Lorenza de' Medici, Diana Kennedy, Jacques Pépin, Julie Sahni, and Anne Willan, among others.

When my wife, Karen, and I moved to New York City, I was lucky enough to land a job cooking at Arcadia. Anne Rosenzweig underscored the importance of understanding your clientele and respecting them and their preferences. In contrast to the wild, spicy dishes at East Coast Grill, and the bold, eclectic ones at Biba, Arcadia's food—while equally creative—is classic and elegant. It involved a daily refinement of my technique.

The most inspirational episode in my cooking career to date was the two-week period I spent in 1992 with Madeleine Kamman at the School for American Chefs at Beringer Vineyards in California's Napa Valley. The other chefs in my class—Mark Gould of

Atwater's (Portland, Oregon), Alan Harding of Nosmo King (New York City), and Chuck Wiley of The Boulders (Carefree, Arizona)—and I lived an idyllic life of cooking, eating, talking and breathing food and wine with the most knowledgeable and passionate person about food I've ever known—Madeleine. (The best thing about having Alan Harding in my class at the School for American Chefs was that he's someone who knows how to have fun while he cooks—see steps 1 and 6 of his recipe on page xxv!)

My outside-of-work education continues. While it doesn't yet rival the size of seasoned chefs', my home library continues to grow at the rate of about two or three cookbooks a month. Karen and I love to visit used bookstores for unusual or out-of-print cookbooks. And during the time we spent working on this book, we had an opportunity to travel widely throughout the United States on the weekends, eating at some of the country's best restaurants. Each meal was an education in itself. Each conversation we had with the leading chefs featured in this book was a graduate-level seminar.

In selecting chefs to be interviewed for the book, we aimed to tap a diverse range of opinions and experiences. After surveying cooks across the country through our publisher, we chose chefs among those they considered to be at the top of the profession. We also strove (often, with difficulty) to represent chefs from different parts of the country, of different backgrounds, cooking different styles of food. (The chefs are typically referred to throughout the text by their names only; for additional biographical information, including their restaurants and locations, see Appendix E which begins on page 305.) We also aimed to transcend popular "glamourized" media images of chefs to portray what it's *really* like to work in a kitchen. While consumers flipping through a cooking magazine might be enchanted by a chef holding a beautifully styled plate of food in an elegant-looking dining room, what they *don't* see is that the chef's smile may be fleeting—and that, as soon as the camera crew leaves, there's a clogged drain, a malfunctioning air conditioner, a late meat delivery, and a sick sous chef to deal with.

This profession requires a tremendous amount of hard work. There is more to being a chef than creativity, just as there is more than creativity to being an artist. As in any other craft, chefs must practice, practice, practice. Perfection is the only acceptable benchmark. Chefs must continue to learn, and must rise to the challenges that will allow them to grow. They must be open to criticism. Work hot. Work cold. Work hurt. Work under intense pressure. And be willing to destroy a canvas or two.

What does it take to become a truly good chef in America? This is the central question we explored, for the sake of other aspiring chefs or the otherwise interested reader. Wherever one might practice this profession—from a four-star kitchen to one more modest—any cook can learn a great deal from the experiences of the leading chefs we interviewed. First, we tried to understand the experiences that were most formative to the chefs' lives and early careers, and these experiences are addressed in the first half of the book. Second, we hoped to gain a sense of the practices that keep leading chefs at the top, which are addressed in the second half.

The paths to the top are as varied as the chefs who have made their way along them. We met introverted chefs whose strength was in creating quiet and elegant spaces in which to serve their refined food, and extroverts whose colorful and loud decor matched both their flavors and personalities—as well as everything in between. The most successful have succeeded in creating restaurants that represent both figurative and literal extensions of themselves, their personalities, and their preferences.

As a cook, I'm overwhelmed by how fortunate I am to have been personally guided and inspired by the 1,000 years' collective experience of the leading chefs you'll meet in these pages. The depth of their knowledge, passion, and generosity—as well as the breadth of their diversity—represent what I love most about this profession.

Despite the immense benefit of having had this experience every day I'm in the kitchen, I realize how much I still have to master. However, through the course of writing this book, I've come to recognize that everything I don't know about cooking—the techniques I've yet to learn, the ingredients I've yet to discover, the dishes I've yet to taste—represents not a deficiency, but a syllabus for a lifetime of learning and experiencing and enjoying that will not only contribute to my development as a chef, but will continue to enrich my life every step of the way. I can't imagine a better way to spend a career, or a lifetime.

Andrew Dornenburg
Spring 1995

Brooklyn Brown Ale Rabbit Rutabega Stew

ALAN HARDING

Nosmo King
New York, NY

"My grandmother used to make wonderful pot roasts in the Alsatian manner—lots of great sautéed onions, spaeztle, and apple sauce. This recipe was inspired by my grandmother."

....

2 bottles Brooklyn Brown Ale (if you don't drink while you cook)

salt and pepper as desired

olive oil

2 large rabbits (3–4 lb) in uniform stewing chunks

1 large rutabagas (softball size) in 3/4-inch cubes

1 1/2 cups pearl onions–peeled

1 1/2 cups white button mushrooms–whole or quartered

1 half orange studded with 3 cloves

4 cups chicken stock (rabbit stock if you're ambitious)

....

1. Start drinking.

2. Season rabbit chunks with salt and pepper and brown in olive oil in the bottom of an ovenproof pot large enough to hold all of the ingredients.

3. Remove rabbit to paper towels to drain and remove excess oil from the pot.

4. Deglaze with 1/2 bottle of Brooklyn Brown Ale.

5. Add onions and sweat (the onions) for 1 or 2 minutes, then add rutabaga and mushrooms for a couple more minutes.

6. Take a short break and enjoy a bottle of Brooklyn Brown Ale; cooking is hard work.

7. Add stock, rabbit, 1 1/2 more beers, and the orange–bring to simmer and place in 325° F oven until rabbit is tender.

8. Serve over rice, egg noodles, or spaetzle with crusty bread and some spinach sautéed in garlic.

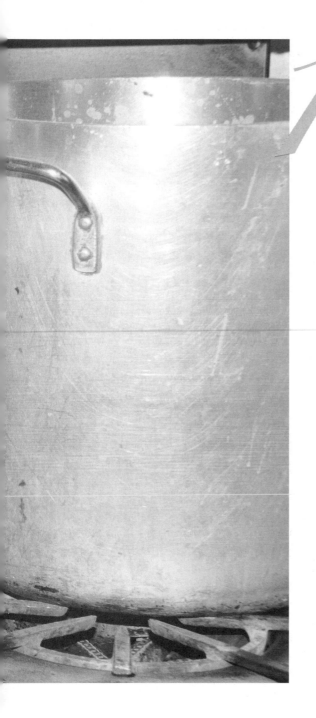

1

CHEFS

Yesterday
and
Today

*" 'A country without a past has no future.'
In a culinary sense, we have to reaffirm our
past because we have one. And if we have
any future, it is our past. We have to understand who we are and where we are."*

—MARK MILLER

Chef-restaurateur Jimmy Schmidt's life is not atypical of the lives of top American chefs like him who alternately wear the hats of chef, owner, host, author, writer, activist, and sometimes even celebrity. Schmidt runs five successful restaurants—the first and most famous being The Rattlesnake Club—in the Detroit area, but he crisscrosses the country to participate in various benefits with other chefs. He's active in leading the Chefs Collaborative 2000, a not-for-profit organization of chefs concerned about the quality of food in America. Before he goes to sleep at night, the author of the cookbook *Cooking for All Seasons* and nationally syndicated columnist uses the quiet time of the late hour to read and write. And, somehow, he—like many of his fellow chefs—usually manages to get by on just four or five hours of sleep a night.

Before reaching this level of success, however, working cooks like me experience "rites of passage" not unlike those one might encounter in boot camp. Our hours are long, the work is physically demanding, and the conditions are, well, *hot*. Our "uniforms" are anything *but*—while most kitchens require cooks to wear the traditional white chef's jacket, these days the pants worn could be anything from the traditional black-and-white houndstooth check to a brightly colored print of red chile peppers. Headgear ranges from a traditional toque (the classic tall white hat) to a baseball cap. Footwear might be tennis shoes or clogs, which are particularly popular among cooks who've worked in French kitchens. Kitchen work during lunch or dinner service is always intense, but the atmosphere may range from a tense calm to loud and frenzied screaming and yelling.

Those able to stand the heat are finding that the growth of the foodservice industry today is opening up greater opportunities for cooks and chefs in the profession. These opportunities carry with them an important responsibility, as the choices made by the next generation of chefs will transform the food of tomorrow. I believe aspiring chefs should recognize this influence and use it responsibly, striving to master their profession. This process starts with an understanding of its history.

Why is it important to understand culinary history? It is the rich tradition of the culinary field that allows this profession to be so much more than standing at a cutting board or a hot stove all day. I have worked with fellow cooks who didn't understand my own interest in the subject. They would ask, "Who cares who James Beard or Escoffier were? Why should I care what anyone did 20 years ago, let alone 200 years ago? I'd rather hear about what's new."

In fact, the media's emphasis on the latest culinary trends adds to the pressure chefs feel to come out with something new and different to attract attention, to define their style, or to satisfy our American desire for innovation. However, how much is ever *truly* new? André Soltner provides an interesting perspective of history's importance: "We've had the same food for 200–300 years—everything we do today was already done before." Could he possibly be right? Think about the wide variety of ethnic and regional cuisines we eat today, the modern demands for convenience and sophistication placed on today's cook, and our concerns about healthful food. Consider these cooking magazine articles: "Foods of the Rio Grande Valley and Northern Mexico," "Italian Cooking," "Russian Recipes," "Fifteen-Minute Meals," "Lentils: A Meat Substitute," "When Unexpected Company Comes," "World-Famous Recipes by the World's Most Noted Chefs," "Creole Cooking," "Delicious Cooking in a Small Space," "Making Gnocchi," "Homemade Timbales," "Making and Serving Curry." Could such variety and such specific needs even have been imagined more than a few years ago? Well, yes. Each article listed appeared in a United States publication between the years of 1895 and 1910!

In addition, how many people are aware that architecturally structured food, covered extensively in the food press in the 1990s as a "new" trend toward "tall" food, was prepared by chefs in the 19th century? As one might imagine, the chefs who pushed food in new directions were real pioneers in their day and thus, not surprisingly, fascinating human beings. Ralph Waldo Emerson wrote, "There is properly no history; only biography." History is simply compelling stories about compelling people, and the people who played a role in culinary history particularly so.

Until recently, the chef's profession was not particularly prestigious. Only in the last 20–25 years have chefs begun to gain the

"Understanding the history of the dish you are preparing will allow you to put a little more of your heart and soul into what you're cooking. I think that's what it's all about."
—JIMMY SCHMIDT

respect and recognition they deserve. Much of the media coverage today stems from their participation in various high-profile charity benefits. But turn to history and you'll see that chefs have long contributed to their communities through food. One example described in the pages that follow includes a chef who fed more than a million people over three months during the Irish potato famine.

As a not-unimportant bonus, an historical perspective allows cooks to give their food greater depth. At the School for American Chefs, Madeleine Kamman would have us think about where and when a dish originated and what the local people might have used to season it in centuries past. In preparing a particular Mediterranean dish, we saw the value of that thinking when we substituted anchovy for salt, and the dish took on a deeper richness and complexity. Understanding the profession's history will make you a better cook—in more ways than one.

Today's cook has a rich and impressive lineage dating back thousands of years, and understanding one's place as a link in a chain to the past—as well as to the future—can help a cook see the profession in a more balanced perspective. The timeline that follows doesn't pretend to be comprehensive—it merely highlights some interesting people, books, and events we hoped might help stimulate the reader's appetite to learn more and feel a stronger connection to the past.

GREAT MOMENTS IN CULINARY HISTORY		
	5th Century B.C.	Chefs play an important role in society from this time forward.
	4th Century A.D.	**Apicius** reputedly writes *De re conquinaria libri decem* ("Cuisine in Ten Books"), considered to be the very first cookbook, in which sauces are prepared in much the same manner as the French do up to 1955.
	Middle Ages	Guilds are formed, with chefs beginning their long tradition of community.
	1380	**Guillaume Tirel Taillevent** (1312–95) writes *Le Viandier*, one of the oldest cookbooks written in French, which provides a complete synthesis

of all aspects of cookery in the 14th century. Its main contribution is considered to be its emphasis on spiced foods and sauces (predominantly saffron, ginger, pepper, and cinnamon), soups, and ragouts, which included the preparation of meat, poultry, game, and fish. (The heavy seasoning served the useful purpose of disguising the taste of stale or rotten food.) He served as the cook of Charles VII of France.

1390   Richard II of England's cooks write *The Forme of Cury* ("The Art of Cookery"), which emphasizes heavily seasoned dishes and recommends the liberal use of almond milk in cooking.

1475   *De Honesta Voluptate ac Valetudine* ("Honest Pleasure and Health"), the first printed cookbook, is published in Italy by **Bartolomeo Sacchi Platina** (1421–1481).

1533   Italian princess **Caterina de Medici** marries the Duc d'Orleans (later Henri II) of France, and arrives in France with her Florentine chefs in tow. They collectively give rise to Florentine influences on the classic French fare, including simplicity, elegance, more delicate spicing, and the addition of new ingredients, most notably spinach.

1651   **Pierre Francois de la Varenne** (1615–78) publishes the first cookbook to give an insight into the new cooking practices of the French: *Le Cuisinier Français*. It is important as the first book to record the advances of French cooking through the Renaissance era, and represents the turning point when medieval cuisine ends and *haute cuisine* begins. Notable is the use of mushrooms and truffles, imparting more delicate flavors, and the use of butter in pastries and sauces instead of oil. La Varenne may also have written *Le Pastissier Français*, the first exhaustive French volume on pastry making.

A 14th-century European guild manual described the early master chef this way: "He is a professional craftsman. He is a cook. He takes fowl from the air; fish from the waters; fruits, vegetables, and grain from the land; and animals that walk the earth, and through his skills and art transforms the raw product to edible food. He serves to sustain life in man, woman, and child. He has the sacred duty through his efforts and art to sustain and maintain the healthy bodies that God has given us to house our souls."

1671	The Prince de Condé's cook **Vatel** (1635–1671) commits suicide by falling on his sword when the fish he ordered for a banquet honoring Louis XIV fails to arrive. (The fish is delivered 15 minutes later.)
1765	The first restaurant (or eating establishment serving restorative broths, known then as "restaurants") opens its doors in Paris, with proprietor **M. Boulanger** hanging out a sign: "Boulanger sells restoratives fit for the gods."
1774	**Antoine Augustin Parmentier** (1737–1813), an agronomist, begins his campaign to promote the potato, at the time regarded as food fit only for cattle or the destitute. A highlight of his efforts includes serving an entire meal—from appetizer and entree to bread and dessert—made from potatoes! Hard evidence that history repeats itself: The night of our visit to Charlie Trotter's, the dinner menu featured a "potato study" of eight courses using potatoes.
1782	The first restaurant, as we know it today, with regular hours and featuring a menu listing available dishes served at private tables, opens by **Antoine Beauvilliers** (1754–1817) in Paris. Its very French name? "The Grande Taverne de Londres" (London!).
1789–99	The French Revolution spurs many French chefs, previously employees of the monarchy or nobility, to flee the country, and many go on to open their own restaurants elsewhere.
1796	**Amelia Simmons** publishes *American Cookery*, the first cookbook written by an American for an American audience, giving voice 

to an "American mode of cooking" and providing the first printed instructions for the cooking of colonial produce such as corn, and specialties such as Indian pudding and johnnycake. One hundred and ninety-three years later, another New Englander, Jasper White, will publish a cookbook with his own recipes for the same.

1800   Scientist Count von Rumford, born **Benjamin Thompson** (1753–1814) in his native United States, develops the stove. Prior to this, cooking was done over open hearths.

1801   When **Thomas Jefferson** (1743–1836), a gourmand and wine connoisseur, becomes President of the United States, he hires the first French White House chef, Chef Julien, and stresses the utmost freshness and quality in produce and other ingredients. His garden features broccoli, endive, peas, and tomatoes (still considered poisonous by some Americans of the day), as well as fresh herbs. He is credited with introducing ice cream, pasta, and new fruits and vegetables to America.

1803–14   The first restaurant guides are published, sparked by the growing popularity of restaurants in Paris.

1820s   Chefs begin to wear the now-traditional large white hats known as *toques* (a white version of the black hats of Greek Orthodox priests).

1825   Seventy-year-old gastronomy philosopher **Jean Anthelm Brillat-Savarin** (1755–1826) anonymously self-publishes *Physiologie du Gout*, in which he challenges, "Tell me what you eat, and I shall tell you what you are."

1833   **Marie-Antoine Carême** (1783–1833), the most celebrated culinarian of his time, known as the "chef of kings, king of chefs," dies. In 1856, he

Carême believed, "Of the five fine arts, the fifth is architecture, whose main branch is confectionary." He saw the ideal cook as having a "discerning and sensitive palate, perfect and exquisite taste, a strong and industrious character; he should be skillful and hardworking and unite delicacy, order, and economy."

posthumously publishes *La Cuisine Classique*, thanks to the help of his student Plumery. As a young cook, Carême copied architectural drawings, upon which he based his patisserie creations which were greatly admired and gained him favor. Through his apprenticeships with the best chefs and pastry chefs of the time—in addition to assisting other leading chefs with special events—he develops in 12 years into their superior. Carême uses his sense of what is in vogue and whimsical to prepare both dramatically presented and elegant dishes, and his work as a philosopher, saucier, pastry chef, craftsman, and author of recipes raises him to the top of his profession. He is credited as the originator of *grande cuisine*.

1846   **Alexis Soyer** (1810–1858), a French cook, publishes his first book, *The Gastronomic Regenerator*. While contemporary chefs like Jimmy Schmidt and Wolfgang Puck popularized the wearing of baseball caps (instead of the traditional toque) as headgear in certain American kitchens, Soyer is known for characteristic headgear of his own: his trademark red velvet cap. Even contemporary chefs who donate their time to charitable events on a regular basis would be impressed with Soyer's contributions to the less fortunate. The same year, Soyer starts a large soup kitchen in London which feeds thousands of people a day, and during the potato famine the following year, he does the same in Ireland, where he feeds over a million mouths in three months. In 1855, he publishes *A Shilling Cookery for the People*, establishing himself as the "Frugal Gourmet" of his time. Long before the creation of American Spoon Foods by Larry Forgione and other contemporary businesses started by today's chefs to sell their prepared products to consumers for

	home use, Soyer markets his own bottled sauces (and so will Escoffier!).
1850s	Traditional French service, in which all the dishes of a meal are arranged artfully at the start of a meal, resulting in cold food, gives way to Russian service (*service a la Russe*), in which the courses are portioned in the kitchen and served on platters in sequence, resulting in hot food.
1863	**Charles Ranhofer** (1836–99) begins his 34-year reign as chef of Delmonico's in New York City, becoming the first internationally renowned chef of an American restaurant. He publishes his cookbook, *The Epicurean*, in 1893.
1889	The opening of the Savoy Hotel in London in 1889, under the leadership of the lengendary hotelier **César Ritz** (1850–1918) and celebrated chef **Auguste Escoffier** (1846–1935) transfers *grande cuisine*, the culinary movement founded by Carême, from the upper-class household to the hotel deluxe kitchen. This marks the age where chefs went from working as servants to becoming entrepreneurs with their own restaurants.
1896	**Fannie Merritt Farmer** (1857–1915), principal of the Boston Cooking School, publishes *The Boston Cooking-School Cook Book*, which has since sold almost four million copies. Hardly slowed though confined to a wheelchair, Farmer makes a major impact through her school, speeches, and writings on cooks' use of measured ingredients in recipes.
1900	The first *Guide Michelin* (restaurant guide) is published.
1902	**Escoffier** publishes the culinary classic *Le Guide Culinaire*. He establishes his place as one of the most influential forces on the foodservice

The Wisdom of Escoffier:

"Society had little regard for the culinary profession. This should not have been so, since cuisine is a science and an art and he who devotes his talent to its service deserves full respect and consideration."

"Not for me is it to point out to what acts of plagiarism the chef must submit. A painter can sign his work, and a sculptor can carve his name upon his, but a dish—how can the chef, its inventor, place his mark upon it?"

"The life of a chef is no idle one, apart from the labor of actual preparation and serving of diverse dishes. His brain must ever be on the alert, and his inventive powers always acute. But there is actual and lasting satisfaction . . . in accomplishing the very best that can be accomplished."

industry by creating the French brigade system, which improves the organization and speed of kitchen operations. In contrast with the stereotypical screaming that goes on in kitchens of his day (as well as before and since!), Escoffier's style as a chef is to walk away from a situation rather than lose his temper, and he forbids both profanity and brutality in his kitchen.

1924   **Fernand Point** (1897–1955), who inherited the restaurant his father had opened two years earlier in Vienne, France, renames it La Pyramide. Point is the first chef to leave the kitchen in order to speak with his customers in the dining room. He is considered a great teacher, and many leading contemporary chefs of France—including Paul Bocuse, Alain Chapel, the Troisgros brothers, Francois Bise, Louis Outhier, and Raymond Thuilier—study with him.

1938   **Prosper Montagné** (1864–1948) publishes *Larousse Gastronomique*—to this day, a culinary bible—with the intention of providing a single reference for the history of gastronomy through the ages, and the spectrum of cooking in the 20th century. The son of a hotelier, he worked his way up through the ranks of the kitchens of some of the most famous restaurants of his day.

1941   *Gourmet* begins publication, elevating food to a serious topic meriting its own journal of record.

1941   **Henri Soulé** (1903–1966) opens Le Pavillon in New York City, the first United States restaurant dedicated to French haute cuisine, which later spawns other great French restaurants (including La Cote Basque, La Grenouille, Le Cygne, Le Perigord) and chefs (including Pierre Franey and Jacques Pépin).

Cuisines of the World Find Their Way to the United States

The following list indicates the decade each type of cuisine first received its own heading in the *Readers' Guide to Periodical Literature*, along with characteristic (*not* comprehensive!) ingredients and/or flavor combinations represented in the recipes included. All names of the types of cuisine are indicated as originally published, however politically incorrect or inaccurate they may be now—further underscoring the fact that "times change!"

Decade	Type of Cuisine	Characteristic Ingredients
1920s	Chinese	garlic, ginger, mushrooms, rice, rice wine, scallion, soy sauce
	French	butter, cheese, cream, eggs, garlic, herbs, olive oil, stock, wine
	Italian	basil, garlic, olive oil, oregano, red wine vinegar, rosemary, tomato (Italian cuisine is influenced by Greek, which is influenced by Oriental cuisine)
	Japanese	garlic, ginger, rice, sake, scallion, sesame oil, soy sauce, sugar
	Jewish	chicken fat, onion
	Mexican	chile, chocolate, cilantro, corn, garlic, lime, rice, scallion, tomato (Mexican cuisine is influenced by Indian and Spanish cuisines)
1930s	Armenian	parsley, yogurt
	Czechoslovak	caraway seeds, sour cream
	Danish	butter, chives, cream, dill, potatoes, tarragon
	English	bacon, dill, mustard, oats, potatoes, Worcestershire (British cuisine is influenced by medieval cuisine)
	Finnish	milk, mushrooms
	French-Canadian	maple
	German	caraway seeds, dill, mustard, vinegar
	Hungarian	caraway seeds, dill, onion, paprika, sour cream (Hungarian cuisine is influenced by ancient Magyar nomad origins)
	Norwegian	sour cream
	Russian	beets, cabbage, dill, mushrooms, potatoes, sour cream
	Scandinavian	butter, cream, dill, horseradish
	Swedish	dill, gravlax
	Swiss	charcuterie (bacon, meats, sausages); (Swiss cuisine is influenced by French, German, Austrian, and Italian cuisines)
1940s	Brazilian	chile, lime
	Greek	cinnamon, garlic, goat cheeses, lemon, mint, olive oil, oregano, tomato
	Hawaiian	pineapple
	Irish	cabbage, oats, oysters, potatoes, rye
	Latin American	chile, corn, garlic, plantains, potatoes, red beans, rice
1950s	Korean	brown sugar, chile, sesame, soy sauce

(continued on next page)

Decade	Type of Cuisine	Characteristic Ingredients
1960s	Argentinian	beef, corn
	Austrian	cream cheeses, onion, paprika, poppy seeds (Austrian cuisine is influenced by German, Italian, and Hungarian cuisines)
	Basque	garlic, peppers, tomatoes
	Chilean	meat, onions, pimentos, seafood
	Dutch	fish, seafood (Dutch cuisine is influenced by Indonesian cuisine)
	East Indian	aromatics, coconut, coriander, curry, mint, saffron, turmeric
	Middle Eastern	cinnamon, dill, garlic, lemon, mint, olive oil, parsley, tomato, yogurt
	Polish	dill, mushrooms, potatoes, sour cream
	Portuguese	cabbage, chile, chorizo, cod, eggs, garlic, olive oil, potato, rice
	Scottish	oats, potatoes
	South Seas	coconut, ginger, red curry
	Spanish	garlic, nuts, olive oil, onion, seafood, sweet peppers, tomato
	Thai	basil, chile, cilantro, coconut, curry, fish sauce, garlic, mint, peanut, sugar (Thai cuisine is influenced by Chinese and Indian cuisines)
	Ukranian	dill, sour cream
1970s	Belgian	beer
	Jamaican	jerk (herbs, peppers, spices)
	Lebanese	bulgar, sesame oil (Lebanese cuisine is influenced by European, Arabian, and Oriental cuisines)
	Moroccan	cinnamon, coriander, cumin, dried lemon, fruit, ginger, onion, saffron, tomato
	North African	cumin, garlic, mint (North African cuisine is influenced by imperial Roman, Turkish, and Jewish cuisines)
	Pakistani	fruit, pulses, rice, spices
	Puerto Rican	ginger, lime, plantains
	Turkish	allspice, bulgar, lemon, olive oil, onion, parsley, walnuts, yogurt (Turkish cuisine is influenced by Muslim, Jewish, Orthodox, and Christian cuisines)

1946   During the beginning of the rise of the television era, **James Beard** (1903–1985), one of the most esteemed and respected food writers in America, and considered the "dean" of American cooking, is tapped for his own cooking show on television because of his experience as both an actor and a cook.

1947   *To a Queen's Taste*, one of the first televised instructional cooking shows in the United States, featuring **Dione Lucas,** debuts.

Decade	Type of Cuisine	Characteristic Ingredients
1980s	African	chile, peanut, tomato
	Black	cornmeal, greens, pig meats (bacon, chitterlings, ham, ribs)
	Cajun	chile, game, seafood, strong seasonings, tomato
	Caribbean	chile, cinnamon, jerk seasoning, nutmeg, okra, rum, seafood
	Creole	alcohol, banana, chile, okra, pineapple, rum, seafood, spices, tomato (Creole cuisine is influenced by African, Caribbean, French, Hindu, and Italian cuisines)
	Dominican	chile, chorizo, coconut, corn, meats
	Egyptian	fruit, pinenuts, turmeric
	Haitian	crushed red pepper, cumin
	Indian (U.S.)	corn
	Indonesian	brown sugar, chile, curry, lemongrass, lime, peanut, rice, soy sauce (Indonesian cuisine is influenced by Indian and Chinese cuisines)
	Israeli	carbohydrates (baked goods, potatoes, etc.)
	Mediterranean	anchovy, garlic, olive oil, parsley, tomato
	Peruvian	chile, corn, lime, onion, tomato
	Philippine	garlic, soy sauce, vinegar
1990s	Australian	fish and shellfish, meat, tropical fruits and vegetables (Australian cuisine is influenced by British and Dutch cuisines)
	Colombian	avocado, corn, onion, pimento, tomato
	Corsican	Broccio cheese, citrus fruits, olives, tomato
	Iranian	almonds, aromatic spices and herbs, rice, saffron, yogurt
	Jordanian	marjoram, oregano, peanuts
	Romanian	garlic, root vegetables, tomato
	Singaporean	chile, cinnamon, coconut, onion, scallion, turmeric
	Syrian	pinenuts, pistachios, pomegranite, red pepper paste
	Tex-Mex	beans, rice
	Venezuelean	banana, beef, corn, red beans, rice
	Vietnamese	basil, chile, cilantro, fish sauce, garlic, ginger, lemon, lime, mint

1948   Two women, one the wife of the president of Yale University, open the New Haven (CT) Restaurant Institute, which eventually becomes The Culinary Institute of America (C.I.A.) in Hyde Park, New York, the first serious cooking school in the country.

1957   **Craig Claiborne** is named food editor at *The New York Times*, subsequently raising restaurant reviewing from a form of promotional advertising to honest critique.

THE 1960s

With new discoveries in science and technology came change, resulting in the advent of fast food, the decline of regional distinctions in food, and the homogenization of the American palate. The 1960s helped usher in a new emphasis on healthy, natural, and organic foods. As more Americans traveled abroad, and as the United States' own ethnic population composition began to shift, there came greater emphasis on the foods and cuisines of other countries. Still, interest in French food was reinvigorated as the "nouvelle cuisine" movement of the young French chefs (including Paul Bocuse and his "band" of chefs) made headlines. Julia Child's presence on TV, with her widely watched series *The French Chef*, exposed Americans to her version of this popular foreign cuisine.

1961	First Lady Jacqueline Kennedy nearly single-handedly revamps White House dining by hiring French-born chef **René Verdon.**
	Julia Child, with co-authors Simone Beck and Louisette Bertholle, publishes her first book, *Mastering the Art of French Cooking*, still cited as an important reference to today's chef.
1963	*The French Chef*, hosted by Julia Child, makes its television debut.
1969	*Fernand Point: Ma Gastronomie* is published posthumously.

THE 1970s

In the 1970s when Jasper White attended The Culinary Institute of America, "the school wasn't anything like it is today, back then. It was attracting a different crowd, more working-class kids who really wanted to become chefs because they thought it would be a great way to make a living. There was no glamour. There were no famous chefs in America in 1975. Not one."

The American restaurant scene was forever changed, however, in 1971 when Alice Waters opened her Berkeley, California restaurant Chez Panisse, which emphasized seasonality and freshness in ingredients, the natural taste of which became the star on the plate. In the years that followed when Waters received national acclaim, she inspired countless American chefs to follow suit, while attracting a new breed of thoughtful, well-educated men and, notably, women into her kitchen and into the profession. The number of leading American chefs who have worked at Chez Panisse is a testimony to its—and Waters'—influence (see page 101).

The news media responded to the newly burgeoning restaurant scene by hiring food critics and covering food more extensively, spurred on by competition from the new food magazines such as *Bon Appetit* and *Food & Wine,* which chronicled the new generation of young American chefs.

André Soltner recalls, "Suddenly, when the star chefs appeared in magazines, the level of respect for chefs became much, much higher. Young Americans were interested because suddenly the chefs were in the limelight. Before, which American wanted to become a cook? But suddenly, they started to go to school and became chefs. I remember the change—the publicity, the people like Bocuse and a few others who were suddenly on the cover of *Newsweek.* Customers—doctors and lawyers—said to me, 'My son wants to become a chef, he goes to The Culinary Institute of America.' Some went to France to train, some came to our restaurant, some went to La Côte Basque, La Grenouille . . . and some became very good. The level of chefs in America changed dramatically."

This decade is also when American cooking started coming into its own, as American chefs and customers rediscovered pride in the cuisine and ingredients of their own country and its regions.

> "The 1970s saw an explosion of nouvelle cuisine, but is that cuisine really completely new? Some of it—the use of exotic ingredients and spices, the shorter cooking times for better texture and nutrition, for example—is new; some is not and is definitely borrowed from the font of ancient cooking. For example, the sauces based on reduction echo the food of Apicius and all the women who for centuries thickened by reduction because they had to keep flour to make bread. It reflects the shrinking of our world through the interpenetrations of diverse cultures, thanks to air travel."
>
> MADELEINE KAMMAN

1971   **Alice Waters** opens Chez Panisse in Berkeley, California.

             Madeleine Kamman publishes *The Making of a Cook,* the first cookbook in the United States to attempt to explain cooking with *why*'s instead of only *how*'s. It is still cited by contemporary chefs as an important reference.

1972   **Leslie Revsin** is the first woman chef to take the helm of a major hotel kitchen when she is named chef of the Waldorf-Astoria Hotel in

Baked Goat Cheese with Garden Salad

ALICE WATERS

Chez Panisse
Berkeley, CA

*"Salad is something that I've been obsessed with since I encoun-
tered the classic Mesclun mix when I visited my friend in Nice 25
years ago. I loved all of the different tastes, textures, and colors
that come together in this salad. We've had goat cheese with garden
salad on the menu in the Café ever since it began 15 years ago,
and some people come here just to have it. It's adaptable enough to
change with the seasons and is a great companion to serve with
fresh figs, olives, walnuts, pears, and many other ingredients. I
prefer it after a meal, although many people use it as a starter."*

. . . .

*3 to 4 2 1/2-inch-diameter rounds of fresh goat cheese,
each about 1/2- inch thick*

1/2 cup olive oil

3 to 4 sprigs fresh thyme

---

*"The more one travels, the
more one realizes that other
cooks are not standing still; they
are progressing. Today anyone
who wants to progress must go
around the world. Each time
that I go to another country, I
come back with many ideas."*

—PAUL BOCUSE

1973

New York City, making the headlines of
Manhattan newspapers.

Calvin Trillin writes in *Playboy*, only half
tongue-in-cheek, that "the best restaurants . . .
are in Kansas City," sparking new attention to—
and pride in—hometown cuisines across the
country.

Madeleine Kamman opens Chez la Mere
Madeleine at Modern Gourmet in Newton

bay leaf, crumbled

*1 cup fine dry bread crumbs
(the bread should be toasted first and then ground)*

2 tablespoons balsamic vinegar

dash red wine vinegar

salt and pepper to taste

*about 4 handfuls garden lettuces (rocket, lamb's lettuce,
small oak leaf and red leaf lettuces, chervil)*

. . . .

Marinate the goat cheese rounds in 1/4 cup of olive oil with the thyme and bay leaf for a day.

Prepare the vinaigrette by whisking the remaining 1/4 cup of olive oil into the vinegars until the vinaigrette is balanced, and season with salt and pepper. Wash and dry the lettuces.

To bake the goat cheese, take the rounds out of the olive oil marinade and dip them in the bread crumbs. Put the cheese on a lightly oiled baking dish and bake in a preheated 450 degree oven for about 4 to 5 minutes, until the cheese is lightly bubbling and golden brown.

Meanwhile, toss the lettuces with enough vinaigrette to lightly coat them and arrange them on round salad plates. Place the cheese in the center of the plates with the browner side up.

Serves 4

Centre, Massachusetts—one of the first, if not the first, French nouvelle cuisine restaurants in the United States. French chef Paul Bocuse proclaims it "the greatest in the U.S.A."

1975 French chef **Paul Bocuse** is named to the Legion d'Honneur by President Giscard d'Estaing—the first chef to be so honored. Six months later, he is featured on the cover of *Newsweek* for an article entitled "Food: The New Wave."

"Every morning I go to the market and stroll among the displays. Sometimes I do not even know what dish I will make for the noon meal. It is the market that decides. This, I think, is what makes good cooking."

—PAUL BOCUSE

Spinach-Wrapped Sea Urchin Roe in Spicy Hollandaise

NOBU MATSUHISA

Matsuhisa
Los Angeles, CA

*"Fifteen years ago, before the sushi boom, most Americans were
hesitant to eat raw sea urchin. Therefore, I wanted them to open
up their eyes and expand their palates to my favorite seafood.
If I made the appearance enticing and heated the sea urchin in a
way that it did not ruin the delicate taste and texture of the
sea urchin, then I was confident in having my American customers
at least take a bite. Once they took a bite, the rest was automatic,
and eventually they were eating it raw."*

Spinach balls

. . . .

3 ounces sea urchin roe

1 shiitake mushroom (finely diced)

6 pieces spinach leaves (large)

1 stalk fresh asparagus (cut in half)

. . . .

1976   **Jeremiah Tower,** then of Chez Panisse, is
inspired by *The Epicurean—A Franco-American
Culinary Encyclopedia,* and features the first
California menu at the restaurant, ranging from
Monterey Bay Prawns to Walnuts, Almonds,
and Mountain Pears from the San Francisco
Farmers' Market.

1977   **Jane and Michael Stern** publish *Roadfood,* celebrating old-fashioned American restaurants.

Sauce

....

1 egg yolk

2 tablespoons melted butter

1 tablespoon Tobanjan

2 tablespoons Beluga caviar or salmon eggs

....

To prepare spinach balls

Mix sea urchin and shiitake mushroom together. Blanch spinach in boiling water for 2–3 seconds, then rinse in cold water. Spread spinach leaf out and fill with mixture, wrap leaf around mixture to form ball. Bake in preheated 450° F oven, and bake for 10 minutes.

To prepare sauce

Beat egg yolk until smooth; add butter and continue beating until blended. Add lemon juice and tobanjan.

To serve

Cut the spinach ball in half. Top each half with a generous portion of the caviar or salmon eggs. Pour sauce around the outside to cover bottom of the plate. Garnish with asparagus. Complete.

Serves one

"Right around the 1980s, there was a major change—from the French model to another model, where everybody was getting back to their roots. Across the country—from New Orleans to California—people started accepting their grandmother's meatloaf as a meaningful food experience, and America started to define its own standards for what a dining experience was."

—Chris Schlesinger

1979   **Paul Prudhomme** opens K-Paul's in New Orleans' French Quarter, launching the national craze for Cajun food and "blackened" fish.

In the 1980s, the French cuisine craze hit America full force, spurred by chefs like Jean Banchet, founder of Le Francais (Chicago); Jean-Louis Palladin of Jean-Louis at the Watergate (Washington, DC); and Georges Perrier of Le Bec-Fin

THE 1980s

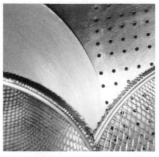

(Philadelphia). There was a melding of French technique and American ingredients that helped give rise to the California cuisine movement pioneered by Alice Waters, Jeremiah Tower, Mark Miller, and Wolfgang Puck. Puck is credited with developing a prototype of a successful restaurant through opening Spago in Los Angeles in 1982, with its emphasis on stylish design, informal service, and memorable food. The dining-out phenomenon of the 1980s created celebrity chef groupies, who came to be known as "foodies," as well as the immensely popular Zagat Restaurant Surveys published nationally by Tim and Nina Zagat.

THE 1990s

The 1990s have begun to witness creative responses to such trends as growing interest both in healthier food and in melding the cuisines of multiple cultures. Jean-Georges Vongerichten, with the publication of his cookbook *Simple Cuisine: The Easy, New Approach to Four-Star Cooking*, illustrated the strides he'd been making at the

Selected American Restaurant Openings: 1960–Present

Year	Chef	Restaurant	Location
1961	André Soltner	Lutèce	New York City
1970	Georges Perrier	Le Bec-Fin	Philadelphia
1971	Alice Waters	Chez Panisse	Berkeley, CA
1973	Jean Banchet	Le Francais	Wheeling, IL
1978	Patrick O'Connell	The Inn at Little Washington	Washington, VA
1979	Jean-Louis Palladin	Jean-Louis at the Watergate Hotel	Washington, DC
	Paul Prudhomme	K-Paul's	New Orleans
	Barry Wine	The Quilted Giraffe	New York City
1980	George Germon & Johanne Killeen	Al Forno	Providence, RI
1981	Michael Foley	Printer's Row	Chicago
	Jackie Shen	Jackie's	Chicago
	Elizabeth Terry	Elizabeth on 37th	Savannah, GA

Year	Chef	Restaurant	Location
1982	Susan Feniger & Mary Sue Milliken	City	Los Angeles
	Wolfgang Puck	Spago	Los Angeles
1983	Larry Forgione	An American Place	New York City
	Cindy Pawlcyn	Mustards Grill	Napa Valley, CA
	Jasper White	Jasper's	Boston
	Janos Wilder	Janos	Tucson
1984	Joyce Goldstein	Square One	San Francisco
	Anne Rosenzweig	Arcadia	New York City
	Jeremiah Tower	Stars	San Francisco
1985	Jimmy Schmidt	The Rattlesnake Club	Denver
1986	Victor Gielisse	Actuelle	Dallas
	Chris Schlesinger	East Coast Grill	Cambridge, MA
	Allen Susser	Chef Allen's	Miami
	Barbara Tropp	China Moon Cafe	San Francisco
1987	Rick Bayless	Frontera Grill	Chicago
	Susanna Foo	Susanna Foo	Philadelphia
	Gordon Hamersley	Hamersley's Bistro	Boston
	Zarela Martinez	Zarela	New York City
	Nobu Matsuhisa	Matsuhisa	Los Angeles
	Mark Miller	Coyote Cafe	Santa Fe, NM
	Michel Richard	Citrus	Los Angeles
	Charlie Trotter	Charlie Trotter's	Chicago
1988	Patrick Clark	Metro	New York City
	Mark Militello	Mark's Place	Miami
	Charles Palmer	Aureole	New York City
	Jimmy Schmidt	The Rattlesnake Club	Detroit
1989	Todd English	Olives	Boston
	Bradley Ogden	Lark Creek Inn	Larkspur, CA
	Wolfgang Puck	Postrio	San Francisco
	Lydia Shire	Biba	Boston
	Nancy Silverton & Mark Peel	Campanile	Los Angeles
1990	Emeril Lagasse	Emeril's	New Orleans
	Wayne Nish	March	New York City
	Susan Spicer	Bayona	New Orleans
1991	Larry Forgione	Beekman 1766 Tavern	Rhinebeck, NY
	Michel Richard	Citronelle (the first)	Santa Barbara, CA
	Chris Schlesinger	The Blue Room	Cambridge, MA
	Jean-Georges Vongerichten	Jojo	New York City
1992	Rick Bayless	Topolobompo	Chicago
	Emeril Lagasse	Nola	New Orleans
	Mark Miller	Red Sage	Washington, DC
1993	Daniel Boulud	Daniel	New York City
1994	Nobu Matsuhisa	Nobu	New York City
	Lydia Shire	Pignoli	Boston

four-star Manhattan restaurant Lafayette to provide maximum flavor with minimum fats through an array of juices, flavored oils, and infusions—techniques going back to the Egyptians.

Norman Van Aken takes credit for coining the term "fusion cuisine," referring to a harmonious combination of foods of various origins, popularized at restaurants ranging from Lydia Shire's restaurant Biba (Boston) to Susan Feniger and Mary Sue Milliken's City Restaurant (Los Angeles). The era of "political correctness" has pushed chefs to participate in a wide range of charitable events, many benefitting such organizations as Meals on Wheels, City Harvest, and Share Our Strength, which also help keep chefs and food in the media spotlight.

President Clinton's White House has also added high visibility to the American food movement, as Alice Waters and others lobbied for an end to French menus with French ingredients served with French wines (the menus written, of course, in French) at White House state dinners. In a letter to the President, Waters and dozens of other co-signing chefs urged him to appoint a White House chef who would promote American cooking, emphasizing local ingredients and organic food. Even celebrated French chef Paul Bocuse admitted that it was "ridiculous" for the White House not to have an American chef. In response, First Lady Hillary Rodham Clinton named her "Kitchen Cabinet" of American chef-advisors, including Larry Forgione of An American Place (NYC), Anne Rosenzweig of Arcadia (NYC), and John Snedden of Rocklands—Washington's Barbeque and Grilling Company (DC) before the Clinton administration's first official dinner. In March 1994, French-born White House executive chef Pierre Chambrin's resignation was accepted. Less than two months later, California-born Walter Scheib, a graduate of The Culinary Institute of America and executive chef of The Greenbrier, had taken over the position.

The influence of leading chefs cannot be underestimated. While they themselves can personally feed only a tiny fraction of the United States population, they train and inspire countless other chefs and cooks who spread their lessons through their own cooking across the country and around the

Letter to President Clinton, on Behalf of Chefs' Coalition for Chefs Helping to Enhance Food Safety

December 8, 1992

Dear President-elect Clinton:

We, chefs from across the country, believe that good food, pure and wholesome, should be not just a privilege for the few, but a right for everyone. Good food nourishes not just the body, but the entire community. It increases our awareness of the sources of life and of our responsibility to preserve all life-sustaining resources. Chefs know this, farmers know this, and with your leadership, the whole nation can be reminded of it. Good food is about seasonality, ripeness, and simplicity. Where there is good food—food that is delicious, wholesome, and responsibly produced—good health readily follows. The broader health of our nation is in peril. By your example at the White House, our hopes for the restoration of the nation's health will be nourished.

By promoting the value of organically grown fruits and vegetables, your table would reaffirm Thomas Jefferson's ideas of a nation of small farmers—caring custodians of the land whose work would greatly benefit from your endorsement. Similarly, a discriminating quest for fish and meat of quality would herald the need to care for our waters, pastures, and the areas surrounding them.

We urge you to select a White House chef who embraces this philosophy. The President's own table would then be a singular expression of long-absent values. Set with honesty and integrity, it would speak profoundly to the American people.

The coalition would welcome any opportunity to work with your office on this appointment and the important issues it addresses.

Respectfully,

Alice Waters for the Chefs' Coalition

Larry Forgione on American Food

I think absolutely, without any stretch of the imagination, the chef in the White House should be American. I think his influence or training should be American food. His fondness should be for American food. His knowledge should be of American foods. And I think when dignitaries and heads of state come to this country, they should only be served American food. I think it has been absurd over the years. The reason that I got involved and agreed to continue to be involved with the White House is that it's about time the head of our country serves the cuisine of our country. When our head of state or dignitaries travel to different countries, and they go to Germany, they get German food. If they go to Japan, they get Japanese food. I mean, dignitaries from other countries come to this country and get what? French food? It doesn't make any sense. It's like the White House is years behind what's going on. Again, this isn't a put-down of French chefs or French food—it's just out of place. It shouldn't be there.

Those two stories in the *New York Times* [on Forgione's participation in the Clinton White House's Kitchen Cabinet of American chefs] got more of a reaction than anything I've ever done in my life. I was called by every television station and interviewed by media from every European country. It was interesting that the rest of the world didn't know that we had American cuisine.

I always turn around and say, "You define French cooking to me, and I'll tell you what American cooking is." What's French cooking? A series of dishes that have French names? It's so hard to describe. What is Japanese cuisine? After being in Japan last summer, I realized that what I thought was Japanese food was a very small portion of what is Japanese food. So it's one of those things that we'd have to accept—that our country is made up of many, many influences, from almost every country in the world. When those settlers arrived in the Americas, they brought with them little parts of their country and heritage, maybe seeds of some of their favorite things, and were met by natives or the people there before them who had left a little bit of their country there.

You look at New England and you say, "What's New England cooking?" Well, the Portuguese seaports that cook food that is sort of Portuguese-Italian is as much New England cooking as anything else. Portuguese seafood stew from Port Judith in Rhode Island is as much New England cooking as a clam chowder. There is the influence of English cuisine, which is boiled dinners, creamed stews, and then you have the influence of the Portuguese settlers. You obviously have the influence of Native Americans. You have the influence of the French settling the area through Canada. You even have the influence of the Tropics, because of the trade triangle that existed. The Boston port would receive rum and spices from the East or West Indies. That's why when you go through old historic cookbooks, you'll find out that powdered ginger is an ingredient in old, old recipes for codcakes The dish that we do at An American Place—one of our most popular desserts—is called the Banana Betty. That's a combination of two very old New England desserts which incorporate gingersnaps and bananas and rum. Well, all those things came up on the trade ships. You find pineapple in a lot of old-fashioned dishes, like pineapple upside-down cake. That's New England. Where did it come from? The pineapples came from the coast, the brown sugar and rum from the Islands.

If you look at the old Junior League cookbooks—well, the Junior League of Richmond, Virginia, could only get the ingredients that were in Richmond, Virginia. Nobody would ever think that curry has anything to do with American cooking. Curry is a very intricate part of Georgia, because Savannah was the port which the ships came from the Indies would come back to. And a dish called "Country Captain Chicken" is a classic dish from Savannah. When the sailors would bring back their pouches of curry powder, their wives would prepare for them this curried chicken dish upon their arrival back in port. So here we have chicken curry during the 1800s in America. So is that part of American cuisine? Or does the [imported] curry not make it American cuisine?

world. Some chefs have branched out into their own business ventures—such as Wolfgang Puck's (frozen) Spago Original California Pizza and Larry Forgione's American Spoon Foods—to make their products available to a wider audience. In a growing trend, major food and food service corporations, from American Airlines to Kraft General

Foods, consult with leading chefs on improving and expanding their own offerings. In addition, the chefs' writing and political activism touch people who might not ever have eaten their food.

Today, the best American chefs are considered world class, and are influencing and even exciting young French chefs. According to Daniel Boulud, a native of France, "Many American chefs are definitely superior—in their cooking, in promoting themselves." He adds, "(When many French chefs) come to America, they get a real kick in the butt."

A Profession Growing by Leaps and Bounds

The restaurant industry employs more than six million people, making it the country's largest retail employer. Chefs, cooks, and other kitchen workers hold over three million jobs in the United States. Job openings in these positions are expected to increase faster than the average for all occupations through the year 2000, according to the U.S. Bureau of Labor Statistics—at a rate of 50,000 to 85,000 cooks a year. These factors led to the profession's being named as one of the top ten careers for the 1990s in terms of growth opportunities.

While workers under 25 have traditionally filled a significant proportion of these jobs, the pool of young workers is expected to shrink through the year 2000. Thus, older career-changers will likely help fill the gap. For example, upwards of 45 percent of the students at the California Culinary Academy come from nonfoodservice backgrounds, and have an average age of 28. Career-changers also represent about 50 percent of the students at the New York Restaurant School.

Further Recommended Reading

Aris, Pepita, ed. *Master Chefs of Europe*. Van Nostrand Reinhold, 1988.

Hobhouse, Caroline. *Great European Chefs*. Van Nostrand Reinhold, 1990.

Jones, Evan. *American Food: The Gastronomic Story*. The Overlook Press, 1992.

Lang, Jenifer Harvey, ed. *Larousse Gastronomique: The New American Edition of the World's Greatest Culinary Encyclopedia*. Crown Publishers, 1988.

Mariani, John. *America Eats Out: An Illustrated History of Restaurants, Taverns, Coffee Shops, Speakeasies, & Other Establishments That Have Fed Us for 350 Years*. William Morrow and Company, Inc., 1991.

Willan, Anne. *Great Cooks and Their Recipes. From Taillevent to Escoffier*. Bullfinch Press, 1992.

Emeril's Portuguese Kale Soup

EMERIL LAGASSE
Emeril's and NOLA
New Orleans, LA

"When I think of my childhood in Fall River, Massachusetts, I remember a happy blur of Portuguese festivals, wonderful celebrations of music, dance, and food from the old country. The feast was known as buon fester, *or "good festival," and the dish that stands out in my memory from the festivals is the* suppische kaldene, *or kale soup. This unusual soup was prepared many ways, often with chorizo, split peas, and mint accompanying the base of kale, potatoes, and stock. When I became chef at Commander's Palace, I made kale soup for the staff, substituting local andouille sausage for the Portuguese chorizo. The response was so enthusiastic, I began to run kale soup as a special on the menu in the spring and fall when the kale is in season in Louisiana. There's even a sweet little Portuguese song about* suppische kaldene, *but I'll spare you."*

. . . .

2 tablespoons olive oil

3 cups chorizo, sliced in 1/2-inch rounds

1 cup chopped onions

2 tablespoons minced fresh garlic

1/4 cup coarsely chopped fresh parsley

3 cups diced peeled potatoes, about 2 large (1/4-inch dice)

4 quarts chicken stock

6 cups kale, rinsed, stemmed, and leaves torn into pieces

2 bay leaves

1/4 teaspoon dried thyme leaves

1 1/2 teaspoons salt

1/4 teaspoon dried crushed red pepper

5 turns fresh ground black pepper

finishing touch: 1/2 cup chopped fresh mint (optional)

. . . .

1. Heat the oil in a large pot over high heat. When the oil is hot, add the chorizo and the onions and saute, stirring once or twice, about 2 minutes. Add the garlic, parsley, and potatoes and cook, stirring occasionally, about 2 minutes.

2. Add the stock and kale and bring to a boil. Stir in the bay leaves, thyme, salt, red pepper, and black pepper. Reduce the heat to medium and simmer until the potatoes are fork-tender, about 30 minutes. Remove from the heat and skim the fat from the top. Makes 14 cups.

3. To serve, pour about 1 1/4 cups of the soup in each bowl and stir in 1/2 teaspoon of the mint, allowing it to infuse for a minute or two. Serve with a crusty Portuguese or French bread.

Serves 8 as a main course

2 EARLY INFLUENCES

Discovering a Passion for Food

"This is not a profession that you
choose. It chooses you."

—Norman Van Aken

> *"A good cook who is born with an interest in gastronomy will naturally become, under favorable circumstances, a more accomplished artist than the individual to whom cooking is an unpleasant task."*
>
> —ESCOFFIER (1846–1935)

You would not be holding this book in your hands if there wasn't something about the idea of cooking that strikes a chord within you. What is the origin of that chord, of that instinctive urge to work with food? Are chefs born or made?

Some chefs are convinced that great chefs are born with that potential. Alice Waters believes, "Most of it's in the genes. The really good cooks seem to just have a natural ability. They don't exactly learn it—it's just in them." Susanna Foo has found that, "A good chef is born with a good palate, just as a good musician is born with good ears."

Other chefs feel that all influences are important. Jean-Louis Palladin feels lucky to have had a Spanish mother and an Italian father. "All that genetic influence was put together in my subconscious." On the other hand, he credits external influences, too, particularly his childhood in the south of France. Almost all of the chefs we interviewed brought up transformational events in their early lives which elevated food to a special level of importance.

This comes as no surprise to Mark Miller, a former college instructor, who says, "Children reach consciousness between the ages of five and seven. Basic personality, taste, and aesthetic ability are formed that early. So it is very important to have a multitude of culinary experiences at an early age. I had those—I was lucky." Lydia Shire agrees, and counts herself as fortunate for having artists as parents, whom she credits with teaching her about aesthetics and design. Shire says, "To be good in this profession, you need to have something really special working for you. It could be how you were reared as a child, what your parents did, what kind of values they instilled in you. Some of this has to start when you're young." Jasper White is even more specific. "Most of the really good chefs that I've met have a connection that started in the embryonic stage," he says. "It has to be instilled—a love for food comes from your family."

In sharing the backgrounds of leading chefs, our purpose is to show that passion and greatness have a variety of origins. While some few were fortunate enough to have eaten in some of the world's finest restaurants as children, others were raised on good (and sometimes even bad) home cooking. The important thing was not always the food itself, but the meaning which was attached to it. "Even eating a hot dog can be a peak experience," points out Chris Schlesinger. Certainly, these chefs' early lives were filled with a wide variety of peak food experiences.

There is no single, straight and narrow path to becoming a chef, and perhaps more than anything, the diversity of the lives of the chefs we interviewed illustrates this fact. The key that unites leading chefs is merely the fact that they absorbed and used what they learned about food, wherever they learned it—cooking at home, learning from relatives or neighbors, growing up on a farm, eating out in restaurants, being raised in a restaurant family, even watching cooking shows on TV.

Early influences establish an encyclopedia of tastes and ideas that becomes a foundation for future work. For example, cooking with raspberries recalls every experience a chef has ever had with a raspberry which has been recorded in his or her memory bank. While other influences may shape and update a particular dish, the influence of the original raspberry is still there. Your own food history and food memory indirectly shape every dish you produce. It's important to be in touch with those memories and to understand how they are shaping the way you cook. Being in touch with the experiences involving food that made food important to you at a young age provides a context for all the ideas about food you will have later. While it's easy to overanalyze food, your experiences bring food back to a personal level, which helps takes your cooking beyond rote. It's also useful to be able to tap positive food memories, as your pleasurable associations with food are what can keep you going when long hours of hard work challenge your dedication.

I still remember weekends spent harvesting walnuts from the four walnut trees at home. Dad would use a pole to knock the nuts off the trees and at the age of six, I would run around with a bucket, gathering them up. We'd pour them by the bucketful into burlap sacks, which we'd store in the cellar. The ones we cracked and ate on the spot weren't anything like the dried walnuts they'd become months later, which were slightly bitter. The fresh ones were sweet and moist, with a thin, tan skin. Even now, I particularly enjoy cooking with walnuts. This is not only because when they're featured on the menu it means they're around for me to snack on in the kitchen, but because my greater knowledge of ingredients and techniques now helps me to be able to use their flavor and texture

Anne Rosenzweig of Arcadia (NYC) always watched Julia Child on TV: "It was the only TV show I was allowed to watch," she explains.

Terrine of Foie Gras, Black Truffles, and Tricolored Pasta with Prosciutto and Fresh Herb-Tomato Sauce

JEAN-LOUIS PALLADIN

Jean-Louis at the Watergate Hotel
Washington, DC

"I was very lucky to have a Spanish mother and an Italian father. During my youth, I was raised with different kinds of food, and only food that came from their farm. They didn't need to buy anything, because everything was there: all the vegetables, fruit trees, the pig, different kinds of poultry, duck and geese for foie gras and confit. One recipe I remember to this day that was very popular in Italy was baked lasagna, and my mother did it very well.

"In my mind, I tried to see if I could create a recipe, doing a different dish while keeping the same meaning. I came up with a terrine of lasagna of different colors with foie gras (because I was practically born inside a duck or a goose) and the treasure of our soil, the black truffle. I am very proud of this recipe, which always reminds me of my mother."

Makes 22 (1/2-inch) slices or 1 (11 x 3 1/4 x 2 1/2-inch) terrine

. . . .

Tricolored Pasta Dough (recipe follows)

1 1/2 lbs. semi-preserved pure duck or goose foie gras, well chilled*

Fine sea salt and freshly ground black pepper

. . . .

Aspic

. . . .

3 (1/4 oz.) packages unflavored gelatin

2 cups cold meat or vegetable consommé

6 quarts water for cooking pasta

1/4 cup coarse salt for cooking pasta

2 tablespoons extra-virgin olive oil for cooking pasta

4 1/2 oz. flash-frozen black truffles, thawed and cut into paper-thin slices

1 recipe chilled Prosciutto and Fresh Herb Tomato Sauce (recipe follows)

a few drops of heavy cream for garnish (optional)

. . . .

© 1989 by Jean-Louis Palladin, *Jean-Louis: Cooking with the Seasons.*

Special utensils

Large, very broad-based pot for cooking pasta (broad enough to cook at least two 12 x 5 inch rectangles of pasta at a time without crowding)

Pâté terrine mold, 5-cup capacity, inside dimension 11 inches long, 3 1/4 inches wide, and 2 1/2 inches deep

2 pieces fairly sturdy cardboard cut to just fit inside the top of the terrine mold, stacked and sealed together with foil to form one sturdy piece

About 2 1/2 pounds of weights

*If available, use the 2 3/4-inch-diameter foie gras log, since its diameter just fits into the terrine mold called for in this recipe.

Method

Prepare the Tricolored Pasta dough. While dough is resting for 1 hour, slice the foie gras. To do this, line a cookie sheet with parchment or waxed paper; set aside. Heat a sharp thin-bladed knife in hot water and wipe dry; then, if using the 2 3/4-inch foie gras log, cut it crosswise into twenty 5/8-inch thick slices, heating and drying the knife before cutting each slice; if using the foie gras of another shape or diameter, cut into 5/8-inch thick slices that are as close in size to the width and length of the mold as possible (so they require a minimum amount of trimming and piecing together when layered in the mold). With a spatula, transfer slices in a single layer to the prepared cookie sheet, being careful to keep them intact. Season tops generously with salt and pepper. Cover and refrigerate.

Next roll out the pasta dough as directed in the recipe. Set pasta rectangles aside.

Now make the aspic by softening the gelatin in 1/2 cup of the consommé for about 2 minutes. Bring the remaining 1 1/2 cups consommé to a boil in a small pot, then remove from heat and stir in the gelatin. Return to high heat and cook and stir just a few seconds until gelatin completely dissolves. Set aspic aside at room temperature while cooking the pasta, then assemble the terrine.

Cook the pasta and assemble the terrine

Combine the water, salt, and oil in the large broad-based pot; bring to a rolling boil over high heat. Meanwhile, prepare a large baking pan of ice water for cooling the pasta once cooked; the pan should be wider and longer than the rectangles and at least 3 inches deep. Cook 1/2 of each color of rectangle, about 2 rectangles at a time, uncovered in the boiling water for 1 1/2 minutes without turning, making sure each rectangle is submerged at least during the first few seconds of cooking (do not overcook). Immediately transfer rectangles with a broad skimmer or spatula to the ice water to cool, being very careful not to rip them

(Continued on next page)

(don't leave them in the ice water more than 15 minutes); then transfer to a cookie sheet lined with parchment or waxed paper, spreading the rectangles flat and leaving them quite wet. The rectangles may be stacked, but keep the 3 colors separated. Replenish water in cooking pot, if needed. When 1/2 of each color of rectangle is cooked, set aside cooking water, ice water, and uncooked rectangles.

Before proceeding, it may be helpful to keep in mind that the assembled terrine will consist of 6 layers of pasta rectangles (each layer is composed of one rectangle of each color), alternated with 5 layers of foie gras and 4 layers of truffles. As you work, trim the pasta rectangles to fit the mold; if you run out of pasta, cook more and continue assembling terrine. Gently reheat the aspic to liquify again if needed.

To assemble the terrine, first pour 1/4 cup of the aspic into the bottom of the ungreased terrine mold, then add a layer of pasta (1 rectangle of each color). Cover pasta layer with 1/5 of the foie gras slices, trimming them to fit the mold and filling any large gaps with the trimmings. Next, add 1/4 cup more aspic or enough to bring the liquid level up to cover the foie gras layer, then add another layer of pasta, then 1/4 of the truffle slices. Continue adding a layer of foie gras, then pasta, then truffles, until all the foie gras and truffles have been used; end with a layer of pasta. After the last layer of pasta has been added, add more aspic to bring the liquid level up to the top of the last layer of pasta.

Once assembled, place mold on a small cookie sheet and cover mold well with plastic wrap. Position the foil-covered cardboard on top to rest directly on the top layer of pasta and distribute weights evenly over the cardboard. Refrigerate at least overnight or until the day of serving.

To finish the dish: one day ahead or early on the day of serving, make the Prosciutto and Fresh Herb-Tomato Sauce; refrigerate until ready to serve.

Prosciutto and Fresh Herb-Tomato Sauce

. . . .

1/4 cup extra-virgin olive oil

1 1/2 cups chopped onions

1/2 cup chopped shallots

2 tablespoons chopped garlic

1/2 lb. prosciutto, finely chopped

6 cups peeled and coarsely chopped vine-ripened tomatoes

2 cups meat or vegetable consommé (preferred) or meat or vegetable stock

1 cup chardonnay wine

1 cup V–8 juice

1 (6 oz.) can tomato paste

3 cups (about 2 oz.) loosely packed fresh basil leaves

15 large parsley sprigs

10 very leafy thyme sprigs

1 tablespoon fine sea salt

about 30 turns freshly ground black pepper

15 dill sprigs (optional)

7 sage sprigs (optional)

....

Special utensils
A very fine mesh strainer or chinois

Method
Heat the oil in a nonreactive 6-quart saucepan or casserole over high heat for 1 minute. Add the onions and shallots and sauté about 1 minute, stirring occasionally. Add the garlic and cook 1 minute. Add the prosciutto and cook 1 minute more. Add the tomatoes, 2 cups of the consommé, the wine, V–8 juice, tomato paste, basil leaves, parsley and thyme sprigs, salt, pepper, and, if using, the dill and sage sprigs, stirring well. Bring to a boil. Reduce heat and strongly simmer for 1 hour, stirring occasionally. Purée mixture in batches in a blender and strain purée through the strainer or chinois, using the bottom of a sturdy ladle to force as much through as possible. Refrigerate until well chilled, at least 3 hours or overnight, before serving. If needed, thin with more consommé just before serving. Makes about 5 cups.

Before serving
At least 2 hours before serving, unmold the terrine as follows: remove weights, cardboard, and plastic wrap. Place mold in a deep pan large enough to have room to spare between the mold and pan sides. Fill pan with 1 1/2 inches of boiling water and let sit for precisely 2 minutes; then remove mold from hot water, heat the blade of a thin flexible-bladed knife, and carefully loosen sides with it. Invert onto a cookie sheet lined with parchment or waxed paper, a cutting board suitable for refrigeration, or a serving platter if you wish to present the terrine to your guests before slicing it. If the terrine doesn't immediately slip out of the mold, loosen sides again or soundly tap mold, right side up, once or twice on a solid surface; invert again, and it should slip out easily. Cover loosely and refrigerate until just before ready to present unsliced to guests or until ready to slice and serve.

To serve
For best results, slice the terrine while well chilled so it will be as firm as possible. Heat a sharp thin-bladed knife in hot water, wipe dry, and carefully cut the terrine crosswise into 1/2-inch slices; reheat and dry knife before cutting each slice. With a spatula, transfer a slice to each chilled serving plate and top with freshly ground pepper. Taste sauce for seasoning, then spoon about 2 tablespoons alongside each slice. If desired, garnish sauce with a drop or two of cream swirled with the tip of a paring knife. Serve immediately. Refrigerate leftovers.

(Continued on next page)

Tricolored Pasta Dough

....

1/4 cup plus 2 tablespoons Parsley Purée

2 cups plus 2 tablespoons finely ground semolina flour

1 teaspoon fine sea salt

1 tablespoon plus 1 teaspoon extra-virgin olive oil

4 large eggs

About 3 3/4 cups all-purpose flour, plus flour for rolling out dough

1/4 cup water

2 egg yolks (from large eggs)

1/2 cup plus 2 tablespoons tomato paste

....

Special utensils
Pasta machine

Method
First make the parsley purée.

Parsley Purée

Makes 3 to 4 tablespoons

....

6 to 7 oz. parsley sprigs (about 2 large bunches)

salt water (1/4 cup coarse salt mixed with 3 quarts water)
for cooking parsley sprigs

ice water for cooling cooked parsley sprigs

2 tablespoons vegetable oil

....

Method

Trim any thick stems from the parsley sprigs; discard trimmings. Bring the salt water to a rolling boil in a large nonreactive pot over high heat. Add the parsley sprigs and cook for 2 minutes. Immediately drain and cool in the ice water. Drain again and squeeze dry. Purée in a food processor with the oil until smooth. Strain purée through the strainer using the bottom of a sturdy ladle to force as much through as possible. Use immediately or cover and refrigerate until ready to use. The purée will keep up to 5 days refrigerated.

To continue the dough

Prepare the basic dough for all 3 (yellow, green, and red) pastas as follows: in the large bowl of an electric mixer fitted with a paddle, combine the semolina, salt, oil, and eggs. Beat at medium speed until well blended, about 1 minute. The dough will still be quite wet and sticky at this point. Flour hands with all-purpose flour and form dough into a ball. Cut the ball into 3 equal portions and wrap 2 of them separately in plastic wrap. Make the remaining portion into yellow pasta dough.

For the yellow dough, break the portion of basic dough into 5 pieces and return them to the bowl of the electric mixer. Add 1 1/4 cups of the all-purpose flour and the water and egg yolks. Beat at medium speed until dough forms a soft supple ball, about 2 minutes; if dough is still sticky, beat in up to about 2 tablespoons more all-purpose flour, 1 tablespoon at a time. Wrap in plastic wrap and set aside.

To make the green pasta dough break another portion of the basic dough into 5 pieces and place them in the electric mixer bowl. Add 3/4 cup plus 2 tablespoons all-purpose flour and the parsley purée. Beat at medium speed until dough forms a soft, supple ball and is an even color, about 2 minutes; if dough is still sticky, beat in about 2 more tablespoons more all-purpose flour, 1 tablespoon at a time. Wrap in plastic wrap and set aside.

For the red pasta dough, break the remaining portion of basic dough into 5 pieces and place in a clean electric mixer bowl. Add 1 1/4 cups all-purpose flour and the tomato paste. Beat at medium speed until dough forms a soft, supple ball and is an even color, about 2 minutes; if dough is still sticky, beat in up to about 2 tablespoons more all-purpose flour, 1 tablespoon at a time. Wrap in plastic wrap and set aside.

Let all 3 doughs rest, covered, for about 1 hour before rolling out.

To roll out the dough

Roll out each color of dough separately. To do this, unwrap 1 of the doughs (yellow, green, or red) and lightly flour with all-purpose flour. Roll through the pasta machine 10 times on the thickest setting of the machine. Fold it in half after each rolling. Next, roll dough through once on each setting, this time without folding in half after each rolling, progressing from the thickest to the thinnest. If needed, lightly flour dough so it doesn't stick, and cut into manageable lengths. Once dough has gone through the thinnest setting, roll it through an extra time. Now cut the dough into about 12 x 5-inch rectangles. Stack and set aside (they don't need to be covered). Repeat with remaining dough, keeping all 3 colors separated. Makes about 3 pounds dough or enough for 1 terrine.

(Continued on next page)

Consommé

Makes about 1 to 3 quarts consommé
For vegetable stock, simply omit the ground beef or fish from the clarification process.

. . . .

1 1/2 to 3 1/2 quarts strained beef, veal, poultry, lobster, or vegetable stock

1/4 cup unpeeled finely chopped carrots

1/4 cup finely chopped celery

1/4 cup finely chopped onions

1/4 cup finely chopped leeks (white and green parts)

1/4 cup unpeeled finely chopped turnips

1/4 cup unpeeled finely chopped tomatoes

2 tablespoons finely chopped shallots

4 large parsley sprigs

1 large garlic clove, peeled and minced

6 oz. scallops or skinned and coarsely chopped fillets of pike, halibut, or flounder or 6 oz. of lean ground beef

1 cup egg whites (from about 8 large eggs)

fine sea salt and freshly ground black pepper

. . . .

in particular dishes in ways which enhance my, and (I hope) others', enjoyment of them. It's always more pleasurable to cook with ingredients you like rather than with those you don't. I find when I cook with walnuts, for example, that whether it's the first or the 21st such dish I've made that night, I can't wait to taste it when it's done and to send it out to the dining room. While I don't expect the customer to enjoy the dish in the same personal way I do, I hope that some of my passion for it comes through on their plate.

Some of the experiences of the chefs we interviewed regarding their important early experiences, which served to influence and inspire their own cooking, follow.

Deep 4-quart saucepan or other large deep pot with a relatively small (about 8-inch) diameter so clarification ingredients can form a fairly thick crust-like layer across the stock as it clarifies
Chinois
Cheesecloth

Method

Skim the stock thoroughly and bring to a boil in the saucepan. Meanwhile, in a food processor, mince together the carrots, celery, onions, leeks, turnips, tomatoes, shallots, parsley sprigs, garlic, and the scallops or fish, if using. Transfer mixture to a large bowl and add the egg whites and the beef, if using; mix thoroughly. Add mixture to the boiling stock and bring to a very slow simmer, stirring gently during the first 2 to 3 minutes of cooking to prevent sticking (disturb the surface as little as possible while stirring so a layer of solids can form across it). Reduce heat and, without stirring, continue very slowly simmering 45 minutes more; keep stock from strongly bubbling so a fairly thick crust-like layer can develop over the surface. Remove from the heat.

Line the chinois with 8 or more thicknesses of damp cheesecloth and ladle consommé through it into a large bowl, leaving crust behind in pan; do not force consommé through chinois, or food particles may also slip through.

Once strained, the consommé should be amber-colored, completely translucent, and free of particles or fat globules. If not, use one or more of the following corrective procedures: skim the surface until clear by laying single sheets of toilet tissue across the surface—just for a second—and then lifting them off; and/or continue straining consommé through the cheesecloth until clear and/or refrigerate until the fat congeals on the surface and it can be lifted off.

Season the finished consommé to taste with salt and pepper. Use immediately, refrigerate, or freeze (in freezer containers or in covered ice cube trays) until ready to use. Consommé keeps well refrigerated for up to about 3 days and frozen for up to 4 weeks.

Cooking or baking at home is, naturally, often the first exposure many children have to cooking. Whether relatives provide role models, or whether experimentation alone teaches the basics, cooking at home is often a chef's first laboratory. Alfred Portale recalls following the recipe for Toll House Chocolate Chip Cookies on the back of the Nestlé Semi-Sweet Morsels bag, and being compelled to modify it to his liking. "For years, I would make them. I remember adjusting the recipe because I liked chewier ones, so I would reduce the amount of flour," he says. How did the young Portale know to do so? He reasoned, "The instructions read, 'If you want a more

HOME COOKING

Kougelhopf

JEAN JOHO
Everest
Chicago, IL

"As a young man I always made kougelhopf on Saturday for Sunday morning's breakfast. This was for two reasons: Kougelhopf is always better the second day, and Sunday morning was the only morning my father had breakfast with the family."

. . . .

1 oz. brewers yeast

3/4 pint milk

2 1/4 cups plain flour

1/2 oz. salt

3 eggs

10 oz. butter

5 oz. sugar

5 oz. pitless sultanas

optional extra: a small glass of kirsch

2 1/2 oz. almonds

. . . .

cakelike cookie, add flour' or something like that, so I just assumed if you took some of the flour out, they'd be chewier. And I was right."

French-born André Soltner recalls, "During the four years of war in Alsace, we were considered a part of Germany [by the Germans], so we couldn't go to the other part of France. But right after the war, as soon as we [were liberated], my mother went to visit an aunt in the south of France for about four weeks, because we'd had no contact with her [during the war]. I was about 13, and

1. First prepare the dough with the yeast, half of the milk, warmed, and sufficient flour to make a dough of average consistency; leave the dough in a warm place.

2. In a separate basin, mix the remaining flour with the salt, eggs, and the rest of the warm milk and knead energetically for about 15 minutes, lifting the mixture with the hands.

3. Add the butter and sugar, softening the mixture in your hands, and knead in the dough, which will have doubled in volume.

4. Continue to knead for a few minutes, cover the bowl with a cloth, and leave to settle in a warm place for about an hour.

5. Knead again, break open the dough, mix in the sultanas (steeped beforehand in kirsch or in water) and then (optional) add a small glass of kirsch.

6. Grease thoroughly the bottom and ridges of the kougelhopf mould, decorate the bottom with almonds which should, if possible, be peeled and wiped, and then place the dough into the mould.

7. Once more, leave the dough to rise until it reaches the top edge of the mould and then place in the oven on a medium heat.

8. If the kougelhopf browns too quickly, cover with a sheet of paper; bake for about 3/4 hour.

Accompany with a Gewurztraminer or a Cremant D'Alsace

Makes 4 to 5 servings

Gary Danko of The Ritz-Carlton (San Francisco) used to love to bake as a child: "My mother saw this tendency to cook, so I spent a lot of time with her, with cookbooks like the Betty Crocker Boys and Girls Cookbook."

I took over cooking for my father and my brother, completely—you know, making dessert tartes, everything. I loved to cook, and my father and my brother loved what I cooked. They'd come home at noon from work and I had everything ready—more food than my mother had, because maybe she was more concerned about budget, and I was not concerned at all. I'm still not concerned! But when my mother came back, she thought I'd spent too much money."

Soltner confesses that at first he wanted to become a cabinet-maker, like his father. "But I had a brother four years older than

Edward Brown of The Sea Grill (NYC) used to "play restaurant" at home when he was nine or ten, with his sisters serving as the waitresses. "I would make omelettes, and snip chives from the garden into the omelettes to order. Cooking was the special thing that I could do."

Lydia Shire on Early Influences

Both my parents were artists, commercial fashion illustrators. I was surrounded by art and by a mother who told me that black was the absence of color. She never liked black, and to this day I don't like black. She got me so excited about things that I love to this day, like lots of color and things that uplift you. I'm happy that my parents started out by teaching me about painting, design, how to look at something, why something is of good quality, why it looks great, why you might put a bit of pepper on this side of the plate but not all over the plate because, as in all good art, it's not asymmetrical.

They were of middle class, of middle income. I would get one new outfit for school, but my mother would go to Best & Company or one of the other better stores, and I would have a real Scottish plaid skirt and that would be it. I would say, "Well, all my friends have seven new outfits," but they were all less expensive or they'd get them at Zayre or some[place] like that. I always say, "I taught my children the difference between cotton and polyester." At Christmastime, my kids never have to return my presents. Why? Because I know what quality is, because I've developed my aesthetic sensibility. Of course, when I was young I didn't understand why, but now I think, "Thank God my parents were the way they were and that I learned those little differences."

My father was Irish, and my mother's Yankee, as in English Yankee. My father was a great cook. He was very soft spoken, very quiet. He was also an alcoholic, but a quiet alcoholic. He used to cut out recipes from *The New York Times* and, after he'd worked all day, he would come home and start cooking. He would make veal scallopine with marsala sauce—he would take fresh mushrooms and cut

me, and at this time it was the eldest brother who was supposed to take over the parents' business. So he became a cabinetmaker, and when I was thinking, at the age of 14, that I wanted to be a cabinetmaker, too, my mother said, 'No way. No two in the same business.' And because I was in the kitchen a lot with my mother, I said, 'No problem for me, I want to be a chef.' And then my parents looked for an apprenticeship for me. Otherwise, maybe, I would have become a cabinetmaker," Soltner says, causing the culinary world to shudder.

them up and sauté them in a pan with a little piece of veal. This was when I was eight years old, so this was back in 1956. If you consider the time, a man would have to be pretty dedicated to want to come home and do those things.

We would have rare flank steak on Saturday night, and spaghetti aglio olio, which is still to this day my favorite dinner in the world. He used to put newspapers on the floor and he would use an old cast-iron pancake griddle and really sear the flank steak. He would press it down a little so that it would stay flat and get really black. Then he would let it rest. I remember him saying, "We don't cut it right now"—he knew instinctively that you shouldn't cut hot meat right away, or else all the juices would come flying out. Then he would always put butter on the meat, so you'd get this great juice.

Because I was the youngest kid in the family, he would pour the meat juice for me into a little Chinese Canton cup (my mother and father had a collection of Canton dishes). I would get to drink the juice, or what we'd call "the bottom of the bowl"—you know, when you make spaghetti aglio olio, some of the garlic kind of sinks to the bottom? I would eat all that garlic up. That's why to this day, garlic is my favorite thing in the world. It's what I crave.

My mother cooked, but she would take all day to make an apple pie. She's a very good cook, but I think because my father shined in the kitchen, he kind of ended up doing all the fancy things. When they would have dinner parties, they would have little linen cocktail napkins—I still have some of my mother's great cocktail napkins. They'd have a real martini pitcher and stirrers for your drinks—I still have some of those stirrers. It's of a day that's gone. That's why my dream now is to open a very fancy cocktail bar with great bar food and little linen napkins and things like that. I think it would be great. It will happen, someday.

FAMILIES OF SERIOUS COOKS

Growing up surrounded by good cooks and, consequently, good food, awakened many chefs' taste buds at an early age. Leading chefs can recall their early food memories in remarkably vivid detail. Jasper White describes his grandmother as "insane" about food. "She was totally passionate," he says. As a child, before weekend trips with his family to visit his grandmother, White would call her to plan the weekend menu. His favorite dishes included apple fritters for breakfast. "My love for food was eating it, not working

Apple Fritters

JASPER WHITE

Jasper's
Boston, MA

"The smell of my grandmother's kitchen in the morning would wake the dead. An early riser, she would start baking and cooking as soon as the sun came up and within an hour, everyone else would be awake, not because of the noise but because of the intoxicating aromas that filled the house. Apple fritters were a special favorite of my brothers and me. We could eat them as fast as she could make them, but she would keep up with us until we could eat no more. My grandmother inspired me to be a chef, like her father was."

. . . .

2 cups all-purpose flour

1 tablespoon baking powder

1/2 cup sugar

1 tablespoon salt

2 eggs

Some Chefs' Best-Loved Childhood Foods*

Larry Forgione	His grandmother's chocolate layer cake
Mary Sue Milliken	Veal tongue
Bradley Ogden	Mom's pot roast, rhubarb pie
Chris Schlesinger	Barbecue
Lydia Shire	Spaghetti aglio olio; rare flank steak
Jasper White	His grandmother's apple fritters

*many have appeared on the chefs' menus

2/3 cup milk

4 large firm green or other tart apples, peeled, cored and sliced 1/4 inch thick

2 tablespoons unsalted butter, melted

vegetable oil for deep-frying

confectioners, sugar for dusting

....

1. Sift together the flour, baking powder, sugar, and salt in a mixing bowl. Mix well.

2. Beat the eggs and milk together and add the flour mixture, stirring until smooth.

3. Fold in the sliced apples and melted butter. Allow batter to stand at least 10 minutes before using.

4. Heat the oil to 375 degrees in a pot suitable for deep-frying. Drop large spoonfuls of batter, the size of a walnut, into the hot oil. Cook the fritters for a few minutes until they are golden brown or even a little darker. Drain onto paper towels. Dust with confectioners sugar and serve at once.

Makes six to eight breakfast or dessert portions

with it," White admits. "I never touched food, really, as a child. All the time I spent with my grandmother, I just sat there and watched her do the cooking. I never cooked. I just ate it, that's all. And still my great love is eating it, you know. That's still the bottom line for me."

Through his grandmother, White developed what he termed an "Italian respect" for good, fresh local ingredients. This included traveling to the "best" apple orchard where, at a young age, he learned to taste the difference in the quality of produce. White attributes his solid connection with food in part to his father, a farmer and hunter. "I don't really particularly like hunting, but I do like game and I do

Mark Miller of Coyote Cafe (Santa Fe) and Red Sage (Washington, DC) recalls that, as a child of four or five, at mealtime he would offer such comments to his mother as, "This sauce is too oily."

know how to hunt and fish, and it was all because of him. I think I had, clearly, a very solid connection to where food comes from and how it gets on the table. That's still the focus of what I do today. Really, the ingredients are everything to me."

Edna Lewis recalls, "In Washington, DC, even during slavery time, some of the diplomats would send their cooks to French cooking schools, and that would create a lot of good cooking around Washington. My aunt had cooked in Washington, and came back and lived three towns away. I used to go and visit her, and her kitchen smelled divine. She was a great cook. I didn't cook at her house, but I just tasted her food and noted what she was doing. She had a dime on the table all the time for her baking soda, and a nickel for her cream of tartar. I think that was pretty common, using a dime and a nickel [to measure out the soda and tartar in a 1:2 ratio to make one's own baking powder].

"They killed hogs, and she would cook the head and the jaw and the liver, and she would boil it all together and add spices and cook it until it fell apart. Then, she would grind it all up and make sausage. It was the best sausage in the world. And she always had a pound cake ready in case anyone dropped in. It was absolutely delicious! So when I left home, I knew what good food tasted like."

ON THE FARM

Chefs who spent time as kids living near or on a farm had a jump on learning, often without realizing it. They learned about product seasonality through the types of vegetables grown and eaten at different times of year. They also learned how to tell when something was ripe, at the same age the rest of us were learning how to tie our shoelaces.

Daniel Boulud grew up in the French countryside, where he became attuned to the seasonal cycle. "There's a season, for example, in late February, early March for baby goat. For about a month and a half we would eat baby goat twice a week. Then after that, there is squab. Than after that, you start to have all the game, the birds. There was a peak for everything."

Seeing how hard his parents worked on their farm, from five in the morning

Granny's Chocolate Cake

LARRY FORGIONE

An American Place
New York, NY

"For a long time, this was the only cake on the menu. We began serving it when we opened An American Place in 1983, and everyone loved it. When I was growing up, it was one of my favorites. We have modified the recipe from the days when my Irish grandmother made a similar cake on request for my birthday every year, but the spirit is the same. When Granny made the cake, she put an inch of fudge frosting between every inch-high layer, which made it a really big cake; eating it meant having as much fudge as cake. The cake should never be refrigerated but kept under a cake dome. If you refrigerate it, it will dry out."

Cake

. . . .

2 1/3 cups flour

1 teaspoon baking soda

1/2 teaspoon baking powder

1/2 teaspoon salt

1 teaspoon vanilla extract

1 1/4 cups buttermilk

11 tablespoons (1 stick plus 3 tablespoons) unsalted butter,
at room temperature

1 1/2 cups sugar

3 large eggs

4 oz. unsweetened chocolate, melted

. . . .

Michael Foley's family had a 400-acre farm on the west side of Chicago. "It was a feed farm with livestock, tree fruit, berry fruit, vegetables. We raised barnyard animals out there. I got quite an education on the farmland."

(Continued on next page)

Fudge frosting

....

6 oz. semisweet chocolate

1/2 cup plus 2 tablespoons water

Pinch of salt

1 1/2 teaspoons vanilla extract

10 tablespoons (1 stick plus 2 tablespoons) unsalted butter, melted

7 large egg yolks, beaten

5 cups confectioners' sugar

....

Preheat the oven to 350° F. Butter three 9-inch round layer cake pans and line them with parchment paper. Lightly butter the paper. Dust the pans with flour and shake out the excess.

Sift together the flour, baking soda, baking powder, and salt. In a small bowl, combine the vanilla and buttermilk.

Using an electric mixer set at medium-high, cream the butter until soft. Slowly add the sugar and continue beating until well blended and light colored. Add the eggs, one a time, beating well after each addition. Add alternating amounts of the dry ingredients and the vanilla-buttermilk mixture to the batter, mixing well after each addition. When the batter is smooth, stir in the melted chocolate. Blend until the batter is smooth and even-colored.

Spoon the batter evenly into the prepared pans. Smooth the tops with a rubber spatula. Bake for 30 to 35 minutes or until a toothpick inserted in the center of a cake layer comes out clean. Let the cake layers cool in the pans set on wire racks for 10 minutes before removing

until nine at night, made Boulud think he wanted a better life for himself. "What I liked was helping my grandmother in the kitchen. That was where I really liked to be. I could feel the warmth in the making of the food, because she was cooking for about 12 people every day, lunch and dinner. What I liked most was helping her peel potatoes and garlic, and tending to all the birds. And I used to love making the goat cheese. It all seemed like fun."

Larry Forgione says he had "the good fortune of growing up in a situation where my paternal grandmother had a completely self-suf-

them from the pan. Peel off the paper and let them cool completely on the racks.

To make the frosting, break the semisweet chocolate into squares and put them in the top of a double boiler with the water, salt, and vanilla extract. Stir the mixture over hot, not simmering, water until the chocolate is almost melted. Remove the top of the double boiler from the heat and stir in the melted butter until the mixture is smooth and blended. Let the mixture cool slightly.

Transfer the frosting to the large mixing bowl of an electric mixer and with the mixer set on the lowest speed, incorporate the egg yolks and then the sugar. Add both gradually and beat well after each addition.

Allow the frosting to cool to room temperature before spreading it on the cake. If you prefer, the mixing can be done by hand, but this must be done gently. Never beat the frosting at a high speed in the mixer or too quickly by hand.

Place a cooled cake layer on a cardboard round or flat serving plate. Use a metal spatula to spread about 1/2 cup of frosting on the layer. Position another layer on top and spread with another 1/2 cup of frosting. Place the last layer on top and smooth any filling that may have seeped from the sides. Refrigerate the filled cake for 15 to 20 minutes until the filling sets.

Remove the cake from the refrigerator and brush any crumbs from the sides and top. Frost the cake with half of the remaining frosting, beginning and ending with the top. Refrigerate the cake for another 15 to 20 minutes. Take it from the refrigerator and frost it with the remaining frosting. The chilled frosting acts as a "crumb coating" and makes the final application easy and smooth. For an extra silky finish, use a metal spatula warmed in hot water and wiped dry to smooth the frosting. Serve the cake at room temperature. Store it under a cake dome or upturned bowl. Do not keep it in the refrigerator.

ficient farm on eastern Long Island. We would go out every other weekend and for summer vacations, so I grew up understanding what strawberries from vines tasted like, and apples off the trees, and corn picked two minutes before you ate it. On the other side, my maternal grandmother was one to get up in the morning, go to church, come back, put an apron on, and spend the entire day preparing lunch or dinner. Even a weekday dinner had to have at least two or three different desserts. Weekends had seven different desserts. So I grew up in one of these situations where everyone

cared about food and took time to make it good."

His favorite dessert growing up? "Chocolate layer cake," he says without hesitation. "On our birthdays, we were allowed to pick what kind of cake we wanted The chocolate layer cake was my birthday cake. It's the same cake that we serve at An American Place today. It's her recipe—minus about two pounds of sugar," he adds.

"My Italian grandmother was a great Italian cook, and a great canner and preserver," Forgione says. "I remember in August, when all the tomatoes [would] ripen at exactly the same time, her entire first floor—her couches, sofas, and carpets—were all covered with drop cloths. There may have been a thousand pounds of tomatoes all over the house. She had two large pots going all day, trying to get those stewed tomatoes into jars before they went bad. We'd help bring them down to the old-fashioned stone storage basement that was nice and cool all year round, and we'd put them on the shelves for her."

While his family didn't have a farm, self-described "country kid" Charles Palmer grew up in a farming town in upstate New York and spent time working on a dairy farm where his duties included slaughtering chickens. Palmer believes that "one of the advantages I have over a lot of chefs is that I grew vegetables, I worked on a dairy farm, I was exposed to slaughtering chickens and rabbits, and hunting and fishing, and that kind of thing. We had big vegetable gardens ourselves—everything from beets, carrots, [and] turnips, to Swiss chard, kale, spinach, green beans, and peas. I remember eating venison, partridge, and pheasant when I was ten years old because, you know, you went out and shot it and then you ate it. We used to eat beet greens while my friends were eating canned peas and Green Giant frozen vegetables. I'd have my friends over and they'd look at the beet greens and say, 'You gonna *eat* that?' "

GROWING UP IN A RESTAURANT

Kids who grew up in or around a restaurant got to learn at an early age about how a restaurant functions. While the rest of us might have perceived some mystery surrounding the inner workings of a

What They Thought They Wanted to Be When They Grew Up

Patrick Clark	Priest or fireman
Larry Forgione	Physical education teacher
Joyce Goldstein	Painter
Emeril Lagasse	Musician
Nobu Matsuhisa	Architect
Patrick O'Connell	Actor
Charles Palmer	Pro football player
Alfred Portale	Jewelry designer
Anne Rosenzweig	Ethnomusicologist
Chris Schlesinger	Plumber or electrician
Jimmy Schmidt	Electrical engineer
Lydia Shire	Artist
Andre Soltner	Cabinetmaker
Jeremiah Tower	Architect
Jasper White	Piano tuner
Janos Wilder	Lawyer

Charles Palmer of Aureole (NYC), who played football in high school, was dared by the home economics teacher to take her class, and Palmer got a group of his friends to do so together: "The kitchen was like a sports arena, very fast-moving, requiring fast thinking, and it was a team thing."

restaurant (as a child, I always wondered what was behind the door with the little window where the food came from), restaurant kids knew there was no mystery—just long hours of hard work. In fact, this sometimes steered them away from going directly into the business in favor of first pursuing other interests.

Victor Gielisse grew up in a family of restaurateurs in the Netherlands. "My grandfather, my father, everybody was in the business. So although it was not automatically assumed that I would go into the business, the option was left open to me."

Gielisse originally tried to pursue another path. But during his first year at technical college for electronic engineering, "I'm sitting there and the teacher says to me, 'Hello, Mr. Gielisse? Maybe if you wake up you would like to join us? Would you mind telling us what you're doing?' And I said, 'I have no idea. I haven't got the faintest idea what I'm doing here.' I was at the wrong school, at the wrong time, and it was just totally wrong. I did not fit in there. So they said, 'What is it you like to do?' And I said, 'I like to cook.' They said, 'You are in the wrong school.' And I said, 'Yeah, I know that.'"

Pearled Barley with Seared Foie Gras, Roasted Granny Apple, and Rhubarb Essence

CHARLIE TROTTER

Charlie Trotter's
Chicago, IL

"Growing up in the Midwest, fresh apples just off the tree were an everyday treat. My mom spent many hours in her kitchen making homemade applesauce, apple pies, and baked apples. The Midwest also has an abundance of fresh rhubarb—the scent of strawberry-rhubarb pie used to be almost overwhelming. My brothers and sister and I spent a lot of time waiting for these treats to come piping hot out of the oven. Being able to utilize these ingredients in my cooking keeps me close to my roots, close to my family."

. . . .

1 cup cooked pearl barley (cooked in water)

5 1 3/4-oz. slices of foie gras

1 Granny Smith apple cut into 1/4-inch slices

1/4 cup Almata apple pieces, finely cubed

1/4 cup julienned Almata apples

1/8 cup julienned rhubarb (lightly blanched in a simple syrup)

1 tablespoon snipped parsley

4 oz. Rhubarb Essence (recipe below)

. . . .

After he began working at a restaurant where his father was at the time, "things started to fall into place."

Rick Bayless was always interested in cooking. While his brother always asked for sports equipment as gifts, 11-year-old Bayless found himself asking his parents for a two-volume set of *Mastering the Art of French Cooking.* "I had watched every single episode of Julia [Child's

Method

Heat the cooked barley over a double boiler. Sear the foie gras slices over medium heat, reserving the rendered fat. In a nonstick pan, sauté the Granny Smith apples on both sides in 1 tablespoon of rendered fat, then roast them in a 350-degree oven for four to five minutes. Remove from oven and blot off excess fat. Sauté the cubed Almata apple pieces until just cooked in another tablespoon of foie gras fat. Sauté the julienned apple in 1/2 tablespoon of the foie gras fat.

Cut one of the pieces of seared foie gras into a fine dice and fold the pieces into the barley, along with the cooked apple pieces and about half of the parsley. Season to taste with salt and pepper.

Place a piece of seared foie gras on each of 4 warm plates. Top with a timbale of barley and a slice of roasted Granny Smith apple. Place a little julienned apple around the top of each slice of apple. Strew some barley around the edges of the plate, along with the rest of the julienned Almata apple and the julienned rhubarb. Drizzle about 1 tablespoon of sauce onto each plate and sprinkle with the remaining parsley.

Rhubarb essence

....

6 tablespoons raspberry vinegar

3 tablespoons sugar

6 oz. peeled and diced rhubarb

2 cups chicken stock

....

Method

Make a gastrique out of the raspberry vinegar and the sugar. Add the rhubarb and briefly stew in the gastrique. Add the chicken stock and slowly reduce down to 3/4 cup; strain.

Serves 4

© 1994 Reprinted with permission. Charlie Trotter, *Charlie Trotter's*, Ten Speed Press.

TV show], since her first season in 1963. I still have all my notes from when I was nine years old, writing the recipes down."

Bayless spent a lot of time at his parents' restaurant—a family-style barbecue restaurant in Oklahoma. "I always worked there in some capacity, even if it was just prepping vegetables or something like that," Bayless recalls. "But I never had any sense of where things were coming from. The meat came in plastic bags, and that was the most we could say about its origins. My grandparents were definitely of the 'have your own garden' and 'can your own food' and 'freeze your own food' school, and I was really drawn to that. When I was seven, my parents had a catering business in conjunction with their restaurant, and I would go out on catering parties and help them set up. I would fill drinks and pass out things like ice cream. I always loved it very much. But the older I got, the more I realized I didn't want to inherit my parents' restaurant, and I didn't want to live in Oklahoma City."

Bayless had other goals in mind. "At the time, I wanted to go out and explore the world," he says. By pursuing this early passion, Bayless eventually put his own stamp on Mexican cuisine. "I loved cultural things. From the time that I was in mid-high school, I knew that I wanted to study Spanish and Latin American culture. I had traveled to Mexico when I was 14, with the Spanish Club at school, and I just fell in love with it."

Judy Rodgers was an exchange student during her senior year of high school in 1973, and was strongly influenced by her surrogate family. "The family I was placed with was the Troisgros family [which owns a three-star restaurant in France]. It was an accident of fate," Rodgers says. "It was still a fairly modest kitchen, pretty old-fashioned, very friendly. It was in an out-of-the-way part of France and there had been hardly any Americans through there, so I was pretty much a curious beast, and they loved it. I spent as much time as I could in the kitchen, in the dining room, marketing with Jean, meeting all his purveyors. He was such a compelling personality, to begin with, and sort of infectious in his approach to his profession.

"It was made clear to me that it was one of the more desirable, pleasant kitchens to work in among the three-stars—they were not at all rough, terrible, screaming chefs. Jean especially took a great interest in teaching and explaining everything to me, because I would copy down every recipe and take notes on everything I saw. They would call me 'Mata Hari.' They all thought I'd become a food writer for sure," she remembers. But Rodgers says she gave no thought at the time to becoming a chef herself. "I figured you had to start as an apprentice when you were 13, plucking feathers off grouse, and that it was too late for me to be a cook. I'd had no relationship with the food industry in America, other than a summer job at a Dairy Queen."

The experience of eating out in restaurants, whether for special occasions only or as a weekly ritual, also influenced many chefs.

Joyce Goldstein recalls hating the food she ate growing up. This was exacerbated by the mandate of the era, which instructed children to "clean their plates" and "drink a big glass of milk with every meal"—something that brought untold misery to the undiagnosed lactose-intolerant Goldstein. "I was a problem eater," is how Goldstein describes her early relationship with food. "Restaurants saved my life." Part of the pleasure of eating out, according to Goldstein, was being allowed to order whatever she liked—including a soft drink instead of milk!

Eating out in restaurants also provided some chefs with their first introductions to ethnic foods, even if not quite at the same level as the food the chefs would eventually come to cook themselves. Barbara Tropp, who is regarded as an authority on authentic Chinese cooking, grew up in New Jersey. "On Friday nights, we went out for Chinese food. If not Friday night, then Saturday night," she remembers. "Instead of celebrating the Sabbath, we'd run away to chop suey."

Nobu Matsuhisa first thought he wanted to become an architect, like his father was, partly because his father's career took him to faraway places. He remembers looking through his father's photo albums at buildings of different shapes and sizes in the cities his father had visited. But a trip to a Japanese restaurant when Matsuhisa was seven years old, where he saw sushi being prepared for the first time, changed all that. "That sushi experience, seeing the sushi man filleting the fresh fish and creating beautiful presentations, reminded me of the beautiful pictures in my father's photo album. I thought being a sushi man or a chef might also take me to different places," Matsuhisa says. (His career has since taken him from the Far East to South America and, finally, to the United States.)

It wasn't always the food that made the biggest impression when eating out, either. Michel Richard still remembers the first time he went to a restaurant and saw the chef wearing a toque. "That's the moment I knew I wanted to become a chef," he swears.

Jean Joho of Everest (Chicago) still remembers a meal he had as a child at Auberge de l'Ill, after his father instructed him "order what you like." Nine-year-old Jean ordered a first course of foie gras, a second course of whole black truffle, and a third course of lobster. "It was a great food moment," he adds, unnecessarily.

No matter what age you are now, you've already learned much about food which can serve you well, should you decide to make a career in this profession. Don't discount what you already know.

LEARNING FROM THE PAST

Lamb with Mint Sauce

CINDY PAWLCYN

Real Restaurants
Sausilito, CA

"This dish is what I always requested of my Mom for birthdays and other special-occasion meals. I was lucky to have a mother who could roast meat and serve it medium rare to medium, not well done. I truly think that the only reason I liked lamb was for her mint sauce which she made the same way her mother had made. Mint was the only fresh herb she grew in her garden."

Lamb

....

1 7–8 lb. leg of lamb

3–4 cloves garlic peeled and sliced

salt

fresh ground black pepper

6–8 sprigs mint (big ones)

2 cups of white wine

....

Preheat oven to 450 degrees. If your butcher hasn't already, trim the lamb leg of excess fat. Cut small slits into the leg of the lamb and insert a slice of garlic. Thoroughly season with salt and pepper. Put the white wine in the bottom of a roasting pan. Place leg of lamb on mint sprigs in the roasting pan. Place in oven and roast at 450 degrees for 15 to 20 minutes until a golden brown. Reduce heat to 350 degrees and continue roasting and basting with wine until an internal temperature of 125 degrees is reached. Rest 25 minutes before carving.

Mint sauce

....

2 cups fresh mint leaves chopped fine

3–4 tablespoons sugar

4 tablespoons vinegar

4–6 tablespoons water

....

Combine all ingredients. Let steep 1–2 hours. Taste and add additional water if too intense.

Take the time to be conscious of it, understand it, and value it. Review your own personal food history, your earliest and most memorable experiences involving food. What was it that made these experiences stand out? The freshness of the flavors? The particular combination of flavors? The setting? Something else? You'll begin to understand what you value in food, as well as the elements other than food that are important in food experiences.

Art museums and galleries often post biographies of featured artists at the beginning of exhibits so that viewers have a sense of the artists' influences, which can enhance their understanding and appreciation of the artists' work. Similarly, understanding the influences and inspirations behind chefs' food can add another dimension to customers' enjoyment of it.

Thinking about food this way will put you in touch with your personal prejudices—the foods you love best, the foods you don't care for, a preference for spicy or rich foods, or foods of your ethnic heritage or American region. These seeds, planted in you years ago, may grow into your eventual direction as a chef.

Elizabeth Terry of Elizabeth on 37th (Savannah) remembers trying escargot for the first time at age 16 at Tour d'Argent in Paris, as well as its most famous dish: "I had pressed duck, and I still have the little card with the duck's number on it," she recalls, referring to the restaurant's practice of numbering its ducks.

Chefs Who Changed Careers to Enter the Field

Chef	Prior Career
Susanna Foo	Librarian
George Germon	Artist
Raji Jallepalli	Medical technician
Johanne Killeen	Photographer
Wayne Nish	Printer
Alfred Portale	Jewelry designer
Alice Waters	Montessori teacher

Wayne Nish's Thoughts on Changing Careers

After graduating from cooking school, he started out at The Quilted Giraffe (NYC): "I think Barry [Wine, the chef-owner, who was formerly a lawyer] selected me because he saw someone similar to himself: a nonfood background, a professional background, a formal education, but a desire to get into the business."

My First Cheesecake

PATRICK CLARK

Tavern on the Green
New York, NY

"From the age of nine, I was always tinkering in the kitchen. I would spend all of my weekly allowance on cream cheese in search of the ultimate cheesecake. By the time I was 17, I found the almost-perfect recipe, which I still make for family and friends. But I always keep tinkering. Just recently, I decided to use vanilla beans instead of the extract, and found that it's so much better that way!"

. . . .

3 pounds cream cheese, room temperature

1 1/2 cups sugar (12 ounces)

pinch salt

1 teaspoon vanilla extract or the seeds of 1 fresh vanilla bean

3 large eggs

1 cup sour cream or heavy (whipping) cream

graham cracker crumbs and butter for crust

. . . .

In the bowl of a mixer, place the cream cheese, sugar, salt, and vanilla bean seeds, if using (if using vanilla extract, add after creaming).

Cream the mixture at medium speed, until light, then add the vanilla extract (if using), and the eggs, one at a time, mixing for 2 minutes after each addition. Stir in sour cream or heavy cream until well combined.

Butter a springform pan (10-inch diameter with 2 1/2-inch sides) and sprinkle with graham cracker crumbs. Pour batter into the pan and bake in a preheated oven about 70 minutes, or until the cake tests done in the center.

Remove to cake rack, and cool completely. Then remove cake from springform pan and refrigerate. Serve chilled plain, or with your favorite fruit or fruit compote.

Serves 16–20

"I would push for some way to figure out how much kids really like food before admitting them to cooking school. In the waiting room [for an admissions interview], have cookies around and see if they steal them. If they steal them, you let them in the school. If they don't steal them, then you don't take them. What's needed is some kind of test to find out—do they want to be in a magazine, or do they really want to work with food?"

—JASPER WHITE

3

COOKING

SCHOOLS

Learning
in
the
Classroom

No matter how strong a chef's inspirations, they are not enough to give rise to greatness. They must be carefully honed and refined through directed effort. The palate, which allowed a chef to first learn what he or she found most enjoyable, must be trained to discern subtleties in flavors and flavor combinations, and to critique as well as taste. Similarly, basic cooking techniques must be mastered, with speed and efficiency developed over repeated efforts, in order to be able to create desired effects. This is what leads chefs into professional kitchens and, increasingly, into professional cooking schools.

Cooking is a profession which places extraordinary emphasis on continuous learning, and today a chef's first formal education often takes place in a cooking school classroom. There are hundreds of cooking schools in both the United States and abroad, offering opportunities to learn about specialties ranging from vegetarian to confectionery to microwave cooking. In fact, *The Guide to Cooking Schools* (ShawGuides) lists more than 700 programs in its 1995 edition. However, a much smaller number are considered to be primarily *professional* (degree, diploma, or certificate) programs, and are the primary emphasis of this chapter.

While many of the country's leading chefs reached the top of the profession without the benefit of a cooking school degree, an overwhelming majority of the chefs we interviewed recommend cooking school as the most expeditious start for an aspiring chef today. Cooking school offers an opportunity to gain exposure in a concentrated period of time to an immense amount of information, from cooking techniques (knife skills, saute, grill) to theory (nutrition, sanitation), to international/regional cuisines (French, Italian, Asian).

A cooking school diploma can also be an important credential in opening doors and demonstrating commitment to the field. "I only hire cooking school graduates," says Patrick O'Connell, who himself doesn't hold a cooking school degree. "If I had to do it again at this point in history, I would probably go to culinary school." Alfred Portale is even more adamant. "I think that if you can go to cooking school, you should. I feel very strongly about it," he says. "It immediately legitimizes you as a professional, and exposes you to a broad base of information, even though not much of it is practical. It certainly puts you at a greater advantage than someone who's self-taught or learns going up through the ranks."

While attending cooking school full-time represents a certain trade-off in terms of the opportunity cost of foregoing a full-time income while at school, the vast majority of chefs interviewed see it as an investment well made. In fact, the cooking school naysayers have little criticism for the cooking schools themselves; they reserve it for the popular misconception that merely attending cooking school can create a chef, which they believe often misleads people without a real passion for food and cooking into the profession. "Cooking schools do an important job," says Anne Rosenzweig, "but the final results depend a lot on the students." Victor Gielisse concurs: "Cooking school gives aspiring chefs a tremendous foundation. But school alone cannot give you a passion for food. It's impossible. Not even the best teacher can do that."

Given the abundance of reputable cooking schools and programs, there is likely to be an option to suit everyone's specific budget, time frame, and other needs. From four-year bachelor degree programs, to certificate programs which can be completed in a few brief months, to one-session cooking demonstrations by culinary experts, there are numerous opportunities to learn about cooking in a classroom. With the hundreds of cooking schools available, it is up to the prospective student to research various options to determine which offers the best fit. In this chapter, the entire scope of the cooking school experience is explored, with recommendations from leading chefs as to how to get the most out of your experience before, during, and after cooking school.

> *"Take as much time as you can to build a foundation laterally, and get as much foundation as you can. As with a building, the deeper and wider the foundation, the higher the building can go. I think you can take the extra time to get more knowledge and to feel comfortable and to realize that because you roasted chickens for a week doesn't mean that you know how to roast chickens."*
> —LARRY FORGIONE

The decision as to whether and where to attend is highly personal and dependent on many factors: How long a program best suits your needs? Is location a factor for you? What is your budget for school? Are you looking to attend full-time or part-time? During the day, or in the evening? (The New York Restaurant School, for example, offers classes 24 hours a day.) While it is not our intention to recommend specific schools, we hope that the insights of leading chefs and the brief information on cooking schools which is included will help guide your eventual decision.

CHOOSING THE RIGHT COOKING SCHOOL

The Culinary Institute of America in Hyde Park, New York, is the country's oldest culinary academy. Originally founded by Frances Roth and Katharine Angell in Connecticut in 1946 as The New Haven Restaurant Institute, the school moved to its current location in 1972 and has produced more than 23,000 culinary graduates. Many are among the country's leading chefs (see page 66). The Institute bills itself as "the only residential college in the world devoted entirely to culinary education," and proudly quotes Paul Bocuse in the school's literature as saying, "[The Culinary Institute of America] is the best culinary school in the world."

Johnson & Wales University opened in 1973 with 141 students, and now has 3,250 students enrolled, with other campuses in Charleston, South Carolina, and Norfolk, Virginia. The school offers associate, bachelor, and graduate degrees in foodservice, hospitality, teaching, education, and technology.

California Culinary Academy is a for-profit institution founded in 1977 to provide technical and professional chef training for individuals desiring an entry-level position or advancement as a cook, chef, or baker. Its 16-month program enrolls more than 500 students and is modeled after the European system of closely monitored apprenticeships.

The New England Culinary Institute was founded in 1980 by Frances Voight and John Dranow in Montpelier, Vermont. The first class had seven students; in 1993, over 500 students enrolled. In 1989, the school expanded to a second campus at the Inn at Essex in Essex Junction, Vermont. Its catalog boasts Jasper White (a Culinary Institute of America graduate) as saying, "New England Culinary Institute offers the most vigorous, hands-on training of any cooking school in America."

The French Culinary Institute was founded in 1984 in New York City, and offers a 600-hour day or evening program in classic French cuisine. The Institute's faculty includes Jacques Pépin as Dean of Special Programs and Alain Sailhac as Dean of Culinary Studies.

If you know the kind of restaurants you'd like to work in after graduation, consider taking the time to ask some chefs at similar restaurants in your area to recommend cooking schools to you. Carefully read all of the literature available from each of the schools you're considering. This alone should address some of your most basic concerns, such as the range of course offerings, and whether the program costs are within your reach. If you're able, plan to spend a day at each of the schools you're seriously considering.

When visiting schools, don't hesitate to ask a lot of questions of administrators, instructors, and even students. Find out whether they offer (or require) an externship program or an international study program. Ask what kind of placement assistance they provide to graduating students and alumni. Find out where some of their recent graduates are working and what the breadth of the school's network is. Who are some of their most successful alumni? Are typical alumni working in the kinds of places you'd like to work in someday? Spend time talking with other students, and decide if they're the type of people with whom you'd enjoy learning and spending time. You'll be happiest at a school that offers a "good fit."

Certain schools, such as The Culinary Institute of America, Johnson & Wales University, the New England Culinary Institute, the California Culinary Academy, and the French Culinary Institute, attract a national (and even international) student body. Other schools, such as The New York Restaurant School, Peter Kump's New York Cooking School, and the Cambridge School of Culinary Arts (MA), tend to attract a greater proportion of their students from their regions, and local chef alumni may show some preference to graduates of their alma maters over graduates of other programs. Still other schools tend to draw more closely from their immediate vicinities.

Schools also differ in their orientation to particular types of cuisine. The French Culinary Institute (NYC) specializes, obviously, in French cuisine. The Culinary Institute of America, which has traditionally offered training in classical French cuisine, has now added classes in Italian and other international cuisines. The Natural Gourmet Cooking School (NYC) emphasizes healthy, vegetarian cooking.

Even many outside the profession have at least heard of the venerable Culinary Institute of America, often by its double-entendre acronym, "the CIA" (by which it is sometimes referred). Founded in 1946, the oldest cooking school in the country has historically offered a 21-month Associate Degree Program in Culinary Arts, in which students master basic culinary skills through hands-on instruction. Coursework includes classes in American and international cuisines, seafood cookery, nutrition, sanitation, charcuterie, and service and hospitality management. All students must also complete an externship semester off campus and work in the Institute's four restaurants. The Culinary Institute of America also offers a 21-month Associate Degree Program in Baking and Pastry Arts, in which students study culinary concepts and then take spe-

"As a woman, you should sit in on classes [at cooking schools]. Interview a professor or two about the philosophy of the school: does it believe women can contribute, that women can reach the top?"
—ELIZABETH TERRY

Endicott College
Beverly, Mass. 01915

Selected Culinary Institute of America Alumni

Class of	Chef	Restaurant	Location
1965	Marcel Desaulniers	The Trellis	Williamsburg, VA
1974	Sanford D'Amato	Sanford	Milwaukee, WI
	Larry Forgione	An American Place	New York, NY
		Beekman 1766 Tavern	Rhinebeck, NY
1976	Jasper White	Jasper's	Boston, MA
	Roy Yamaguchi	Roy's Restaurant	Honolulu, HI
1977	Gary Danko	The Ritz-Carlton	San Francisco, CA
	Susan Feniger	Border Grill	Santa Monica, CA
	Bradley Ogden	Lark Creek Inn	Larkspur, CA
		One Market Restaurant	San Francisco, CA
	Chris Schlesinger	East Coast Grill	Cambridge, MA
		The Blue Room	Cambridge, MA
1978	Dean Fearing	The Mansion on Turtle Creek	Dallas, TX
1979	Charles Palmer	Aureole	New York, NY
1981	Alfred Portale	Gotham Bar & Grill	New York, NY
1982	Michael Chiarello	Tra Vigne	St. Helena, CA
	Todd English	Olives	Charlestown, MA
		Figs	
1983	Edward Brown	The Sea Grill	New York, NY
1984	Caprial and John Pence	Westmoreland Bistro	Portland, OR
1987	Monique Barbeau	Fuller's	Seattle, WA

cialized coursework in baking, pastry, patisserie, and breads and desserts.

The Culinary Institute of America also has two Bachelor of Professional Studies degree programs in Culinary Arts Management and in Baking and Pastry Arts Management. The new programs are designed to build upon the associate degree programs and require two years of subsequent study, with courses in leadership and management, marketing, communications, finance, ethics, foreign languages, history and culture, and advanced cooking. Students are expected to research a senior thesis in food. The programs also include a six-week food and wine seminar at the Institute's Napa Valley (CA) campus.

Other leading schools include the College of Culinary Arts at Johnson & Wales University in Providence, Rhode Island. Like the Culinary Institute of America, it offers a four-year bachelor's degree program in addition to its two-year associate's degree program, which emphasizes progressive individualized development, environmental and nutritional awareness, sanitation and food safety, marketing and merchandising, financial controls, production, and a six-month cooperative education experience. The New England Culinary Institute (NECI) in Montpelier, Vermont, has its students spend 75 percent of their time—starting the first day of class—in a hands-on environment, cooking and managing The New England Culinary Institute's ten food service outlets, which are open to the public. The New England Culinary Institute students also spend two out of four semesters in a paid internship program, which allows them to work in any food service establishment in the world that meets the school's standards. The California Culinary Academy in San Francisco offers a 16-month career program emphasizing classic and modern techniques, which is modeled after the European system of closely supervised apprenticeships, and features three student-staffed restaurants open to the public.

For those unable or unwilling to dedicate two to four years to their culinary educations, another option is a school such as Peter Kump's New York Cooking School, which offers a three-month program in the techniques of French cooking. Upon completing the course and passing practical and written examinations demon-strating mastery of those courses, a diploma is awarded. The school also offers a three-month Career Pastry Program. Upon completion of either program, students can extend their training by participating in the school's extern program, which places students in the professional area of their choice for an additional six weeks. In addition,

Alma Maters of Leading Chefs

Chef	Restaurant	Alma Mater
Patrick Clark	Tavern on the Green New York, NY	New York City Technical College Brooklyn, NY
Bobby Flay	Mesa Grill, Bolo New York, NY	The French Culinary Institute New York, NY
Mark Franz	formerly of Stars San Francisco, CA	California Culinary Academy San Francisco, CA
Emeril Lagasse	Emeril's, NOLA New Orleans, LA	Johnson & Wales University Providence, RI
Mary Sue Milliken	Border Grill Los Angeles, CA	Washburne Trade School Chicago, IL
Wayne Nish	March New York, NY	The New York Restaurant School New York, NY
Jimmy Schmidt	The Rattlesnake Club Detroit, MI	Modern Gourmet (Madeleine Kamman) Newton, MA
Lydia Shire	Biba, Pignoli Boston, MA	Le Cordon Bleu London, England
Hiroyoshi Sone	Terra St. Helena, CA	Tsuji Cooking School Osaka, Japan
Allen Susser	Chef Allen's Miami, FL	New York City Technical College Brooklyn, NY

the school will arrange apprenticeships in France which will allow students to work at Michelin-starred restaurants and fine pastry shops in France.

Don't think that if you can't attend school full-time you can't receive a fine education. "If you don't have enough money, you can still attend part-time," emphasizes Dieter Schorner. Schorner, along with other experienced chefs who cooked in restaurant kitchens by day, taught classes in the evening at New York City Technical College, a vocational college based in Brooklyn. "I found some of the most dedicated teachers at this little college," he says. There are more than 300 vocational schools and community colleges offering programs in culinary arts listed in *The Guide to Cooking Schools* (ShawGuides).

A brief word about programs in hospitality management: such an education can certainly prove valuable to aspiring chefs, particularly to those who aim to become executive chefs or chef-owners. Cornell University in Ithaca, New York, offers both four-year bachelor's degree and two-year master's degree programs in hospitality management. As the college's literature on its School of Hotel Administration states, "If your goal is to become one of America's great chefs, we can get you started, but we won't teach you to cook." While their course offerings include selections such as Culinary Theory and Practice, such schools place most of their emphasis on the teaching of management skills through courses in such areas as communication, finance, food and beverage management, human resources, information technology, law, management, marketing, operations, real estate management, and tourism. Having some training in these subject areas becomes increasingly important as you move up the ladder in a kitchen, and an advanced degree is something to consider seriously if you see your ambitions as one day expanding beyond the kitchen walls.

If you're aiming for a competitive program, getting in presents the next hurdle. Some of the top schools aren't able to admit everyone who applies. At other, less-competitive programs, merely submitting an application and application fee is basically all it takes. Given the increasing demand for trained cooks and chefs, many cooking schools have been expanding their programs to be able to accommodate more students.

The admissions process, depending on the school, may be simple and straightforward, or relatively more involved. The Culinary Institute of America, for example, requires a completed application form, an application fee, and a high school transcript, as well as transcripts from any postsecondary studies and at least two letters of

**ADMISSIONS
REQUIREMENTS
AND PROCESS**

Crabcakes

DEBRA PONZEK (CIA '84)

formerly of Montrachet
New York, NY

"My recipe for crabcakes was given to me by two old friends of the family. They owned a restaurant in Greenwich Village, and were the first people to help me get started investigating culinary schools and pursuing my culinary career. I have such wonderful memories of going to their restaurant with family and friends and enjoying their wonderful crabcakes."

....

2 eggs, beaten

1/2 cup mayonnaise

1–2 tablespoons Dijon mustard

1 pound lump crabmeat, cleaned

2 tablespoons chopped parsley

1/4 cup chopped scallions

1 tablespoon chopped cornichons

2 cups fresh breadcrumbs

1 teaspoon Old Bay Seasoning

pinch cayenne pepper

....

In a bowl beat the eggs; add the mayonnaise and the mustard. Toss lightly with the cleaned crabmeat. Add the parsley, scallions, and cornichons. Gently fold in the breadcrumbs. Add the Old Bay Seasoning and the cayenne pepper. Form into desired size, and coat lightly with fresh breadcrumbs. Panfry until golden brown. Serve alone or with a mixed green salad.

reference from employers, food service instructors, or Culinary Institute alumni. The application form itself asks whether applicants have traveled extensively in or outside the United States, attended seminars/lectures on the food industry, and read books and/or magazines about the foodservice industry. In addition, applicants must submit an essay explaining why they wish to enter the foodservice field, what research on the industry they have done, details of their foodservice background, and why they're interested in attending The Culinary Institute of America.

The New England Culinary Institute requires applicants to submit a written personal statement on their background and experiences, why they have decided to seek a career in the culinary arts, and their reasons for applying to the New England Culinary Institute. Also required are three letters of recommendation; copies of high school, vocational school, or college transcripts; along with the application form and an application fee.

At Peter Kump's New York Cooking School, no previous professional experience is necessary, but a minimum of two years of college is required. Applicants are asked to submit a completed application and a copy of college transcripts, as well as a down payment of the total cooking school fees. If students are not admitted to the program, the down payment will be refunded, minus a nonrefundable registration fee.

While some local cooking schools will have less rigorous application processes, most schools will require you to apply well in advance of your desired date of attendance, so plan ahead.

Some schools, such as the New England Culinary Institute, see prior work experience as a plus but not a prerequisite. Many cooking schools, however, require work experience in a kitchen as a condition of admission. The Culinary Institute of America requires a minimum of three to five months of foodservice experience that includes exposure in a professional kitchen. This is for the prospective student's benefit as much as it is the cooking school's. Both

BEFORE ATTENDING COOKING SCHOOL

parties have a vested interest in seeing students who enter success-fully complete the program, and not everyone who's attracted by the perceived "glamour" of the profession finds that the reality of the work is a good fit. Emeril Lagasse offers high school students who have expressed an interest in cooking a chance to spend some time in his restaurants. He finds that more than half of them change their minds after they see what kitchen work is really like. Is cooking something you could come to love as a profession? It's best for all concerned that a reality check be taken sooner rather than later.

Because of all the benefits that accrue to a student who works before attending school, this is something that should be consid-ered seriously by everyone thinking about attending cooking school, whether the school requires it or not. Larry Forgione says, "I think people really ought to think about whether this is what they really want to do before they jump into it with both feet. I might suggest stepping in with one foot—working weekends at a place, hanging out at a restaurant to understand what the restaurant busi-ness is all about." While the glamorous image of restaurant business might help to attract people to the profession, only those who have actually worked in a kitchen know the intense effort involved.

In addition to practical experience, other preparation can pro-vide an edge at cooking school. If you can't work full-time in a kitchen, consider getting some part-time experience working for a caterer, gourmet store, or as a waiter or waitress. Spend as much time as you can reading about food and cooking, if you don't already. Charles Palmer recalls, "When I decided that I was going to go to The Culinary Institute of America, I read about food and cooking so that when I got there, I found that I was more knowl-edgeable than most. Every night, I would read *Larousse Gastronomique*. I read any cookbook that I could get my hands on. I especial-ly liked the Time-Life series because it really explained things so that you could understand." In addition, restaurant experience before cooking school offers an opportunity to determine what area a student might want to specialize in—for example, cooking on the line, or pastry.

You may, in addition, have prior academic or work experience in a field unrelated to cooking. Prior experience can be a great help in preparing you for the rigors of a tough cooking school program and difficult first jobs. You are likely to have already developed study habits and writing skills. Also, food is so basic that few fields don't offer some degree of overlap—from art to science to history. Alfred Portale's work in jewelry design certainly hasn't hurt his reputation for artistic presentation, and Barbara Tropp's academic training has helped her to succeed as both a chef and an author. If you have already invested time and energy in another field, you are likely to ask good questions and have a clear idea of what you are looking to get out of your education.

AT COOKING SCHOOL

While at cooking school, it's important to make the most of your opportunity. Several leading chefs noted the tendency of some students to put more effort into their social life at cooking school rather than into the important learning process that takes place both in and out of the classroom. This can be a tragic mistake. Alfred Portale, who graduated first in his class, recalls: "I started at The Culinary Institute of America a little older than most of the students there. I had good experience, and was very, very serious. For a lot of the students, it's their first time away from home, and they can't really get over that part. They go crazy partying, and it takes them a whole year to calm down. And by then it's too late."

In addition to using classroom time as an opportunity to ask questions and learn as much as possible, it's important to take advantage of extracurricular learning. Volunteer to assist professors and visiting chefs with special events, and make an effort to get to know them. Aside from the knowledge they can pass along, these interactions get you noticed, and may spawn leads on future jobs.

Some chefs found that the most important lessons they learned came outside the classroom. "I spent a lot of time in the library [at The Culinary Institute of America]," says Gary Danko. "And I came across this book called *The Making of a Cook* [by Madeleine Kamman], which made so much sense to me. It went into the how's and why's of cooking—like how to make a hollandaise sauce, and if

"Learn the basics. You must understand the products, the ingredients, how to season and taste, the actual cooking, the composition of dishes, and food presentation."

—JEAN JOHO

The Culinary Institute of America

Through illustrating various cooking school curricula, it's easier to discern the process of skill development. As in the mastery of any subject, you first learn the basics and work toward the complex. Starting with the mastery of basic knife skills and product and equipment knowledge, students move into more sophisticated applications. You don't start out baking ten-tiered wedding cakes. The same set of basic skills and knowledge are important to learn no matter where one attends cooking school.

As an example, we've outlined below the courses required for a two-year associate's degree in **culinary arts** at The Culinary Institute of America. The first semester includes Introduction to Gastronomy; Culinary Math; Nutrition; Sanitation; Meat Identification; Meat Fabrication; Product Identification and Food Purchasing; Culinary French; and Culinary Skill Development. The second semester includes Introduction to Hot Foods; Supervisory Development; Seafood Cookery; American Regional Cuisine; Oriental Cuisine; Charcuterie; Breakfast Cookery; Lunch Cookery; and Advanced Garde Manger. The third semester consists of a required 18-week externship. The fourth semester includes Baking Skills Development; Cost Control; Patisserie; Menus and Facilities Planning; Management of Wine and Spirits; Business Law; International Cookery; and Advanced Culinary Principles. The fifth semester includes Classical Banquet Cuisine; Introduction to Table Service; and Catering Seminars, as well as practical dining room and kitchen experience in the school's four restaurants: St. Andrew's Cafe, the Caterina de Medici, The Escoffier Room, and American Bounty.

In contrast, the two-year associate's degree in **baking and pastry arts** requires a different curriculum. The first semester includes Introduction to Baking Science; Baking Math; Sanitation; Baking I, II, and III; and Pastry I. The second semester includes Pastry II and Pastry III; Patisserie I; Costing Examination; Baking Practical Examination; and Patisserie II and III. The third semester consists of a required 18-week externship. The fourth semester includes Nutrition; Ice Carving, Display Work and Showpieces; Cost Control I; Supervisory Development; Cost Control II; Cooking Fundamentals for Bakers; Menus and Facilities Planning; Management of Wine and Spirits; Business Law; Product Identification and Food Purchasing; and Advanced Culinary Principles. The fifth semester includes Bread and Desserts in St. Andrew's Cafe, the Caterina de Medici, and the American Bounty; Entrepreneurship; Costing Examination; Baking Practical Examination; and Advanced Patisserie.

---

it breaks, how to correct it—and that was something that I wasn't learning in the classroom at that point.

"When I went to another cooking school, before transferring to The Culinary Institute of America, the first thing I noticed was that every instructor was saying, 'Now this is how you make the best [blank],' and the next was saying, 'No, no, no, *this* is how you make the best [blank].' All of a sudden, the confusion starts. But as you learn cooking, and you do different things, and see different people's styles, that influence becomes part of your style. And eventually that style will become your cuisine."

Danko advises, "Be serious when you go to cooking school. Make sure you have some books to draw from, and that you spend some time and really pick the instructors' brains. Ask them every question you can. Spend extra time cooking with instructors. Volunteer for things. Because to me, that's where the real learning comes from, putting in the extra time. And, as Madeleine Kamman would always say, 'Get an education. Don't just go to cooking school.'"

Many chefs we interviewed emphasized how much their in-class learning was complemented by their outside work in a kitchen while attending school, and suggested that students maximize their learning by working while attending school. Allen Susser says, "I think you need to see the real side of the ideal things you're cooking in the school kitchen." Mary Sue Milliken goes so far as to recommend that students work full-time while they attend cooking school: "If the schedule is too rigorous, this is probably not a good career choice."

Working while attending school can serve many purposes. It can reinforce what you are learning in the classroom, and point out what you are not. Jasper White advises working during cooking school "because then you can start applying things every day, and retain a lot more." It can give you extra practice on your knife and other skills, and allow you to pursue other interests in food, such as ethnic cuisine or catering, that may not be covered. White loved his work at the Waccabuc Country Club in Westchester County, NY: "We did buffets on Sundays—I got to use a lot from school that I wouldn't have had a chance to use otherwise."

Any experience is what you make of it—you don't have to work  at a four-star restaurant in order to learn. Susan Feniger worked at a fish market in Poughkeepsie, NY while attending The Culinary Institute of America. A former coworker of mine worked at the sandwich counter at a wine and cheese store while attending cooking school, in order to educate himself about cheeses. I know another

"If there's one thing I wished I'd studied at school, it's mechanics. It's very hard to fix your stoves, your kettles, your dishwasher, and all that. Chef-restaurateurs need to be versed in the mechanical aspects of the machinery they work with—otherwise, it's $50 or $60 for a visit to hear, 'Well, you're going to need a new compressor, son. . . .'"
—VICTOR GIELISSE

Potato Gnocchi

TODD ENGLISH (CIA '82)
Olives, Figs
Charlestown, MA

"My grandmother taught me how to make these potato gnocchi. She learned from her mother, and she from her mother. I distinctly remember her bent old fingers working ever-so-gently with the dough. She instructed me that, when made properly, they should be as light and fluffy as a kiss from an angel."

. . . .

2 russet potatoes (peeled and cut into chunks)

1/2–2/3 cup water

3 egg yolks

salt

freshly ground black pepper

1 1/2 cups all-purpose flour (extra for dusting work surface)

. . . .

1. Boil potatoes in salted water (enough water to cover). Cook until soft (20 minutes). Drain well (10 minutes or more) in a colander.

cooking school student who chose to work in catering instead of a restaurant because of the flexibility in scheduling, which allowed her to learn and practice her culinary skills without the intense pressure of daily service at a restaurant. She was also able to see a wide variety of food at the catering company—from 200 wontons to an entire theme dinner centered around the early settlers in Boston. There is a price to pay for all of this—less sleep, not to mention less energy and time for other school activities. While the burden of such a workload might give pause to some, leading chefs seemed to be in agreement with Nietzsche's principle: "That which does not kill me makes me stronger."

2. Dust a clean work surface with flour. Mash potatoes through a ricer onto work surface (make a pile with potatoes).

3. Add egg yolks, salt, and pepper. Add flour (small amounts at a time) and knead gently—only to incorporate.

4. On a floured surface, form a strip of dough 1/2 inch wide, 2–3 feet long. Cut strip into 1/2-inch pieces. Roll into balls.

5. Using two forks, roll dough balls the full length of the fork prong, pressing at the end to create a pocket in the middle and a fork mark at the end.

Please note

It is best to work with ingredients when they are still warm. It is also very important not to overwork dough—knead dough only to incorporate ingredients. Dough can be prepared ahead of time and then frozen. Be sure to sprinkle with generous amounts of flour before freezing and do not stack.

To cook

1. Bring a pot of salted water to boil. Drop gnocchi in water.

2. Cook approximately 8 minutes—they will float to the surface when done.

3. Remove from water and toss with sauce.

EXTERNSHIPS

An externship is a period of time spent working in a restaurant for the purpose of gaining practical, on-the-job experience, and may be paid or nonpaid. Some schools mandate serving an externship as a requirement for graduation, while others offer it as an option to students. Certain schools even offer a chance to work abroad or at leading resorts. It's important to research the options available through the school you're interested in and, if there's a particular restaurant you'd like to serve an externship with, to take an active role in doing all you can to pursue it. Find out which faculty or administration members have the strongest ties to the restaurant and speak with them, write a letter to the chef, or possibly offer to work for free until the time your official externship commences.

Every experience is different. Some restaurants have students cook on the line, while others allow externs to do only basic prep work. André Soltner requires that The Culinary Institute of America students he takes into his kitchen at Lutèce (NYC) commit to a minimum one-year externship, which maximizes both the student's learning and his restaurant's ability to benefit from it. If an externship is offered or required, make the most of it. Work in the best kitchen you can get hired into. If you make a good impression, you may find yourself with an offer for permanent employment, and at worst you'll end up with a good reference for future jobs. At the New England Culinary Institute, 70 percent of second-year internships turn into first jobs.

One extern I know was passed over for a permanent pastry position due to his inexperience, yet kept coming in on his own time to keep his skills sharp while looking for a job at another restaurant. When the pastry chef left unexpectedly, he was hired into the position. Another extern received an offer to join a restaurant as *garde manger* because of her excellent work habits and attitude (including coming in early, staying late, working fast, and taking direction well). While she had no experience, her work habits spoke volumes about her potential and she was given a chance to prove herself.

AFTER GRADUATION

Chefs emphasize the importance of viewing graduation from cooking school as merely a starting point in one's education. André Soltner puts it this way: "I think cooking schools give students the basics they need. But they are not accomplished chefs. They are just coming out of school. A doctor, after his four years, goes to a hospital not as the chief surgeon but as an intern. We have to look at cooking school graduates as what they are." Schools and parents were attributed with feeding students' expectations. "Parents send their kids for two years at The Culinary Institute of America and then think they are André Soltner or Paul Bocuse," Soltner notes. "But they are not."

Cooking school graduates might find themselves tempted with offers to become full-fledged chefs upon graduation—welcomed by

students, at least in part, due to the sometimes substantial debt incurred through financing cooking school. However, leading chefs speak discouragingly of the notion of accepting a job as a chef too soon. In her speech to a graduating class at The Culinary Institute of America, Debra Ponzek used the opportunity not to pump up graduates' hopes and expectations but to implore them, "Don't take a chef's job!" She explained, "It's hard to go back, once you realize there are things you didn't learn. Many people want to make the jump [to a chef's position] too quickly." Patrick Clark agrees. "Don't look for glory right away. When you get there, it's harder."

Some chefs advise that after graduation you should work with your "idols," in order to continue your education. Upon graduating from The Culinary Institute of America, Alfred Portale answered an ad and was selected to work at the food shop that Michel Guérard was opening at Bloomingdale's. He recalls: "Here I'm just out of school, and I'm standing in a kitchen with Michel Guérard, the Troisgros brothers—all these huge French guys, all my idols. It was thrilling. I learned all the butchering and the charcuterie, the poaching and the smoking, and the stuffing and the sausage making, and all that kind of stuff that young cooks dream about. After putting in a year with these guys, they invited me to France. So I spent a year working first at Troisgros, and then with Guérard. I had a car and toured France, spending the last six weeks in Paris, going out every day and every night, going to every bookstore, every cooking store, just learning and submerging myself in everything."

After graduating from The Culinary Institute of America, Gary Danko began a dogged cross-country pursuit to track down Madeleine Kamman, to persuade her to let him study with her. While Danko says she expressed reservations about working with a newly-minted culinary school graduate, he set out to change her mind. "I pulled up in my car the first day of class with all these local products that I'd been working with—goat cheese, guinea hens, ducks, geese, lamb, you name it. She saw that I was very serious about cooking and she sort of took me under her arm."

Jimmy Schmidt of The Rattlesnake Club (Detroit) spent a year in France studying wine. "It really developed my ability to taste."

CONTINUING EDUCATION

Just because you graduate from cooking school doesn't mean the learning process ends. In this profession, it should never end. You don't have to earn a cooking school degree to benefit from time spent in a classroom learning how to cook. Patrick O'Connell attended a Chinese cooking school on Saturdays for six months. Susanna Foo, who entered the restaurant business mid-career, found the eight-week stint she spent at The Culinary Institute of America invaluable. "After The Culinary Institute of America, I decided I only wanted to use fresh vegetables that tasted fresh, the way they did when I was growing up," says Foo. "I went back to the restaurant determined to meld Chinese ingredients with French technique, and started to re-create my kung po sauce, black bean sauce, curry sauce, and other sauces."

If your goal is not necessarily to earn a degree but to learn about cooking from chefs themselves, there are a growing number of venues available offering classes with, and demonstrations by, leading chefs and other food authorities. For example, De Gustibus is a popular program at Macy's (NYC) run by Irene Feldman Sailhac, which has featured such chefs as Daniel Boulud, Anne Rosenzweig, and André Soltner. Susan Feniger and Mary Sue Milliken of Border Grill (LA), Raji Jallepalli of Restaurant Raji (Memphis), Georges Perrier of Le Bec-Fin (Philadelphia), and Allen Susser of Chef Allen's (Miami) are among the chefs we interviewed who offer cooking demonstrations in their restaurants.

While I was cooking during the lunch shift at Biba, I made it a point to attend Boston University's Seminars in the Culinary Arts in the evening, where I was able to take classes with local chefs such as Jody Adams and Gordon Hamersley, and visiting luminaries like Julia Child, Lorenza de'Medici, Julie Sahni, and Anne Willan. The Boston Public Library sponsored a Cooks in Print series which, in lecture format, offered wonderful opportunities to learn about food from leading chefs like Jasper White. The Schlesinger Library at Radcliffe College also offers panels of leading culinary experts on various issues, from food safety to customer service, which are open to the public. To find similar kinds of programs in your local areas, check with adult education and continuing education programs, with your local library, or with local chapters of national associations such as the International Association of Wine and Food.

Swiss Onion Soup

SUSAN FENIGER (CIA '77)

Border Grill
Santa Monica, CA

"When I was a teenager, my boyfriend's mom used to make this dish. It was extremely comforting and the surroundings we often dined in were, too. In front of a big fire, we'd sit on the floor and talk and eat. I have to say that is how I see food and its importance—bringing people together to share and be comforted in many ways."

Unlike some onion soups where the cheese forms a tough, stringy mass at the top, the cheese in this hearty soup grows softer and sweeter as it simmers in the milky broth. It may not look great, but the taste is superb. You can refrigerate this homey soup for as long as 6 days with no loss of quality. When gently reheating it, remember to keep stirring.

. . . .

8 tablespoons (1 stick) unsalted butter

3 medium onions, thinly sliced

2 teaspoons salt

1/4 teaspoon white pepper

1/2 day-old French bread or 6 slices white bread

1 teaspoon granulated sugar

1/2 gallon milk

1 pound good-quality Swiss or Gruyère cheese, diced

. . . .

Melt butter over moderate heat in a large heavy stockpot or Dutch oven. Cook onions with salt and pepper until soft but not colored, 15 minutes.

Cut bread into medium dice and add to pot along with sugar. Stir constantly for about 1 minute, so bread absorbs butter.

Add milk and bring to a boil. Add cheese, stir, and reduce to a simmer. Cook, uncovered, stirring occasionally, about 1 hour 15 minutes. Serve immediately.

8 to 10 servings

Reprinted with permission. © Mary Sue Milliken and Susan Feniger, *City Cuisine*, William Morrow and Company, Inc., 1989.

Recommended Reading

A Guide to College Programs in Hospitality and Tourism. The Council on Hotel, Restaurant and Institutional Education (CHRIE). New York: John Wiley & Sons, Inc., 1993.

The Guide to Cooking Schools— 1995: Cooking Courses, Vacations, Apprenticeships and Wine Instruction Throughout the World. Coral Gables, FL: ShawGuides. New editions published annually.

Many cooking schools also sponsor continuing education programs for working chefs, where one can spend anywhere from a day to a month learning more about cooking. The Culinary Institute of America even offers courses on videotape. The School for American Chefs, sponsored by Beringer Vineyards in St. Helena (CA), awards scholarships to working chefs for two weeks of advanced culinary study with Madeleine Kamman.

Nancy Silverton took a break from her career to attend Lenôtre (the namesake school of noted French pastry chef Gaston Lenôtre), in France, to study pastry. "I was working at Michael's, which at the time was considered one of the top restaurants in Los Angeles, and my desserts were very well regarded. I went to Lenôtre and thought I might end up teaching them a few things." Silverton was surprised and humbled to find herself in classes with pastry chefs, some of whom owned their own pastry shops and who had been working in the field for 30 to 40 years. Silverton admits, "That's when I first came to realize that you never learn it all."

If you do decide to pursue cooking school, as recommended by the majority of chefs we interviewed, the most important point to keep in mind is to stay focused on what you're hoping to get out of it. Work for at least a year before attending, in order to confirm your interest, before making such an important investment in your career. This will give you a more realistic view of the profession and also make you more focused once you're at school. If an externship is offered, take advantage of it. Work at the best restaurant you can get into, and learn and absorb everything you can. And, once you graduate, beware the paradox of "commencement": you're not a master chef yet—you've just taken the first important step in beginning to acquire an important base of knowledge on which to build. As Jimmy Schmidt says, "Remember: a building is only as strong as its foundation. If you don't have a strong foundation, you can never erect a skyscraper."

Chocolate Chip Cookies

NANCY SILVERTON

Campanile
Los Angeles, CA

"All my life, I've waited for a recipe for the perfect chocolate chip cookie—crisp, buttery, with a cracked surface and a plump interior with hand-chopped high quality chocolate. I wanted it to hold its shape all the way to the edges. Even when cooled, I wanted it to have the rich, incredible aroma of a freshly-baked cookie.

"The downside of this story is that I can't take credit for formulating this recipe—it belongs to Michelle Guyer, a pastry chef who worked at Campanile. The up side is that I get to eat them every day!"

....

8 oz. chocolate (Valrhona is the best)

8 ounces plus 2 tablespoons unsalted butter

1 cup sugar

3/4 cup brown sugar

1 egg

1 teaspoon vanilla

2 1/2 cups all-purpose flour

1/2 teaspoon baking soda

1/4 teaspoon baking powder

1 cup walnuts

....

Chop the chocolate coarsely and chill in the refrigerator for 2 to 3 hours. Using the paddle attachment of an electric mixer, beat the butter on medium speed until it whitens and holds peaks, about 3–5 minutes. Add the granulated sugar and brown sugar, beating until well blended. Whisk the egg and vanilla extract together and beat them into the butter mixture, scraping down the sides of the bowl as necessary.

Sift together the dry ingredients (flour, baking soda, and baking powder). Beat half the flour mixture into the butter mixture, scraping sides of bowl; then add the remaining flour mixture, mixing until just combined. Beat in the chopped walnuts and the chilled chopped chocolate. Wrap dough in plastic wrap and chill until firm, about 2 hours.

Preheat the oven to 325 degrees. Roll the dough into 1 1/2-inch balls and place on paper-lined cookie sheet 2 inches apart. With the palm of your hand, lightly press down on the ball. Bake until the cookie has risen and cracked, about 8 to 10 minutes. Do not overbake.

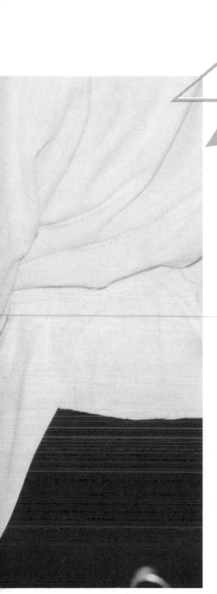

4

APPRENTICING

*Learning
in
the
Kitchen*

*"In any good cooking, you have to be humble
in front of the ingredients and you have to be
humble in front of the fire. You have to daily
deal not with what you've learned but with
what you don't know. If you're not a curious
person, if you're not a humble cook, there's a
lot you simply don't learn."*

—BARBARA TROPP

It takes diamonds to cut diamonds. And the best training comes at the hands of the world's best chefs, both here and abroad. The previous chapter noted that many cooking schools offer or even require a period of practical work experience referred to as an externship, and apprenticing can be thought of as serving an extended externship. Both are valuable for the same reason: They offer opportunities for hands-on learning through practical experience, as there is only so much one can learn about professional cooking in a classroom. There is nothing like the pressure of paying customers in a dining room waiting for their food to teach speed and timing. In fact, some chefs decide to forego cooking school altogether in order to work their way up through the ranks of a kitchen, learning as they go.

Apprenticing has its roots in a long European tradition which originated in France. For years, the young French cook learned by becoming an apprentice, sometimes at as young as 13 years old. Apprenticed to a chef able to teach them the business of cooking, young cooks worked their way up from peeling vegetables to running a kitchen. The French system has remained virtually unchanged through the years, except that apprentices now start relatively later (at 14 after earning a *Certificat d'Etuds*, or at 16 after junior high), while keeping up with regular school a few days a week while they work. Also, the sometimes violent discipline which characterized apprenticeships of years past has reportedly calmed into mostly good-natured hazing.

Ten to 20 years ago, many ambitious American chefs made their way to France to spend time in the kitchens of Michelin-starred restaurants as a sort of "finishing school" experience. Patrick Clark recalls, "If you didn't have European experience, restaurant owners wouldn't bother with you. There were no great American chefs back then." Today, given the proliferation of truly excellent restaurants in the United States, aspiring chefs need no longer look beyond domestic borders for the opportunity to work with world-class chefs.

While the American Culinary Federation now administers a three-year national apprenticeship training program for culinary students, the United States does not have the same widespread apprenticeship arrangement on a par with the European system. André Soltner notes, "There are not enough restaurants here that can take the time, and the laws do not allow us to do apprenticeships the way we used to. You cannot hire young people—they have to be 16, at least." Larry Forgione adds, "I don't think, given the economics of restaurants, that we have the ability to have layers and layers of people to walk you through everything all the time. The way kitchens are structured today, I don't think that they can teach you completely." In the United States, then, such learning takes place informally, with cooks taking the initiative to volunteer to work inexpensively or even for free in a desired kitchen. As experience is gained and skills developed, apprentices may be able to work their way into regular, paid staff positions.

Learning about the historical tradition of apprenticing can help you understand more about a chef who is a product of it, as well as appreciate the apprenticing process in its current form. The European-born chefs we interviewed typically began their apprenticeships between the ages of 14 and 17. They commonly spent six days a week, for ten or often more hours a day, in some of the world's leading kitchens, under the watchful eyes of some of the world's leading chefs. If you've ever wondered where some of these chefs got their drive and knowledge, imagine all that they were exposed to before they even turned 21.

THE EUROPEAN APPRENTICE SYSTEM

André Soltner got his start as an apprentice in the mid-1940s. He was 14 when he started, at a salary of 500 old francs—about a dollar—a month to work 16 to 18 hours a day. Soltner recalls, "Chefs then were not stars. Nobody knew the chef; they knew the restaurant, they knew the owner, but they didn't know the chef. Looking back now, I know my chef was a very good chef. I still analyze what he taught me, what he said to me, over those three years. He always said, 'The dish needs what it needs.'

"I remember when my parents signed the contract," says Soltner. "The chef said to my parents, 'I own him—he's mine!' He was a little kidding, but he meant I was his. He did with us whatever. Today you cannot understand. Even kicking us—I mean, I got a few good ones. He almost knocked me out once or twice. My chef

Jean Banchet worked with legendary French chef Fernand Point for a couple of years in his mid-teens. He recalls, "If you were late three times, you were fired. No excuses."

was a very good man. He had a big heart. But he was very tough, and he was very severe with us."

Soltner considered his chef a good man because he was kind after he punished his apprentices. "I was a small kid, and crying, and the next day I'd be a few hours late. He'd say, 'Bubi'—he called me 'Bubi'—'Thursday, you'll have lunch at my house.' That meant I couldn't go home to my parents [as Soltner typically did on his day off] and he could make up."

Soltner also acknowledges that his chef was a good teacher and prepared him well for the *Certificat d'Aptitude Professionelle* exam which is required of all apprentices after serving their three years. "I was first in the region, I think, because of how he taught me." After passing the exam, the young cook is considered a *commis*, a paid position. Soltner remembers that even 30 years after finishing his apprenticeship, he visited his chef whenever he went back to France. "That means I respect him very much."

A generation later in France, Daniel Boulud lived alone at the age of 14 in a small place owned by his uncle, while serving his apprenticeship. The owner of the restaurant where he worked liked him, but the chef was frustrated to not have full control over the young Boulud. "They were very tough in France when they wanted to crush you. He once chased me around the stove with a ladle," recalls Boulud, with amusement.

Later, during his apprenticeship, Boulud would fill in for cooks at other restaurants (for example, when cooks injured themselves and were unable to work). He described the pranks the tightly-knit fraternity of French chefs would play on one another and on each other's young cooks: "They would send you with junk that was nicely wrapped, and tell you to take it to a certain restaurant. Once you were there, the restaurant would catch on and tell you that they'd love to keep it, but that they really thought it should go to another guy, so they'd send you on your way to the next chef. Or they'd send naive cooks around from restaurant to restaurant asking for a 'parsley curler' or another piece of [nonexistent] equipment."

The first time Boulud met legendary French chef Paul Bocuse, who was well known for his playful antics, Boulud was on his way to a catering job with his boss. While Boulud's boss was attending to other business, Bocuse gave Boulud a tall glass of blanc cassis (a strong, black currant liqueur) while he waited. Not wanting to offend Bocuse, and wanting to seem like one of the guys, Boulud drank up. However, by the time his boss returned, young Boulud was completely drunk and unable to work.

Antics aside, Boulud believes the apprenticeship system has many merits. "In the past [as an apprentice], you did your best to assist the chef or owner, and I think this is the best passport to life. They would open any door. What's important is to create a bridge between places you've worked and never to disconnect the bridge. My cooks come back to ask me for advice, or about looking for a job, or about what salary they should ask for in a new job. I think it's very good because these people worked very hard for me, and gave everything they had for me, and I think in return I owe them for that support."

Jean-Georges Vongerichten recalls of his apprenticeship in the early 1970s, "At first, I never saw the stove. I really learned about the products. We had all these wild animals coming in, like hare and pheasant. I was plucking pheasants, cutting chickens, and cleaning meats and fish. The first year I learned what a good carrot is like and what a bad carrot is like, and all the seasonal foods. I was trained like that, so when I see someone in the middle of August having pheasant or hare or venison, it doesn't sound right in my head.

"Some days you'd spend 17 or 18 hours in the kitchen. Two or three days in a row of that, before Christmas, with so much preparing and things, you'd say, 'Why am I doing this? My friends are running around chasing girls, and I'm at the stove.' It was tough.

"After my apprenticeship, I stopped for two months, just to think about whether it's what I wanted to do or whether I should move on to something else. I was just 19, and I had my whole life to do something else. But when I stopped for two months, I missed it so much—touching the food and working with the public every day."

Former White House pastry chef Albert Kumin started his three-year apprenticeship at the age of 15 in a pastry shop in Switzerland. "It was a better type of pastry shop in a town called Wille. I started scrubbing pots and trays for two months, and then I would weigh and measure ingredients," he recalls. "After that, I got to make almond paste. You would cook the almonds in boiling

A French Culinary Family Tree—and Selected American Branches

Chef/Teacher Restaurant (Location)	Influenced	Who Influenced	Who Influenced
Fernand Point (1897–1955) *La Pyramide (Vienne, France)*	Paul Bocuse *Paul Bocuse*	Jean Banchet *Le Francais (Wheeling, IL)*	Vincent Guerithault *Vincent Guerithault on Camelback (Phoenix)* Yoshi Katsumura *Yoshi's Cafe (Chicago)* Jackie Shen *Jackie's (Chicago)*
	Hubert Keller	Fleur de Lys (San Francisco) Georges Perrier *Le Bec-Fin (Philadelphia)* Jovan Trboyevic *Le Perroquet (Chicago)*	Susan Feniger Mary Sue Milliken *both of Border Grill (Los Angeles)*
		Jean-Georges Vongerichten *Jojo, Vong (New York City)*	
	Francois Bise *L'Auberge du Père Bise*		
	Alain Chapel *Mionnay*		
	Louis Outhier *L'Oasis*	Joachim Splichal *Patina, Pinot Bistro (Los Angeles)* Jean-Georges Vongerichten *Jojo, Vong (New York City)*	
	Jean and Pierre Troisgros *Troisgros*	Jean Banchet *Le Francais (Wheeling, IL)* Alfred Portale *Gotham Bar & Grill (New York City)*	
		Judy Rodgers *Zuni Café (San Francisco)*	
(Others)	Georges Blanc *Georges Blanc*	Daniel Boulud *Daniel (New York City)*	

Les Prés d'Eugénie

Daniel (New York City)
Patrick Clark
Tavern on the Green (New York City)
Alfred Portale
Gotham Bar & Grill (New York City)

Tom Colicchio
Gramercy Tavern (New York City)
Diane Forley
Verbena (New York City)
John Schenk
Monkey Bar (New York City)
Tom Valenti
Cascabel (New York City)
David Walzog
Arizona 206 (New York City)

Paul Haeberlin
L'Auberge de l'Ill

Jean Joho
Everest (Chicago)
Hubert Keller
Fleur de Lys (San Francisco)
Jean-Georges Vongerichten
Jojo, Vong (New York City)

Gaston Lerôtre
École Lenôtre

Michel Richard
Citrus (Los Angeles)
Nancy Silverton
Campanile (Los Angeles)

Jacques Maximin
Hotel Negresco

Hubert Keller
Fleur de Lys (San Francisco)
Alfred Portale
Gotham Bar & Grill (New York City)
Joachim Splichal
Patina, Pinot Bistro (Los Angeles)
Jacques Torres
Le Cirque (New York City)

Traci Des Jardins
Rubicon (San Francisco)

Joël Robuchon
Joël Robuchon

Hiroyoshi Sone
Terra (St. Helena, CA)

Roger Vergé
Le Moulin de Mougins

Daniel Boulud
Daniel (New York City)
Hubert Keller
Fleur de Lys (San Francisco)

Chocolate Crème Brûlée

JACQUES TORRES

Le Cirque
New York, NY

"Two weeks after I started my apprenticeship at age 15, my mom brought me to the doctor. I wasn't feeling well and had some unexplained discomfort in my stomach. After a long discussion, she deduced that I was eating too much chocolate! Valrhona chocolate was the first truly fine chocolate that I experienced, and I was instantly addicted. Since Le Cirque is famous for its Crème Brûlée, I was anxious to add my signature by combining the legendary recipe with my favorite chocolate. To me, a dessert is more interesting when it has contrasts. In the Crème Brûlée, I like the differences in the textures, creamy and crunchy, and the tastes, bitter and sweet. The lightness of the chocolate mousse complements the heaviness of the cream. I still have a sweet tooth and Chocolate Crème Brûlée remains one of my favorites."

Crème brûlée

....

2 cups heavy cream

1 vanilla bean

1 egg

1/2 cup sugar

4 yolks

1 banana, diced

....

Preheat oven to 200°F. Scald the heavy cream and vanilla bean. Mix the egg and sugar. When the cream is hot, slowly pour into the egg mixture. Discard the vanilla bean and mix well with rubber spatula. Pour into a mini muffin pan and sprinkle with the diced bananas. Bake for about 40 minutes [or until set]. Let cool and put into the freezer.

Chocolate mousse

....

2/3 cup heavy cream (liquid)

9 oz semisweet chocolate (chopped in small pieces)

2 cups heavy cream (to be whipped)

....

Heat the 2/3 cup heavy cream to a boil. Slowly pour over the chopped chocolate. Mix well. Be sure all the chocolate is incorporated and melted. Fold in the 2 cups whipped cream and be careful not to over mix. Place the mousse into a piping bag fitted with a large tip. Using a large muffin mold, fill each mold to half. Unmold the frozen crème brulées and place one in the center of each large muffin mold. Fill the remainder of the mold with the remaining chocolate mousse. Top with a small round of sponge cake. Place in the freezer.

Garnish

....

4 sheets phyllo dough

5 tbs. melted butter

1/4 cup powdered sugar

5 tbs. cocoa powder

....

Preheat the oven to 400°F. Line a half size sheet pan with parchment paper. Place a sheet of phyllo dough on the pan and brush with melted butter. Sprinkle lightly with sugar and lightly dust with cocoa powder. Repeat the process with phyllo dough, butter, sugar, and cocoa powder. Bake at 400°F for about 6 minutes.

Presentation

Unmold the chocolate crème brulée and reserve in refrigerator to defrost. When defrosted (about 1 hour), center the dessert on the serving plate. Decorate with broken pieces of phyllo. Sprinkle the phyllo crumbs around the plate's edge. Dust lightly with confectioners' sugar and serve.

water, and then you would peel them, 50 pounds of almonds. The first time I worked more than a day on it, peeling them one by one. But you get smarter with time—I got it down to an hour or so. You learn when the other people laugh at you, and then they show you how to put them in a bag and rub them up and brush them off. But first they have to make a joke out of you."

Kumin describes the Swiss apprenticeship system of his time (the 1930s) as not very different from the French system: "One day of school, and six days of work." Learning on the job required special traits. "You had to be very nosy so the chef would show you something. You learned a lot in school, but in many kitchens nobody knew the recipes but the boss. In my time, the secrecy of recipes was much, much greater than it is today. When somebody had something special, they didn't want to give it to you. Now, it's like an open book."

Victor Gielisse trained in his native Holland, where the apprenticeship process was similar. "My chef was an animal in the sense that he was so passionate about what he did. I went in at 10 [A.M.] and left at 10:30 [P.M.]. We both rode the same bus in and out of work—God forbid if I should miss that bus, or if I wanted to go to a movie in the afternoon [during the standard break between lunch and dinner service]. The chef would do his stocks and sauces in the afternoon, in the time off. This is when I picked up most of his skills—what we use a strainer for, why some stocks are less gelatinous than others—all this, I picked up in the off-hours when he was on his own.

"He was a hard individual. This business makes you hard. It is tough. I can only look back and say, 'Why was he so hard?' Kitchens in those days were in the basement—no air conditioning. It was hot as hell."

When spending time cooking in Italy, Gielisse was instructed by another chef to wash his car. "I didn't say, 'Hey, I'm not washing your car.' I said, 'Well, chef, what do you mean?' He said, 'You wash my car. Otherwise, you work two lunch shifts for two days.' I washed his car. And then he took me to Milano, to the Italian pasta factories. I wanted to ask, 'Can I wash your car tomorrow so we can go somewhere else?' "

On the other side of the globe in Japan, things were not so different for Nobu Matsuhisa, who became an apprentice in his native Japan at the age of 18. "In my first three years as an apprentice, I

Carpaccio with Green Peppercorn Dressing and Summer Salad

VICTOR GIELISSE

Actuelle
Dallas, TX

"Perhaps the picture that stands clearest in my mind, and made a lasting impression, was the food served at a small restaurant called Grotto in 1971 in Northern Italy, en route to Lago Di Como, in a village called Chiavenna. The robust flavors, crisp and refined, cooked to perfection, served in rustic, simple, country surroundings, yet serene and comforting, displayed the innermost passionate skills of a craftsman who loves his trade. The Carpaccio and the Summer Salad intend to reflect these feelings—the simplest of foods expertly prepared. These dishes are constantly part of our menu at Actuelle and remind me to be passionate about the food we serve, and to respect the food's overall integrity."

. . . .

3/4 cup olive oil

1/4 cup red wine vinegar

2 Tbs parsley, finely chopped

1/2 tsp garlic, finely chopped

1 Tbs oregano, fresh, chopped

1 20-oz. sirloin strip

. . . .

In a bowl, combine olive oil, vinegar, parsley, garlic, and oregano. Lay the sirloin in the marinade and turn until well coated. Marinate for four hours.

Pre-heat grill to high heat. Remove meat from marinade and pat dry with a towel. Brown the strip very quickly on both sides then set it on a rack and place in a 500-degree oven for 3 minutes. Remove from oven and refrigerate immediately.

(Continued on next page)

Once thoroughly chilled, trim the outside brown crust completely and slice the sirloin into paper-thin slices.

Arrange the slices on chilled plates, spoon some sauce over each portion of beef, and serve with rye melba toast.

Green peppercorn dressing
....

3/4 cup olive oil

1/2 cup parsley, chopped

1/2 cup capers, drained

1/2 cup green olives, pitted

1/2 cup Dijon mustard

1/2 cup white vinegar

1/3 cup green Madagascar peppercorns

12 cornichons

2 garlic cloves, chopped

....

In a food processor, blend all ingredients until just combined, 5–10 seconds. Serve with carpaccio.

washed a lot of dishes and sharpened a lot of knives—I wasn't even allowed to touch the fish." In the Japanese kitchen, mistakes were simply not tolerated and, as in France, physical punishment was not unheard of—"Some cooks got knocked in the head or chased after." In those days, the restaurant would board the sushi chefs, in some cases with ten guys sharing a single room. Matsuhisa says, "My early restaurant experience included everything from serving tea to washing the chefs' blankets and underwear."

In addition to giving him an opportunity to acquire practical skills, Matsuhisa credits his apprenticeship with imparting real knowledge—including how to cook from the heart. "You can have the same exact ingredients go into the same exact dish, and you can

Actuelle summer salad

....

2 lbs young green beans, washed

1 lb white mushrooms, julienned

1 oz truffles

4 tomatoes, cut in wedges

16 artichoke hearts

....

Snap off ends of beans and string them. Cook in large quantity of boiling water. Make sure that the beans remain crunchy. Once beans are cooked, cool under cold water and drain at once. Pat dry.

Place beans in a salad bowl. Top with julienned mushrooms and truffles. Surround and alternate with the tomato wedges and artichoke hearts. Season with vinaigrette and freshly minced chives.

Vinaigrette

....

1/2 cup walnut oil

1/4 cup red wine vinegar

2 shallots, finely chopped

salt and freshly ground pepper

2 Tbs fresh chives, minced

....

always tell which was made by the amateur and which was made by a professional," he says. "I learned so much just by watching, watching very closely."

Before cooking schools became the more standard training ground, many contemporary American chefs started out by working in the kitchens of some of the leading restaurants in the United States Certain restaurants seemed to spawn great chefs, such as Chez Panisse in Berkeley, California (see page 99).

"APPRENTICING"
IN AMERICA

Chefs without Cooking School Diplomas

Chef	Restaurant(s)	Location
Rick Bayless	Frontera Grill Topolobompo	Chicago, IL
Joyce Goldstein	Square One	San Francisco, CA
Gordon Hamersley	Hamersley's Bistro	Boston, MA
Raji Jallepalli	Raji	Memphis, TN
Zarela Martinez	Zarela	New York, NY
Mark Miller	Coyote Cafe Red Sage	Santa Fe, NM Washington, DC
Patrick O'Connell	The Inn at Little Washington	Washington, VA
Susan Regis	Biba Pignoli	Boston, MA
Judy Rodgers	Zuni Cafe	San Francisco, CA
Anne Rosenzweig	Arcadia	New York, NY
Jackie Shen	Jackie's	Chicago, IL
Susan Spicer	Bayona	New Orleans, LA
Elizabeth Terry	Elizabeth on 37th	Savannah, GA
Jeremiah Tower	Stars Star Cafe	San Francisco, CA San Francisco, CA
Barbara Tropp	China Moon Cafe	San Francisco, CA
Alice Waters	Chez Panisse	Berkeley, CA
Janos Wilder	Janos	Tucson, AZ

"The Alice Waters School of Cooking"

Selected Chefs Who Have Spent Time in the Kitchens of Chez Panisse

Alice Waters
Chef and Co-Owner
(1971–Present)

Lindsey Shere
Pastry Chef and Co-Owner
(1971–Present)

Jeremiah Tower
Chef (1972–78)
Chef-owner of Stars and Stars Cafe

Mark Miller
Cook (1975–79)
Chef-owner of Coyote Cafe and Red Sage

Jonathan Waxman
Cook (1978)
Later opened Jams and Table 29

Deborah Madison
Pastry Cook (1970s)
Founding Chef of Greens

Michel Troisgros
Cook (late 1970s)
Replaced father at the helm of Troisgros

Judy Rodgers
Cook (late 1970s)
Chef-owner of Zuni Cafe

Mark Peel
Pastry Cook (1980–81)
Founding Chef of Spago; Chef and co-owner of Campanile

Joyce Goldstein
Cafe Chef and Manager (1981–83)
Chef-Owner of Square One

"If you had anything to do with Chez Panisse from 1971 to 1980, you had a ticket. You had a certain amount of attention, especially in the Bay Area."
—JUDY RODGERS

In the United States, the reasons to apprentice are varied. The investment of time and money involved in attending cooking school may be prohibitive to some aspiring chefs. Others may find they prefer a more hands-on approach to learning. Still others are lucky enough to happen upon a chef willing to teach and to overlook an occasional mistake.

All of the above played a role in my own decision to forego cooking school in order to keep working, as I made the transition from the front of the house to the kitchen. After I asked Chris Schlesinger, a Culinary Institute of America alumnus, about cooking schools, I jumped at his offer to instead teach me what I needed to know. He let me work into the kitchen slowly, starting one or two days a week and gradually increasing my schedule until I was cooking full-time.

I started from ground zero. I owned only one cookbook, *The Joy of Cooking*, and only one knife. I heard the names "Escoffier" and "Madeleine Kamman" for the first time. Chris gave me a copy of Escoffier's *Le Guide Culinaire* and told me to go out and buy *The Making of a Cook*. I also learned that most chefs owned their own knives which they kept stored in their own knife bags. As I heard the cooks around me come into work and discuss the food pages of *The Boston Globe* and *The New York Times*, I developed the habit of reading both papers over coffee first thing every Wednesday morning. I learned which chefs were the most respected and why, and I started my passionate search of what else successful cooks had ever read or done in their lives, so I could become inspired to incorporate some of the same habits into mine. I also learned to adapt the spirit of modesty exemplified by Chris, who used to tell me: "I've been cooking 15 years, and I don't know shit about cooking." (Since that time, he has published three books and opened two more restaurants, and I believe he still has the same humble attitude.)

Passion and humility play integral roles in starting in a kitchen as an apprentice. You must have the passion to convince a chef to take you on, and that you—as an untrained cook—will be worth the chef's and staff's time and effort to teach you. The length of time you are willing to commit may also be a factor. You can demonstrate your humility by showing respect for the food and the entire staff. Even the dishwashers who have been working longer than you may know more.

The best way to land an apprenticeship is to speak with the chefs at the restaurants you're interested in about your willingness to work for free while you learn the business. You may have to try many restaurants, and some more than once, but persevere. As Emeril Lagasse puts it, when he was seeking his own apprenticeship in France, "The wheel that squeaked was the one that usually got the oil. Sometimes I would go to places twice a day and knock on the door and try to explain to the chef how much I really wanted to work there."

While chefs certainly like the idea of free labor, recognize that it represents a significant commitment of time and energy to teach you. Demonstrate to a chef that you bring some basic skills to his or her kitchen, whether knife skills, baking experience, knowledge of cooking, or something else. For those interested in apprenticing in pastry, consider bringing in something you baked yourself as a sample of your capabilities. If a chef tells you that he or she is unable to take you on at the moment, use the opportunity to ask the chef what books they might recommend you read, what local classes you might take, or anything else you might do to increase your value to the restaurant.

Alice Waters accepts apprentices only on an extremely selective basis, which typically means a strong recommendation from another chef she knows and respects. "I do like to have people come in and help, and especially young kids," she says. "We had two extremely rewarding people come last summer, and I feel like we changed two lives. I think that they will forever go out and spread the good word, and that makes it all worthwhile."

If a chef agrees to take you on, sit down with him or her to assess your skills and goals. Realize that your development as a cook will take time, and express your willingness to start anywhere you're needed. Set a time frame to talk again about next steps, such as moving into a regular staff position down the line. Meanwhile, do your best to demonstrate that you learn quickly, handle criticism constructively, and know enough to ask good questions. Working your way up means

Crustillant of Crab with Razorback Caviar and Blackberry Chutney

RAJI JALLEPALLI

Raji
Memphis, TN

"This dish on my menu is one of my very favorites, which I refer back to fondly like an old book of poems or a diary of fond memories. Shortly after Jean-Louis Palladin visited me in Memphis, he asked me to come and spend a few days in his kitchen. I still remember the joy and exhilaration I felt about the energy in his kitchen—to me, it is one of the last culinary temples of the world. It is there that I learned the importance of originality, respect for standards and quality, and I was delighted to go home with that precious inspiration. I remember assuring Jean-Louis that out of respect to him I would not copy anything that I had seen in his kitchen. But he got slightly hurt and said that for a French chef to have somebody copy his work was a form of flattery. He felt that with my imagination and creativity, it would take a completely new turn, and he was curious to see what it would be. I sent copies of the menus I developed, and he was very pleased with this dish and many others that I sent him. A couple of years later, when I found out that he had my Lobster with Coconut Milk Soup on his menu, I thought I had died and gone to heaven!"

For crustillant
....
1/4 lb. goat cheese
1/2 lb. crabmeat, small lump

a few fine fennel leaves

2 cups crushed ultrafine vermicelli or shredded phyllo

1 cup clarified butter

2 tsp. Arkansas Razorback caviar

. . . .

For chutney

. . . .

3 tbsp. peanut oil

1/4 tsp. mustard seeds

1/4 tsp. cumin seeds

1/2 cup blackberries

1 pinch turmeric

1/2 tsp. salt

4 fennel sprigs for garnish

. . . .

1. To make crustillant, mix goat cheese, crab, and fennel leaves thoroughly and shape into four balls. Roll them in vermicelli or shredded phyllo until totally covered. Drizzle with clarified butter until completely covered. Bake in preheated 500°F. oven for 2 min., until golden.

2. To prepare chutney, heat oil, then add mustard and cumin seeds. When they start to pop, add blackberries, turmeric, and salt. Stir berries gently, being careful not to break them, until soft. Set aside.

3. Plate crustillant and top with a dab of caviar. Spoon chutney on the side. Garnish with fennel sprig.

Yield: 4 portions

 you also must be much more aggressive and structured about your education outside the kitchen. Although, starting at the bottom, you may learn very good technique and speed, you must seek out on your own the how's and why's of what you are doing. Chefs and coworkers do not always have the time to explain more than the minimum a cook needs to know in order to accomplish a particular task. Much of my own on-the-fly learning came with the caveat, ". . . and I don't have time to tell you why it works best this way—just trust me that it does and do it that way." I learned the techniques, but I didn't learn the theory behind them until I went home and did some reading on my own.

It's also important to seek out opportunities to work with food you are unfamiliar with. While at cooking school there may be required classes covering diverse areas of food, from baking to Italian cuisine, a self-taught cook must take responsibility for this self-education. A cook who strives to become better educated may come in early to assist the pastry chef, or spend a day off working for free in a bakery learning the art of bread making, or volunteer to help at local cooking classes to broaden skills and knowledge. Other avenues for self-education are explored in Chapter 8.

Anne Rosenzweig got her start in a kitchen by working for free for nine months. She was the only woman there and did experience some hazing, yet she persevered and eventually worked her way into a paid position. She says, "My first chef became a mentor and schooled me, and I got a great education from him. I think I learned more than if I had gone to cooking school."

As mentioned previously, the American Culinary Federation's Educational Institute (ACFEI) also sponsors a formal National Apprenticeship Training Program for Cooks, through which more than 17,000 apprentices have passed since the program's founding in 1976. The three-year program allows aspiring chefs to 'learn as they earn,' by working 40 hours a week and spending an average of 15–20 hours a month in classroom instruction. For more information, contact the ACFEI in St. Augustine, Florida at (904) 824-4468.

Some Americans still find the idea of apprenticing in a European kitchen alluring, and are motivated to find a *stagiaire*'s (essentially, a French term for an apprentice) position. The initial contact can be made either through an intermediary or directly. Cooking schools with contacts abroad (such as Peter Kump's New York Cooking School) can make these arrangements. Otherwise, prospective apprentices can contact chefs directly by letter.

Georges Blanc, chef of the three-star restaurant in Vonnas, France, which bears his name, for example, brings in stagiaires for three- and six-month commitments. (At this writing, only 20 restaurants hold the Michelin Guide's highest three-star designation.) Several former stagiaires mentioned that they found the food quality between three-, two- and one-star restaurants surprisingly close, so you shouldn't assume you won't learn anything unless you're accepted to work at a three-star restaurant.

After working in "All-American" places, Emeril Lagasse decided that he needed to take a break and would go to Paris. "I wanted to understand more of the chemistry, and more of the religion, if you will, of fine cooking," says Lagasse. "I just went. I didn't speak the language. I didn't have any money. I just went over there and banged on doors, washed a few dishes, and just got my butt kicked. I did whatever I could do to work, making a little money where I could, for about two months." After a subsequent stint in Boston, Lagasse went back to France where he briefly served as a stagiaire at La Castrant and Tour d'Argent.

Janos Wilder landed a job in a Michelin-starred restaurant in France this way: "I bought a Michelin Guide and sent letters along with my resume to every single restaurant listed, asking for a chance to work in their kitchen. The following months brought me some of the most beautiful letters you've ever seen, on creamy engraved stationery with brightly colored stamps, all saying essentially, 'No way!' Finally, I received a letter from the chef at a tiny one-star restaurant in Bordeaux. It happened that he was visiting Los Angeles, and was willing to visit me in Santa Fe. I cooked for two days, preparing his dinner. At the end of the meal, he said, 'Well, you need to come to France.' It was music to my ears."

Allen Susser moved to Paris for a year to work at The Bristol Hotel after graduating from cooking school, and found his eyes

Sugar Cane Kebobs of Rabbit

ALLEN SUSSER

Chef Allen's
North Miami Beach, FL

"Rabbit was one of my first—what I thought to be then—"exotic" meats that I not only had an opportunity to cook, but to taste. It was my first year as an apprentice at Le Bristol in Paris. In my first few days in Paris, I spied many rabbits hanging, skinned in the market butcher shops. Then, my day came—20 whole rabbits arrived in the back door of the kitchen. I knew the time had come to learn about rabbit. I had to skin, butcher, marinate, and roast them for a banquet party that night for the Interior Ministers. From disgust to delight in a day's hard work, I found rabbit to be wonderful and wholesome. As the dignitaries dined on the prime cuts, the cuisiniers all dined on rabbit stew—and we all enjoyed the rabbits with great pleasure."

....

3 Tbs ground allspice

1 tsp ground cinnamon

1/2 tsp ground nutmeg

1 Tbs ground coriander

4 whole chopped scallions

2 Tbs chopped garlic

1 tsp tamarind pulp

1 cup red wine

were opened to a whole new level of appreciating food. He recalls, "I loved the way that foods were handled, the way they were treated as part of the culture, not just as a food product. It just changed the whole focus of food for me. It was a matter of respect for food, for the way chefs were treated, for the way restaurants, food, and wine

1/4 cup olive oil

1 tsp salt

1 tsp chopped scotch bonnet

1 pound rabbit loin

30 pieces sugar cane sticks*

4 cups red bean ragout

1/4 bunch cilantro

....

*The sugar cane adds a unique raw sweetness to the tropical preparations of the intense flavors of foie gras. To make 1/4 the sugar cane sticks, cut the sugar into 3 inch lengths. Trim the bark from the cane and cut into lengths about inch x 1/4 inch wide.

To prepare the rabbit: Combine the allspice, cinnamon, nutmeg, coriander, scallion, garlic, tamarind, red wine, 2 tablespoons olive oil, salt, and scotch bonnet. Clean and trim from the rabbit loin. Cut each into 1 1/2 inch thick medallions. Marinate with the seasoning in a ceramic bowl for 2 hours.

To prepare the kebobs: Skewer each rabbit medallion with a sugar cane stick. Move the rabbit to the center of the cane kebob.

To cook the kebobs: Heat a small heavy bottom saute pan red hot. Remove it from the stove top and place 4–5 kebobs in the pan at a time. It will sear and smoke immediately. Return the pan to medium heat and sear the rabbit for almost 1 minute. Turn it over and cook the other side for another minute. Remove it from the heat and keep warm while continuing to cook the remaining rabbit.

To serve: Warm the red bean ragout and divide it among the plates. Serve 5 kebobs on each plate. Garnish with a branch of cilantro.

Serves 6

Michelin Three-Star Restaurants—1995

France: (20) L'Ambroisie, La Tour d'Argent, Lucas-Carton, Taillevent, and Joël Robuchon in Paris; Lameloise in Chagny; Les Prés d'Eugénie in Eugénie-les-Bains; L'Auberge de l'Ill in Illhaeusern; A la Côte Saint-Jacques in Joigny; L'Auberge de l'Eridan in Lake Annecy; Paul Bocuse in Lyon; Louis XV in Monte-Carlo; Boyer-les-Crayeres in Reims; Troisgros in Roanne; Pierre Gagnaire in Saint-Etienne; La Côte d'Or in Saulieu; Buerehiesel and Le Crocodile in Strasbourg; L'Espérance in Vézelay; and Georges Blanc in Vonnas; **Great Britain:** (4) Chez Nico, La Tante Claire, The Restaurant, and Waterside Inn; **Germany:** (3) Im Schiffchen, Residenz Heinz Winkler, and Schwarzwaldstube; **Spain:** (3) Arzak, El Racó de Can Fabes, and Zalacaín; **Benelux:** (2) Bruneau and Comme Chez Soi; **Italy:** (2) Antica Osteria del Ponte and Gualtiero Marchesi; **Switzerland:** (1) Fredy Girardet.

---

were considered a significant part of the national culture. That's something that wasn't going on in the [United States] in 1976."

Special work permits are not needed to serve as a stagiaire in France in non-paid positions, and a regular passport and tourist visa are sufficient. For positions which pay a small salary, a special visa is required, which limits your working stay to a few months. Some restaurants may be able to recommend local housing or nearby youth hostels, and all typically provide meals to staff members.

THE FRENCH KITCHEN

In his earlier years as a cook, Larry Forgione wanted to work in France, so he wrote to a Parisian chef he'd read about. However, the chef had since moved to London to the Connaught Hotel. Forgione went anyway: "Once you got inside the hotel's kitchen, you wouldn't have known whether you were in London or Paris." Working as a stagiaire in a French kitchen—no matter where it's located—involves learning to adapt to this unique culture.

The first requirement for serving as a stagiaire is being able to subjugate all ego. "You've got to be willing to do whatever it takes," says Emeril Lagasse. "I knew that I was going to get kicked and screamed at, but I also had a vision and was very focused on why I was there, which was to learn. I think the biggest thing it accomplished for me was learning not to be intimidated because I wasn't European, and that Americans were just as good, or could be just as good, as anyone else in the craft. Because the thing that I figured out was that it's a craft. It's doesn't matter if you're white, black, male, female, green, purple—it's a craft. And what you can explore and learn and build on the foundation of that craft—that's what makes the difference."

Knowing at least basic kitchen French, and preferably more, is an asset. You should at the very least know the names of equipment and ingredients, be able to ask basic questions, and understand simple instructions. The better your language skills, the easier the time you're likely to have. Janos Wilder admits. "My French during my apprenticeship was not very good—often we would communicate by writing in flour that had been sprinkled on the counter and then wiping it off." Luckily, most things can be demonstrated in a kitchen.

A stagiaire might start out cleaning and prepping vegetables, learning the perfectionism of a highly rated French kitchen. Of an entire head of lettuce, only four or five of the best leaves might be used. Stagiaires typically assist those in charge of a particular station, such as meat, fish, garde manger and vegetables. Stagiaires might also be assigned a special project for the kitchen: one sta-

Aioli

JEREMIAH TOWER

Stars
San Francisco, CA

"The most dramatic difference between hand- and machine-made mayonnaise can be tasted in aioli (garlic mayonnaise) made in a mortar and pestle (not the smooth chemist's variety but one of semi-rough marble). The texture is like velvet, the flavors are subtle, and the result is more digestible.

"It was Richard Olney who showed me the best way to make aioli. Later I made the red pepper version, rouille, for Julia Child in her house at Plascassier in the south of France in 1978, when a group including the English novelist Sybille Bedford, Richard Olney, and other friends gathered, and Julia let me cook. Put in a fish soup, the rouille was a sensation. Yet another version of aioli can be made by adding sea urchin purée—the result is transcendental."

. . . .

4 cloves garlic, peeled

2 egg yolks

1/4 cup fresh white bread crumbs

1/2 teaspoon salt

4 tablespoons fish or chicken stock, depending on final use

2 cups olive oil

. . . .

Work the garlic, egg yolks, bread crumbs, salt, and a little stock in a mortar or food processor to a paste. When the paste is smooth, start adding the oil slowly, working it all the time. Add as much oil as it will take without breaking; then add stock to thin it to the desired consistency.

Makes 2 1/2 cups

giaire recalls cleaning more kilos of cèpes (mushrooms) than he could stand, and plucking countless chickens and ducks.

The ratio of diners to cooks is far smaller than in the vast majority of American restaurants. At the height of the season, Georges Blanc might have as many as 15 stagiaires in addition to his regular staff to put out perhaps 100 dinners. In contrast, at Arcadia in New York, for example, three cooks would produce as many, or more, dinners. With such a large kitchen staff, there is more labor and time available to ensure that everything is done perfectly.

Stagiaires are not assumed to know much, so it is essential to be assertive in communicating your knowledge and taking the initiative to help out. During dinner service, however, stagiaires reported simply observing, and taking it all in: the precision of the cooking, the artfulness of the plating. This is the time that you will probably learn the most.

The culture of the French kitchen is different from that of most American restaurants. There is typically little or no talking allowed during the day, and none at all during service. However, there is lively conversation when the staff sits down before service to eat dinner together, which likely includes wine, a cheese course, and even dessert.

Your glamorous image of working in a Michelin-starred kitchen for a few months should be tempered by a realistic sense of what to expect. Stagiaires are not likely to ever have the opportunity to cook, and your day will involve a minimum of 12 hours of peeling and plucking. No matter what the state of your linguistic skills, you may find that some of the lessons you learn, delivered at high decibels, may even transcend language. "I learned a lot from my French experiences, and more about what *not* to do," admits Alfred Portale. "This happens when you put up a plate on the line and the chef grabs it and says, 'This is [!*#?$!]' and 'You're a [!*#?$!]' and 'You'll never be a cook!' and all this other nonsense."

Any nonmale and/or non-French stagiaire should not expect to be welcomed with open arms. Given the centuries-long all-male tradition in most French kitchens, women should not necessarily expect to work with enlightened colleagues. However, former women stagiaires have mentioned that they found it easier to work with younger cooks, or at somewhat less-competitive (e.g., one- or

two-starred) restaurants. And "younger"
is not merely a relative description; with
French apprentices starting out so
young, Americans can find themselves
working side by side with 15-year-old
colleagues. One former stagiaire com-
mented, "It's not hard to stand out next
to them, because at 15 their immaturity
is apparent. You're able to do better in
part because you have more riding on what you're doing, and
you've invested time and money to get this opportunity."

Still, most stagiaires say they'd do it again. The exposure to
great French food and the experience of living and working in
France are incredibly motivating, prompting one former stagiaire to
remark, "Being in France, seeing the products, experiencing how
they feel about their food and restaurants—you just can't read
about it. You have to experience it."

LAST WORD ON APPRENTICING

Whether you apprentice in the United States or abroad, the key
criteria in selecting a kitchen should be the quality and reputation
of the restaurant. But, particularly when making the choice to
apprentice abroad, choose a cuisine and culture that appeal to you.
Many chefs have chosen to study the cuisines of countries other
than France. For example, French-born chef Jean-Georges
Vongerichten's time spent cooking in Thailand later contributed to
his decision to open his French-Thai restaurant Vong (NYC).
Whether you're interested in Italian, Mexican, Thai, or some other
cuisine, do your research into the chefs who are best respected for
cooking that type of food, and contact them to offer your services.
Travel guides to other countries almost always list the best restaurants in a particular city, and these can be used as a guide to finding
apprenticeship opportunities abroad. Within the United States, the
Zagat Guides list the best restaurants in major cities across the
country, and using their food ratings (as opposed to popularity ratings) can help guide you to some of the best kitchens.

Once you get there, it's simple (if not necessarily easy). Watch.
Listen. Absorb. Learn.

Warm Blue Cheese Soufflé in Phyllo Pastry

GARY DANKO

The Ritz-Carlton Dining Room
San Francisco, CA

"Early in my professional career, I had the opportunity to live and work in Napa Valley and Sonoma County. My challenge was to create and prepare menus for special winery events, formulating dishes that complement vineyard-designate and reserve bottling.

"Entertaining with winemakers often means a five- to seven-course menu to accommodate the succession of variously styled wines. As a result, I endeavored to repopularize the savory course. From English tradition, the savory—two small bites, usually with cheese—is served after the entree when guests linger over wine. Proper wine selection, to create a fitting comparison with each dish, is a hallmark of my time spent in the wine country."

. . . .

4 sheets phyllo pastry

1/4 cup walnut or hazelnut oil or clarified butter

. . . .

Brush phyllo with butter and stack; cut into 4" x 4" squares. Brush small cupcake tin with butter and press into form, making a small cup. Flatten corners to form petals. Chill.

Filling

....

4 oz Blue Castello cheese or triple creme blue cheese

1 oz cream cheese

1 egg

1 oz heavy cream

1 medium basil leaf, chopped

pinch rosemary leaves, chopped fine

salt and pepper to taste

....

Mix well until smooth and blended. Pour into formed cups. Bake at 350 degrees until cups are golden and the mixture is lightly puffed. Serve with a small salad of mesclun, dressed with vinaigrette.

Serves 6

5 GETTING IN

Starting at the Bottom

*"I spent a month in France cook-
ing for customers' dogs. On
Sundays, I might cook for 30 or
35 dogs in one day. I'd make them
fillet either raw or cooked—and
veal, fish, potatoes."*

—JEAN-GEORGES VONGERICHTEN

I feared I wouldn't even have a shot at ever becoming a successful chef because I hadn't grown up in the French countryside or gotten my start cooking in a three-star restaurant at the age of 14. I was surprised and pleased to learn that this was not the case for most of the chefs we interviewed, either.

Dieter Schorner got his start salting pretzels. Allen Susser got his start selling hot dogs at a Playland amusement park. Chez Panisse alumni Mark Miller and Judy Rodgers both got their start in ice-cream parlors—Miller at Friendly's, and Rodgers at Dairy Queen. Clearly, humble beginnings do not preclude great success.

This chapter tracks the process of what aspiring chefs go through in order to line up their first job, and what their work life is like when they're first starting out.

STARTING AT THE BOTTOM

First jobs are an important learning experience. Not the least of the lessons to be learned includes developing the right attitude. Great success is often not the result of doing only one thing right. More frequently, it is a matter of getting all the minute details right, every time. No job—from sweeping floors to washing dishes to polishing doorknobs—should be considered beneath a cook. As Hiroyoshi Sone points out, "You need to know how to do something yourself in order to teach someone else how to do it."

In years past, just working in a kitchen—in any job—was seen as being in a position of servitude and thus "at the bottom." In France, Georges Perrier's mother was a doctor and his father a jeweler, and neither took well to the idea that young Georges wanted to become a chef. Perrier recalls, "When I told my father, he screamed bloody murder." Patrick O'Connell remembers, "People would say things like, 'You're working in a restaurant? What's a bright person like you doing in restaurants?'" When the father of Chris Schlesinger used to mention that his son was attending cooking school at The Culinary Institute of America, Schlesinger says people expressed their condolences that he "wasn't smart enough to get admitted to college." Susan Regis recalls how upset her mother

Chefs' First Food-Related Jobs

Rick Bayless	family restaurant
Lissa Doumani	dishwasher
Michael Foley	family restaurant
Larry Forgione	family catering company
Joyce Goldstein	own cooking school
Rick Katz	doughnut shop
Emeril Lagasse	washing pots and pans at a bakery
Edna Lewis	cooking at Cafe Nicholson
Mark Miller	Friendly's Ice Cream
Mary Sue Milliken	working in a bakery
Wayne Nish	cooking for a fraternity
Patrick O'Connell	cooking frozen hamburgers at a carry-out
Judy Rodgers	Dairy Queen
Chris Schlesinger	dishwasher
Dieter Schorner	pretzel salter
Lydia Shire	making salads at Maison Robert
Hiroyoshi Sone	dishwasher
Allen Susser	selling hot dogs at an amusement park
Barbara Tropp	China Moon Cafe
Charlie Trotter	The Ground Round
Norman Van Aken	busboy at a Holiday Inn
Alice Waters	Chez Panisse
Jasper White	bar on the New Jersey shore

"I tell [my cooks] that there's a huge body of cooks out there, and this little fine line at the top, where all the best cooks are. I say 'You want to be right at the top, above that little fine line, and there are two ways to get there. You can be a super-genius and be gifted with unbelievable talent. Or, you can work harder than everybody else.' That's how I did it."

—ALFRED PORTALE

was when she chose to work in a kitchen full-time. "She would say something along the lines of 'My Skidmore daughter is *not* going to go work in a kitchen. What would I tell the ladies at the club?'" Regis herself struggled with misconceptions and negative connotations about restaurant work: "In college, I'd studied women's literature, and should have realized that women have been the pillars of cooking in the world. My interest makes sense in that context."

Since then, leading chefs have gained celebrity status and, to the uninitiated, being in the kitchen of a top restaurant as a cook has the illusion of glamour. In reality, however, the people who cook your dinner likely arrive at the restaurant by 1 P.M., or perhaps even earlier. Their day begins by hunting for equipment like containers and cutting boards: squeezing into a tight place to work; roasting bones and vegetables to make sauces; reducing stocks;

Biba Baked Beans

SUSAN REGIS
Biba and Pignoli
Boston, MA

"Baked beans were often synonymous with blustery Saturday nights growing up in New Hampshire, an hour north of Boston. Unable to resist them hot, I would scald my tongue more often than not . . . ah, but relief was not too far off, as I loved them cold the next day just as well . . . a slightly modernized version equally intoxicating as those memories . . ."

. . . .

1/2 lb. kidney beans

1/2 lb. Great Northern beans

1/2 lb. cannelini beans

3 med. Spanish onions

1 carrot, chopped in 1/2" cubes

1/2 lb. smoked bacon (Shaler & Weber)

1/2 c. olive oil

8 cloves garlic, chopped

1/4 cup toasted cumin seeds

3 jalapeno peppers, chopped

8 ripe plum tomatoes (cut into medium size dice)

---

assembling their *mise en place*—all the ingredients that go into every dish they'll make that night; and preparing the ingredients (such as slicing and portioning vegetables). One cook may also spend 30 minutes making "family meal" for the kitchen and dining room staffs—anything from soup to pasta to marinated grilled pork chops. The people who cook your lunch probably get in around at 7 A.M. and, in addition to the previous scenario, might also receive, inspect, weigh, and store produce, meat, fish, poultry, and specialty

8 oz. can crushed red tomatoes

1/2 c. maple syrup

1/2 c. brown sugar

1/2 c. cider vinegar

2 bay leaves

zest of 1 orange

2 T. black peppercorns, crushed

1 bunch fresh cilantro, chopped

8 lb. country or meaty pork ribs

. . . .

Rinse beans after soaking and reserve.

In a heavy-duty large stockpot, saute the onions, carrot, and bacon over low heat for 10 minutes in olive oil. Add the garlic, half the cumin seeds, the jalapeno and cook an additional few minutes. Add the pre-soaked beans, both tomatoes, maple syrup, brown sugar, cider vinegar, bay leaves, orange zest, and 1 T. of crushed black pepper. Cover the beans with 8 cups of cold water, adding half of the chopped cilantro. Cover and bring to a slow simmer.

Meanwhile, marinate the meaty pork ribs with 1 T. toasted cumin seeds, half bunch of cilantro, 1 chopped jalapeno, and 6 cloves of slivered garlic, sauteed lightly in olive oil. Ribs should be cut in double thick pieces (2 ribs each) and rubbed or tossed with the marinade. Sprinkle with 1 T. crushed black pepper. Marinate for 2 hours.

Salt & pepper the ribs and then saute them in 2 T. olive oil in a heavy skillet till brown on both sides. Remove.

When the beans have simmered approximately 1 1/2 hours, check the liquid amount, making sure it is ample. If necessary, add more liquid. Add the ribs and cook till the beans and ribs are tender. Season with salt and pepper, and 1–2 T. of cider vinegar, according to taste. Serve the beans with a portion of the ribs. Garnish with sprigs of fresh cilantro.

items; check to see that key equipment is working (and call in a repair order if it is not), and perhaps answer the phones until a manager comes in.

It's hard to understand what working as a cook is like until you spend your first week in a professional kitchen. The work is physically hard—a bag of sugar or flour can weigh 25 or 50 pounds. A pot is heavy to start with—then try adding vegetables, 40 pounds of bones, and water. Even with the help of another person, it's hard to

Tripe Stew with Spaghettini

HIROYOSHI SONE
Terra
St. Helena, CA

"I used to hate tripe. Now it's my favorite. This dish has been on my menu at Terra for five years. The first restaurant I worked for was a great Italian restaurant in Tokyo. I was a dishwasher and a prep cook. Once a week, the chef gave me tripe to clean. It took about 45 minutes, and the smell was so strong I couldn't stand it! But I thought, 'some day I'm gonna be a chef—and somebody's gonna clean tripe for me!' I learned so many things from this chef—of course, how to clean tripe, but also how to cook the tripe. Thank you, chef!"

Ingredients for 6
....
1 gallon water

1 cup rice wine vinegar

2 lbs. honeycomb tripe

1 stalk celery

1 sprig thyme

3 bay leaves

1 Tbsp. black peppercorn
....

Put water, vinegar, and tripe in large stockpot. Bring to a boil. Skim. Add rest of ingredients, simmer 30–45 minutes until tripe is tender. Drain water. Cut into 1/2" x 2" rectangles.

lift or move. At the end of the week, the hand that holds your knife is calloused and fatigued, and if you were not careful, your lower back might be sore. A week is often five or six days, eight to 12 hours a day. The end of the work day, if you work the dinner shift, may not come until 11 P.M. or midnight. In terms of what it takes to work in a kitchen, Mark Miller says, "Physical abilities come first,

Sauce

....

1 carrot, diced

1 onion, diced

1 stalk celery, diced

3 cloves garlic, chopped

1 tsp. red chili flakes

Olive oil

1 Tbsp. fennel seeds

1 Tbsp. cumin powder

1 cup white wine

3 cups tomato purée

2 cups chicken stock

Salt, pepper

1 1/2 lbs. spaghettini

1/2 cup Parmesan cheese, grated

2 Tbsps. basil, chopped

2 Tbsps. parsley

....

In a large saucepan, sauté carrot, onion, celery, garlic, and red chili in olive oil until vegetables turn light brown. Add fennel seeds, cumin, and white wine. Reduce wine by half. Add tomato purée, chicken stock, and cooked tripe. Bring to a boil. Skim. Salt, pepper, and cover with parchment paper. Put in 350°F. oven. Cook about 30 minutes.

Cook spaghettini in salted water. Drain water. Toss with tripe sauce and Parmesan cheese, chopped basil, and parsley.

personality is second, and I would say cooking skills are third down my list."

Your time at work varies from relatively calm to frenetic. If you get in early to replenish your supply of *mise en place*, it can be smooth. *Frenetic* occurs when your preparation was insufficient to deal with a barrage of orders, either all at once in a single "hit," or

> *"Cooking ability doesn't make you a chef. There are thousands and thousands of people who cook at home who are actually much better. Could they run a restaurant? No. Could they deal with the pressures, could they actually, physically, do it? No. There are a tremendous number of other things involved."*
>
> —MARK MILLER

unrelentingly over the course of a busy night. The pressure is not only the result of the sheer volume of meals that must be produced, but also from the overseeing chef, as well as self-imposed pressure to make everything perfectly. In the midst of your chaos a critic or a VIP may come in, requiring special attention, which can back things up and add additional pressure. On top of this, imagine the occasional burn or cut sustained in mid-shift. A burn makes its presence known everytime you grab a pan from the back of the stove, or reach into the oven. You're aware of a cut every time you bang your finger or take a pinch of salt without thinking.

The scenarios described do not necessarily take place amidst ideal conditions, either. A restaurant kitchen is a very different place from its dining room, and the more formal the restaurant, the starker the contrast between the two. Walking into a restaurant kitchen in the middle of service can be like walking into Dante's *Inferno* at the height of heat and frenzy. You might work in front of six blazing burners during the dinner rush, and ovens are typically turned on to 500°. On the other hand, a pastry cook may occasionally try to escape the heat to finish off a delicate dessert, like chocolate truffles, by working with a coat on and an apron wrapped around it in the walk-in refrigerator. And every kitchen has its own individual temperament. While there are some kitchens in which no one is allowed to raise their voice or use profanity, there are also many kitchens in which yelling is a daily occurrence.

"TEMPERAMENTAL CHEFS"

So what kind of person does it take to handle this pressured scenario? Research on the types of temperaments attracted to various careers gives some indication as to the personalities disproportionately drawn to the cooking profession. Keep in mind that there are, of course, many examples of successful chefs who don't fit the "typical" profile. As Elizabeth Terry points out, "This is a field with a tremendous tolerance for individual differences. There's amazing flexibility and space for creativity." Still, "you either have something for this business, or you don't," says Chris Schlesinger. "You have to love feeling pressure, working the line. That hollow feeling in the pit of your stomach has to be something that motivates you. We had a cook walk off the line last Saturday night who couldn't handle it. Other people tolerate it, but don't like it. And other people laugh at it. They're the ones who love it."

People who are attracted to cooking on the line (not necessarily those who become chef/owners, where extroversion predominates) tend to be introverts, people who are energized by spending time alone, who tend to listen more than they talk. This is not so surprising, considering that while teamwork is essential to a well-run kitchen, most of the work a cook performs is done at his or her own station, independently. "I like to cook by myself—I had to learn how to be a team player," admits Elizabeth Terry.

People drawn towards cooking also tend to be intuitive, creatively oriented people who trust their own instincts, and value imagination and innovation. They also like to learn new skills, because good cooking draws on creativity and is a constant learning process "Chefs are born possessing certain balances of the left and right brains, allowing them to master both technical and creative skills," says Jimmy Schmidt. "While a chef is not born knowing how to sauté, for example, technique and discipline are developed through attending school, working, watching, and experimenting. All of one's experiences are added to a mental resource file, which actually helps make the creative idea appear."

They also tend to like living spontaneously, and enjoy adapting to new situations. This is crucial to good cooking, as cooks often develop daily specials in order to take advantage of the ingredients that are in peak condition that day and use their creativity to come up with new and better ways of serving them. "Being a good cook has nothing to do with rote," echoes Joyce Goldstein. However, unlike artists, for whom the concept of time is relatively unimportant, Dieter Schorner sees chefs as "industrial artists who have a very, very rigid time schedule. When somebody orders a wedding cake for 300 people for a certain day, it has to be ready. You can't say when they come to pick it up, 'No, no, it will be ready tomorrow or the next day—I didn't feel inspired to make it today.' It is great discipline you need to achieve these things."

Developing a thick skin also helps. There will always be someone around with more knowledge and experience than you, and how their lessons are communicated to you will vary. The key is to associate feedback—whether in the form of constructive criticism as to how a dish you're making could be improved, or high-decibel

"The best chefs are sensualists who are given to wretched excess."
—JOYCE GOLDSTEIN

"Do you love to eat? That's the main thing. Do you love people? Are you willing to please people? You must be respectful of and nice to customers and employees. You must be generous and giving. This is our religion, it's all we do."

—MICHEL RICHARD

screaming about what a so-and-so you are for being so ignorant to do something the way you just did it—with becoming a better cook. The criticism may hurt you, but it should never break you. As pastry chef Albert Kumin advises, "It's most important when you're starting out that you learn to accept correction professionally. If the chef complains, then it means something is not right. Accept it—don't take it personally."

Additional skills help propel a chef up the ladder. "Because you're a good and skilled cook doesn't make you a chef, even if you've got a palate and can make a menu," Alice Waters points out. "You need to be wonderful with people, and you need to be a manager. You need to be able to evaluate how people can work together, how to get the best out of them, and how to inspire them. You must know when to push and when to pull back. You must also serve as a bridge in relating the food to the public, because the whole thing is not just about being a chef in the kitchen, it's about feeding people. You have to have a real nurturing side, at least to be a chef [at Chez Panisse]—I want someone who feels strongly and cares deeply about who's out there in the dining room." Mark Miller agrees. "Most people in food are generous. You have to take care of people. You have to give. It's not about accumulating—it's a different kind of personality."

KITCHEN OPTIONS

Every kitchen is different. Many factors determine what working in a particular kitchen will be like, such as the number of cooks; the style of food (classical French versus casual barbecue); the type of restaurant (major hotel dining room versus small independent restaurant); and the geographic location (both regional and urban versus rural).

A small kitchen may consist of one to three cooks and a dishwasher. Its advantages include the necessity of taking on more responsibility, which provides a cook with broader exposure. However, a cook may not see as wide a variety of food. A large kitchen may save cooks from doing all of their own prep work while serving a larger number of meals—you might be involved in serving hundreds of entrees during lunch or dinner.

Working in a hotel probably provides the widest sheer variety of experiences. Through exposure to banquets, breakfasts, lunches,

Garlic Soup

SUSAN SPICER

Bayona
New Orleans, LA

"This is one of the first recipes I developed on my own when I first started cooking. It was inspired by an old boyfriend of mine who used to spend a lot of time in Mexico and would come back talking about sopa de ajo. I researched lots of different versions and came up with this one. It has been my single most-popular menu item for a long time and I still love it. (My dishwashers used to have to peel all the garlic—now it comes peeled in gallons! Quite a breakthrough!)"

. . . .

2 lbs. onions, roughly chopped (approx. 4 cups)

2 cups garlic, peeled & chopped

2 tbsp. olive oil

2 tbsp. butter

1 1/2 qt. chicken stock

1 tbsp. fresh or 1 tsp. dry thyme leaves

1/2 loaf stale French bread, in chunks

1 pt. half and half (or cream)

Bouquet garni tied together with butchers' string (or cotton string)

10 3" stems of parsley

1 bay leaf

. . . .

Sauté onions & garlic in butter and olive oil, stirring frequently, over low to medium heat until a deep golden color is reached (about 30 minutes). Add chicken stock, thyme, bouquet garni, and bread. Simmer 15–20 minutes. Remove bouquet garni. Puree in blender. Strain through medium strainer. Heat and add half and half. Salt and pepper to taste. The soup is better the second day, as it mellows out overnight.

Yield: 8 servings (6 oz. each)

dinners, room service, and baking, there are ample opportunities to learn. Typically, hotel kitchens are the biggest and most formally structured of all kitchens. Another possible advantage of working in a hotel is travel; it's possible for executive or consulting chefs to travel or transfer nationally or internationally within leading chains. Hotels typically pay a notch above what restaurants do, and offer benefits to employees. Many are also unionized.

Chefs who have opened restaurants in small cities or towns or in the countryside agree on one thing: it's difficult to find good help. For those looking to break into the business, there's less competition to battle in convincing a chef to take you on and train you. This presents an opportunity for talented and ambitious cooks in these areas, because with dedication, interest, and self-motivation you'll find you can become indispensable quickly. However, there are also likely to be fewer great restaurants to approach. Urban areas offer more restaurants, including some of regional, national, or even international renown. Having name restaurants on your resume opens up more options when it's time to relocate to another restaurant or another city. Large cities offer the greatest concentration of restaurants and, therefore, potential job opportunities, representing the widest range of cuisines and types of restaurants. Also, other learning opportunities abound, as leading chefs from across the country often travel to major cities for special events or book tours. Working in a top restaurant, however, doesn't necessarily mean receiving top pay. Because working at a top restaurant is considered a learning experience and a career stepping stone, there is often an inverse relationship between pay levels and the status of the restaurant. You must consider this trade-off as an investment in your education.

Given countless options, how should you decide where to pursue a job? To pastry chef Albert Kumin, the answer is simple: "If you're interested in opening up a pastry shop, then you should start your career in the pastry shop field. If you're interested in restaurants, you should choose a restaurant of the type you feel comfortable in. For myself, not to be snobby or anything like that, I always had the ambition to work

in fancy-type hotels and restaurants. When I was young, I always looked for the right job, even if it meant making less money. It's still important today to make the right moves."

Allen Susser agrees. Susser spent two years at Le Cirque (NYC) earning $5 an hour, which represented a step backward in terms of what he had been earning previously. Still, he found the sacrifice worthwhile. "The important thing to me was to be around the right type of restaurant, the right type of food, and the right type of chef who would be able to teach me—that's where the value was. It didn't matter what I started out doing. I had a nice bachelor's degree from FIU, and I thought that, even after four years of school, it was more important to still learn rather than to look for dollars," he says. "That's really where I think today's students are way off base—most of them, when they graduate, are looking for dollars instead of looking to be in the right place to learn for a few more years."

Alfred Portale stresses how important it is to choose first jobs carefully: "You really need to make the right choices in terms of your career. Once you start, it's critical that you get the right experience. Don't get off track and start working at some kind of crappy restaurant. Set your sights on the best, and try to get yourself the best experiences. I'm a product of all my different experiences. I see so many people who needed the money or went for the title or for various other bad reasons got into a series of kind of 'mid-restaurants' and now they're trapped. They can't come out. When you're starting out early, it's good to get a lot of varied experience. But as you mature, and you grow as a cook, you should commit to a place for a minimum of a year. It's better to see one-year stints at several restaurants than someone who's worked for four years at one."

Judy Rodgers cautions that people sometimes choose restaurants for the wrong reasons. "People get very wrapped up in working in a prestigious restaurant, as opposed to choosing a restaurant and getting a job where they're actually going to learn something," she says. "Just when a restaurant chef becomes very famous is about the worst time to go there. That's when they have the least time for you, and they already have their close coterie already wrapped around them who aren't going anywhere, and they don't really have time to teach people anything." Rodgers believes cooks can learn more from people who are either up-and-coming, or who take a lot

"I don't hire robots. I hire people who can think and actually enjoy working on a day-to-day basis. And as an employer, I like to be able to provide the type of atmosphere which is conducive to their creativity as well."

—RAJI JALLEPALLI

of pride in their work but are not necessarily well known. "They're not as busy all the time, so they get to take more care with things. When my cooks are moving on after three years with me and ask me, 'Where should I work?' I tell them, 'You don't need to work at Chez Panisse. Work someplace where you can work closely with the chef, if that's what you're interested in.' "

WRITING YOUR RESUME

So, how do you go about landing a job? The first step is to write your resume.

The goal of a resume is to convey your experience, enthusiasm, and a positive attitude. After listing any prior restaurant jobs—and this applies especially if you're new to the business and need to stretch a little to fill a whole page—think beyond to other previous work or study that could increase your value to a restaurant. Play up experiences that have augmented your overall food knowledge. Did you ever work on a farm? Sell produce at a stand? Pack meat? I spent a summer canning salmon and salmon roe in Alaska, which taught me a love and respect for salmon. Mentioning this experience on my resume has prompted many interesting discussions with chefs I've interviewed with, and sometimes made me stand out in their memories. Don't hesitate to sell skills which might have been acquired in a previous career, where there is some degree of applicability. I was surprised that a former bank teller I met who was looking for a job in pastry didn't think it relevant to point out her math skills!

Also list your educational experience. Mention culinary classes you have taken and with whom, so that an employer knows about your specific food interests (e.g. pastry, *garde manger*, etc.). Even if you didn't graduate from a cooking school, mention any classes or seminars you've attended to demonstrate your genuine interest in food and in expanding your knowledge.

LANDING AN INTERVIEW

Do your homework. Drop by the restaurant to take a look at a copy of the menu. Read reviews that have appeared on the restaurant in local newspapers or city magazines (*Chicago, New York*) or even national magazines such as *Gourmet*. While "dressing up" isn't necessary, you should make an effort to look neat and presentable. Use the restaurant's level of formality to gauge how formally or casually

The Job Application at Al Forno

At Al Forno in Providence, Rhode Island, applicants are handed a four-page written questionnaire to complete before being considered for a job. While the first page is biographical, the other three pages ask for answers to such questions as:

"What is crème brûlée?"

"What is radicchio?"

"Who is Alice Waters?"

"Who was James Beard?"

"What is blanching?"

"What is grilling?"

"What is the proper way to open wine?"

to dress. (I'll never forget the look on the host's face at Le Cirque when I dropped off a resume wearing a black leather motorcycle jacket. I also learned to find out whether there is a separate kitchen entrance.) Find out as much about the chef's background as you can and, finally, do some self-examination: What are you seeking to learn from the chef? What do you hope to bring to the restaurant, to be shaped under the chef's vision? Why have you chosen this particular restaurant?

Try to drop off your resume when the chef is at the restaurant. Call ahead to find out the best time for you to stop by and the best time to catch the chef in. If the chef is unavailable when you arrive to drop off your resume, ask when the best time might be to try to call the chef to follow up. (Make sure to ask for the kitchen telephone number, which is often different from the reservations line.) Getting through to a chef can take the perseverance of a sled dog in the Iditerod. I wish this were not an exaggeration. From the moment they first walk through the door, chefs have purveyors calling, people requesting donations or their participation in charity events, in addition to all the usual and unexpected demands of running a restaurant. It may take time.

Typically, the best time to catch a chef is between lunch and dinner service, but not always. That's why you must be politely aggressive about finding out his or her particular schedule.

After finishing his apprenticeship and his mandatory year of military service in France, Jacques Torres was looking for a job with a friend, walking past the biggest, grandest-looking hotel in Nice, the Hotel Negresco. The friend laid a $10 bet as to whether Jacques had the nerve to go in to apply for a job. After an interview in personnel, Jacques found himself face-to-face with Chef Jacques Maximin in the kitchen office, telling him he was unemployed. "The chef said to me, 'Listen, I have 25 guys here, and I don't do any sentiment. If you are good, you stay, and if you are no good, you go.' I said fine. He said, 'Come back in an hour with a jacket and pants.' I went outside and told my friend that I just got hired, went out to buy a jacket and pants, and went back and started working an hour later. I stayed at that hotel for eight years."

Barbara Tropp is frank about what she looks for in applicants, echoing what other leading chefs had to say on the topic: "The people whose applications we look at first are the people who've worked in restaurants that are like ours: Anne [Rosenzweig], Lydia [Shire], Jasper [White] can all send me somebody. If we can find someone who fits a New American-cook mold, in terms of passion and curiosity and emphasis on freshness, that works better for us than someone who has trained in a Chinese or an Asian restaurant [who may have cooked with MSG or canned water chestnuts]. As an example, someone who's done a year at Postrio [Wolfgang Puck's restaurant a few doors down the block] can come here because they're wanting a smaller environment. We know that their training has been impeccable, that they have learned to taste, that they have learned to cook, that the emphasis isn't on garnishes, isn't on ego—it's about the food."

What's most important in an interview is your attitude. You will typically be asked about your responsibilities at your last job, including how many covers (the number of meals served) you did each shift. You might be asked how you liked the chef you worked for and why you are changing jobs. Or what books you are currently reading, and what kinds of food you like to eat on your day off. Or maybe what you cook for yourself.

The chef will be listening for your attitude toward food and toward your work: whether you speak with passion about ingredients and your work or whether you're blasé, whether you talk first about the schedule you want before you talk about the food. Cooking is about food, not schedules.

André Soltner never hesitated when he said he looks for "good spirit, and willingness to learn—from there on, I can go anywhere. I don't need a chef who comes in who thinks he is Escoffier. Or Paul Bocuse. I do that myself," he jokes. "I don't ask them too much," he continues. "I look at them. I try to get the feeling that they want it. That's about all."

"I always choose attitude over experience," says the largely self-taught Charlie Trotter. "It's a judgment call, but you base it on talking to somebody. People give me resumes, and I think, 'What am I supposed to do with this?' I hate resumes. I've never had a resume in my life. I want you to tell me what you're all about, I want you to

"You have to be so earnestly devoted that if you were any more devoted it would be perverse, and any less, it would not be enough."

—CHARLIE TROTTER

What the Top Chefs Ask in Job Interviews

- What is your philosophy of cooking? (Georges Perrier)

- Where have you worked before? (Georges Perrier)

- Where have you traveled? (Alice Waters)

- What did your grandmother cook for you? (Alice Waters)

- What do you cook for yourself? (Alice Waters)

- What do you want to do with your life? (Norman Van Aken)

- What are your five- and ten-year goals? (Norman Van Aken)

- What do you think of waiters? (Norman Van Aken)

- What books have you been reading lately? (Lydia Shire)

- What do you think your strengths are? (Lydia Shire)

- How many cookbooks do you have, and which are your favorites? (Mark Miller)

- Tell me about a food experience from your childhood. (Mark Miller)

"If you say you're interested in the Southwest, I'll ask, 'Have you been to Latin America or South America? What books have you read about Latin America? How much history about Latin America do you know? How many friends of yours are Spanish? If I hear 'no, no, no, no,' I say, 'You don't even know what it is—how can you possibly be interested in it? How can you possibly be interested in something that you don't know anything about?' "

—MARK MILLER

"I don't look for a lot. I want people who are happy to work here, who have the fire, the flame. I don't care if they don't know anything."

—JEAN-LOUIS PALLADIN

tell me what you're made of. I want you to tell me: why cooking? Why in the world do you like to do this?"

Understanding the types of people that haven't succeeded in their kitchens in the past helps chefs know what to watch out for. "Often I see the most technically capable and talented people, the naturals, fail miserably in the field due to their interpersonal skills.

This is what we look for most in hiring people: that they're not in any way going to be a prima donna," says Patrick O'Connell. "We spend a lot of time interviewing them about their previous work experiences. 'Did you like your boss? Did you like the restaurant?' Every time they say a negative thing, like 'That manager was such an idiot.' is a strong point against them.

"We feel that people develop and create a pattern throughout life, and if they've had a negative experience at a restaurant, it's as much their fault as it is the restaurant's. They chose it—they should have chosen better. Why would you choose a disorganized mess to go and work for? It reflects as poorly on them as it does the restaurant. So we try to find people who reflect a classic illustration: 'I loved my previous employer and would still be there, but they went bankrupt, and I stayed there one month after all my paychecks bounced to do what I could to help them, and it was only after the fifth check bounced and I couldn't pay my rent, or else I would still be there.' Wow! That person has the capacity to be a devoted, loyal, trusting person who could be a really strong asset to the root synergy that you're trying to build. The applicant has got to learn to play the role of the interviewer, to put themselves into the head of the employer, either the chef that they're going to be hired by or the restaurant proprietor."

An important way to convey your interest is by expressing an understanding of the goals of the restaurant or the chef you're trying to impress. Larry Forgione says, "The first thing I ask anyone [in an interview] is 'Why do you want to work at An American Place?' Our starting pay rate is always less than the market rate, so that sort of shows me that you want to work here—and not just come here because I'm paying the same thing that everyone else is paying. But after you've been here, then we move you quickly up to the average New York rate. We don't take advantage of people; we just use it as a ploy to see if you're really interested in working here." Forgione wants to know that you've heard of An American Place and understand its influence. "I want to see that you want to be part of that movement to better American cooking or the image of American cooking, that some day you would like to go back to where you came from and open a little American restaurant, or something like that."

To be successful, it's important to have mastered the art of "kitchen speak." Nancy Silverton admits she looks for people with at least a basic kitchen vocabulary, either from cooking school or from extensive reading. "That way, if someone says, 'My sauce is breaking—hand me that whisk!' we're not likely to have the response from someone new on the job be, 'What's a whisk?' "

It's fine to have high ambitions, even when you're starting out at the bottom. "I only want to hire people to work for me who want my job," says Alan Harding. However, sheer ambition can prove fatal without the proper addition of humility and respect. Gordon Hamersley laments, "I'm amazed and shocked at the attitude of some of the people who come in to apply for work, who want my job and want me to pay them more than I pay myself."

TRAILING

If the interview goes well, it is common to be asked to "trail" (work for free) in a restaurant for a few shifts to see if the chemistry works—for both the restaurant and you. While being asked to work without pay may sound strange, it's actually a very good system. After a single shift, you may find that you'd really rather work in a larger or smaller restaurant, or that the food being cooked is not a style you're interested in. In any case, you have an opportunity to preview what it would be like to work at the restaurant as a regular employee.

Alfred Portale years ago replaced Daniel Boulud as sous chef of the Polo at the Westbury Hotel in New York after returning from France. "I made a crucial mistake there that I've never repeated," admits Portale. "I didn't work an evening in the kitchen before accepting the position. I knew the first day that I'd made a mistake, once I walked into the kitchen." Portale believes it's important for a cook changing restaurants to get to know the food, the cooks, the chef, and the standards. "As a result, every single person who has ever worked at Gotham has always trailed first. How else can you make a decision whether you want to work with these people? You come in, you work in the kitchen, you meet the cooks, you talk to them, ask questions, see the food, see the condition of the walk-in, the quality of the products, understand the pace, understand the job."

These lessons came hard learned. "I didn't last there," says Portale, who was fired after four months at the Polo. "It wasn't a good fit between me and the chef."

There are certain guidelines for trailing in a kitchen that you should keep in mind. When you are trailing, you are there to

watch, help, and learn. The best thing to do is talk to the cook you will be following to find out the best way you can be of help. And understand that when it gets busy, often the best thing you can do is step back and let them cook. The customers always come first—not your training.

Ask the cook if you can learn a dish that you can do for the shift, so that you can demonstrate your technique and your ability to learn quickly. As you learn one dish perfectly, ask for another. The whole time you should be watching all the stations' dishes. You do not want to be intrusive, nor do you want to appear comatose. Be humble and respectful of your teacher, and remember that you are in their territory. Help where you can, and often. While preparing *mise en place* and during slow times you can ask questions about the food. But talking too much, bragging about your prior experience, or bad-mouthing other restaurants will not win you any respect.

Depending on the size and stature of the restaurant, you may only get a few minutes to speak with the chef. Think in advance about what you would say to maximize that opportunity. Be complimentary about specific things you admire in the restaurant, be brief, and don't waste the chef's time.

By the last day of trailing, you should know most of the station and be able to work during some of the milder rushes of business without much problem or correction. You will not be expected to know anything perfectly or by heart.

Since you are working for free during the period you are trailing, you typically are not asked to work the whole shift. If you are told to leave before the shift is over, feel comfortable about leaving. On the second or third shift you work, you should help the person who is teaching you to clean their station, and you should leave when they leave.

When cooks come in to trail, Charles Palmer wants them to get a sense of the kitchen and of Aureole's food, while he tries to get a sense of their personality and ambition. Palmer says, "I expect cooks to come in and hustle. I want to see them carrying things up and down the stairs, not standing around with their hands in their pockets."

The restaurant may bring other cooks in to try out if they are actively seeking to fill a position, so you will need to follow up. By now, you know when to call the chef. Communicate how much you got out of the experience and what you liked about the food. Then cross your tongs and hope for an offer.

If you are not made an offer, be courteous and ask for feedback. In some markets and at certain times, there can be a lot of talented and experienced people competing for the same position, so don't assume an offer wasn't forthcoming because you made a mistake. Chefs tend to know one another, so it pays to inquire whether the chef knows of anyone else who may be looking for cooks. Always be gracious and thank them for their time and the opportunity to work in their kitchen. Never burn any bridges unnecessarily—there is a lot of turnover in kitchens, with cooks changing jobs every year or two in many cases. Maybe you'll even get a call back the next day with an offer when the chef's first choice decides to accept a job at another restaurant!

The teamwork environment necessary in a kitchen starts with understanding the positions in a kitchen and how they interrelate. Every kitchen is different. The accompanying sidebar represents typical positions in a medium-sized restaurant kitchen. Large or small, a kitchen staff is a team and every member of the team is important and should be treated with the same respect.

A classical French restaurant is likely to be structured somewhat differently, more closely along the lines of the French "brigade" system originally developed by Escoffier. The stations may be referred to as the sauté, or fish, station; the broiler/grill, or meat, station; vegetable station; pantry and hors d'oeuvres; and pastry/desserts. There is also likely to be a saucier responsible for making all sauces, which is an esteemed position.

The emphasis on continuous learning in this profession carries over to the kitchen, where advancement depends upon mastering the techniques and dishes of one station before moving on to the next. It makes sense to consider how to get the most out of your experience in a restaurant, and how to use your experiences to help you advance through your career as a cook.

The Positions of a Kitchen

Dishwasher A dishwasher washes not only dishes, but pots, pans, and cooking utensils. They are often responsible for maintaining the floors, cleaning and organizing storerooms, and taking care of garbage. They may also put away deliveries and do light prep work in the kitchen. When you're cooking on the line and need a favor, they're sometimes the only ones around who can free themselves to help, for example, by running to the walk-in for needed items. In the restaurants where I've worked, dishwashers butchered quail, opened oysters, and washed greens. They are invaluable and treated with much respect.

Prep Cook In many ways, prep cooks are the backbone of a restaurant. They serve to perform labor-intensive small tasks (such as chopping vegetables for *mire poix*, peeling garlic, cleaning salad greens), saving the more experienced cooks' valuable time. They may sometimes butcher less-expensive cuts of meat, clean racks of lamb, or strain stocks.

Pastry Assistant Sometimes there is a person who will set up and plate desserts during service. A pastry assistant also helps the pastry chef in a number of other ways. This position requires speed and delicate hands, especially when the restaurant is trying to turn (make room for new parties at) tables during the 8 P.M. mid-dinner service rush.

Garde Manger This station is most often responsible for hot and cold appetizers, such as salads, and desserts. Although garde manger is often considered a starting position in a kitchen because there is typically less technique needed for the food, its importance should not be discounted. The plates that come from this station are responsible for a customer's all-important first and last impressions of a meal.

Hot Line The cooks on the hot line produce the entrees, typically at two or more stations, including sauté and grill, described below. The hot line requires a cook to have experience with the delicate cooking temperatures of meat and fish. Often, cooks on the hot line are required to prepare their own sauces and to create daily specials. These cooks typically work with the most expensive ingredients used in the restaurant, which adds to the pressure of not overcooking or burning the food.

Sauté Cook This person sautés entrees on top of the stove, and may or may not finish them in the oven.

GETTING A GOOD START

To start out on the right foot in a new job, you want to be the first person to arrive for your shift every day. If you are not set up on time, you will feel like an amateur, and look disorganized. This will not put you in the frame of mind you need to perform at your best.

A cook starting out needs to proactively make the most of on-the-job learning. Identify a "mentor" who is willing to teach you and give you feedback on how you're progressing. Keep a notebook

Grill Cook This person grills meat, fish, or vegetables, while preparing side dishes on the stove.

Vegetable Cook This person works on the hot line in conjunction with the grill and sauté postions, and puts up the side dishes that are served with the entrees.

Rounds Cook This person holds what is often considered to be the most challenging position in the kitchen—that of filling in for each of the other stations on the particular cook's day off.

Sous Chef The sous chef assists the chef in running the kitchen. In cases where the chef is also the owner, the sous chef may hold primary responsibility for managing the kitchen while the chef manages the restaurant as a whole. There may be more than one sous chef in larger restaurants (for example, a day sous chef and a night sous chef). Again, the job varies from restaurant to restaurant. However, sous chefs typically work with the most expensive ingredients and may portion meat or fish. They often order food and supplies, train the staff, inspect work, answer questions, and may also expedite during service. (The expeditor calls out the orders as they come into the kitchen.) When they expedite, it is their job to taste the food and to see that it all goes out perfectly, as the chefs envisioned. They are responsible for the pacing of the food to the table. A sous chef typically has some of the longest hours of any cook in the restaurant, and may also fill in for sick or injured employees.

Pastry Chef In a medium-sized restaurant, the pastry chef may bake breads for the restaurant, as well as prepare custards, ice cream, sorbets, cakes, and candies. Pastry is far different from line cooking, primarily because pastry chefs are spared most of the minute-to-minute pressure of cooking on the line. A pastry chef typically works independently, and starts the day early in order to be finished by the time lunch service begins. The work involves a wide variety of cooking and baking techniques as well as a greater knowledge of culinary math and sciences, not to mention patience.

Chef The chef is responsible for hiring, firing, overseeing cooking and cleaning, and managing all aspects of the daily operation of the kitchen. They're typically the ones to make the call to bring in a repair person to fix the broken refrigerator or clogged drain. They write the menus. They set the tone of the kitchen. They also cook. And, typically, they receive the press mentions and, hopefully, the accolades. By the end of the next chapter, you should know how you can eventually work your way into their shoes (or clogs).

of kitchen essentials, such as lists and diagrams of *mise en place*, recipes and steps for executing each dish. Establish a daily plan that you can execute the same way every day. A good cook always has a pen and pad handy for a prep list and a diagram of the setup of his or her station, which will change with menu changes. Arrange the ingredients at your station in accordance with the steps necessary to assemble each dish. Establish your daily schedule: you'll want to do the same job at approximately the same time every day, so you'll know when you're running behind (or "in the weeds," in restaurant slang).

Jean Banchet emphasizes the importance of learning discipline: "You must be on time, you must be clean, you must write in a journal every day what you do. Write down recipes and everything you see."

Your goal is to be standing in front of a clean station when service starts. Heaven help the cook who hasn't prepared enough food for service. Sometimes, however, no matter how well you prepare, your station may take the bulk of orders, and you will find yourself low on or out of food. If you have done everything properly to prepare, your fellow workers will jump in to help you if they can. Even the chef may help out with sympathy.

Every kitchen has its own division of responsibilities. There is nothing wrong with wanting to take on extra work and to help coworkers, but never lose sight of why you were hired: to work your own station and fulfill your own duties. It looks bad and hurts the restaurant if you take on too much too soon before you have mastered your duties. Recognize when you're too comfortable in a station and need to move to another station (or another restaurant).

Susan Feniger and Mary Sue Milliken describe their stint at Le Perroquet in Chicago, where the two met, as "the best education we could have ever gotten. The restaurant was run with food costs of about 25 percent, serving dishes like vegetable mousses with two scallops." The two also recall learning about the time-honored principle of not wasting anything in a kitchen, through examples such as saving and clarifying duck and chicken fat for use in sautéing on the line, a process which also imparts more flavor in cooking.

Joyce Goldstein advises beginning cooks: "Make yourself invaluable. Pay attention. And taste, taste, taste."

AS YOU ADVANCE

When you have mastered your own station, start learning the station next to yours, so you can jump in to help when you're not busy and the other cook needs a hand. This will benefit both the restaurant and your career. It increases your value to the kitchen, and it clearly makes you a better cook because you are learning twice as fast.

After several months spent mastering the responsibilities of your station, start looking at the other stations in the restaurant to see where you would like to work next. Most often, a person will stay at a particular station for a year, but obviously there are exceptions to the rule. If you work at several stations around the kitchen, you will get the maximum exposure to the restaurant's food. When you've mastered your station to the point that you're always set up on time, and you can run specials successfully and smoothly, it may be time to change positions. You want to be challenged, so that you don't fall into cooking by rote. When you find yourself reaching this point, speak with the sous chef or chef about the possibility of changing stations.

In the restaurant business, there's always something more to learn. Tired of Italian? Move to a restaurant that cooks Southwest food. Similarly, you can also move to a larger or smaller restaurant, a more formal or more casual restaurant. You will never learn everything in a restaurant, but when you've moved nearly as far along the learning curve as you can, you can start thinking about moving on. Although there are no hard and fast rules, this generally happens after a year or two at a restaurant. After gaining a few years of basic experience, you may also decide change restaurants for more opportunity. For example, at your current restaurant there may be others higher on the list than you to move into a sous chef's position.

As you advance in your career as a cook, you will largely be "moving through the kitchen," spending time in many of the positions of a kitchen. Finding your way through the profession means establishing a very personal agenda. Michael Foley says, "The only way I think you can be happy with the routine of 'chop, slice and dice' is if you set up a program of goals for yourself. I don't care what trade you're in—you have to set goals. The goals have to be related to the industry, such as learning as much as you can about fish or meat. You should set up a program to learn as much as you can about your trade. Then you should learn as much as you can about operations, how to work a station properly. Always put your goals into a time frame. Don't say, 'I want to be a chef in five years.' Rather, say, 'I would like to learn how to cut fish and meat' and realize that that alone is going to take you five years."

Lissa Doumani remembers a colleague at Spago who would start every morning by boning two cases of chicken. "I finally said to

"I don't really have any horror stories to tell about being a woman in a man's profession. While working [in her first job as a cook], every three or four weeks I'd open my paycheck and I'd have another ten-cent pay increase. I started at $2.62 an hour—then it would be $2.72, then $2.82. . . ."
—LYDIA SHIRE

Fish Oriental

JACKIE SHEN
Jackie's
Chicago, IL

"This is a healthy recipe that I frequently use because it is a low fat, delicious, and easy dish to prepare. This is also my mother's favorite recipe."

....

2 8-ounce salmon fillets

2 stalks of green onion, cut in half between the white stem and the green (slit the white stem part into 3 slivers)

1 thumb of ginger, peeled and sliced thin

4 T. Kikkoman soy sauce

4 T. white wine

1 t. sesame seed oil

4 pieces mini corn (canned)

2 oz. dried shiitake mushroom, which has been soaked first in warm water to soften, with the water then squeezed out

4 T. vegetable oil

2 pieces Szechuan peppers

....

Brush baking dish with sesame seed oil. Lay down salmon fillets. Top with all remaining ingredients except the vegetable oil and Szechuan peppers. Bake in a 450-degree oven for 10 minutes. Heat the oil with Szechuan peppers until the peppers turn black and the oil smoky. Pour the hot oil on top of the salmon and liquid in the baking dish. (This step must be handled carefully so that the hot oil doesn't burn you.) Serve over white rice.

him, 'Lord, Kazuto, you've got to quit boning chicken! How can you do that?' He said something that made a great impression on me, which was that each time he does one, he tries to do it better than the last one. There's always something you can improve on. Somehow, you can try to make it more perfect. And as long as you always do that, it's not monotonous, because you're always trying to better yourself."

There is a lack of glamour to certain moments in this business— the time spent doing dishes, sweeping, or mopping tend not to be highlighted in restaurant reviews, chef profiles, or cooking school catalogues. I still remember hosing down the floor at the East Coast Grill one Sunday night at 11:30 P.M., thinking about all my friends who were asleep at that moment, and how the restaurant life was definitely not "normal." But what makes it all worthwhile is looking beyond specific chores to the overall sense of accomplishment: the satisfaction you feel over the few dishes you put up over the course of the night that you knew were done perfectly, the fun of having spent the day with a group of like-minded people, and the amazement of how fast the time flew when you were engaged in doing something you love.

"Young people today don't want to work too hard. I don't think they are that serious. They can't understand that if you want to accomplish something and improve on yourself, you've got to stick to it. You can't just go home, put your books down, and go out and have a good time. It's serious work. If it requires you to stay there all night to get it under control, you have to do that. You don't walk away."

—EDNA LEWIS

"If it does take 10 or 15 years for you to learn this profession, don't think you're stupid. You need time and dedication. Be patient. Don't take the elevator—take the stairs."

—MICHEL RICHARD

6

DEVELOPING

AS A COOK

The
Next
Level

Once a cook has developed basic kitchen skills and good work habits (which is much easier to say than it is to do), further development takes place over a period of years through work at higher and higher levels, ideally under the watchful eye of a skilled chef. You build speed. You develop a larger repertoire of skills. You refine your techniques. You learn to grasp and translate the chef's idea of a dish more easily. You're more comfortable using new or exotic ingredients and better able to apply familiar techniques to working with them. You are able to develop more sophisticated specials. You begin to learn your own preferences in cooking, and to develop a sense of your own style as a cook—even while you're cooking someone else's cuisine.

As you grow as a cook, the way you think—or care—about a particular dish will also evolve. A prep cook cares that the vegetables are sliced uniformly. A line cook cares that they're cooked through. A sous chef cares whether they're seasoned properly. And the chef cares not only whether the other cooks are doing everything right, but whether the customer will find the dishes delicious enough to come back and order them again.

Therefore, the key to advancement is to make yourself invaluable to a restaurant, which can be accomplished in two ways: through your cooking skills and through your management skills. The best cook doesn't always advance the fastest if he or she can't work with other cooks and command their respect.

Even after Alfred Portale had developed a solid cooking background, he recognized his need to develop management skills. He recalls, "I was always frustrated as a cook when I felt that I had the most efficient way of doing something and the guy working next to me didn't think so and wouldn't listen to me. Just because you have the title of sous chef or chef doesn't necessarily mean that people will follow you. You must learn how to motivate them, how to inspire them."

EARNING THE TITLE OF CHEF

Jasper White believes in planning a career. "I think it's realistic to want to be a sous chef after five to seven years, and to be a chef in ten years," he says. "Once a year, you should reevaluate where you've been and where you're going, and whether you're moving toward those goals."

When you've mastered being a sous chef and you have developed both a strong voice for your own food and a thorough knowledge of how a kitchen is run, you may be ready to become a chef. Chefs have made that transition in several ways. You may fall into an opportunity to do so, or you may seek one out.

However, even if an offer to become a chef is forthcoming, it doesn't necessarily mean it's the right time. After graduating from The Culinary Institute of America and spending 16 months working at a French restaurant in Nashville, Edward Brown jumped at the opportunity to become the chef of a new restaurant in town. He recalls, "While they were thrilled with what I was doing, I wasn't learning anything new"—a chef's worst nightmare. "I realized I hadn't done the right thing."

Soon after, he received a call from a former classmate who was about to start working with Christian Delouvrier at The Maurice (NYC). Invited to join them, Brown says, "I left my job and my girlfriend, and was in Manhattan in ten days" to go back to working the line—and continuing his on-the-job education.

Charles Palmer also recognized his need to keep developing his cuisine out of the spotlight. He made a stint as chef of the Waccabuc Country Club part of his career plan at the age of 21, explaining, "I had plenty of money to work with, and I was able to develop my own style of cooking while not having to worry about being reviewed." Two years later Palmer was asked to replace Larry Forgione at The River Cafe (NYC) when Forgione left to open An American Place (NYC).

Sometimes chefs played a hand in creating their own luck by doing their jobs to the best of their abilities. Anne Rosenzweig got her break when she was working as the pastry chef and brunch chef at Vanessa. While the restaurant itself received only a lukewarm review, Vanessa's brunch and desserts received raves, and Rosenzweig was tapped to become the restaurant's chef. Nobu Matsuhisa was 23 years old and working as a sushi chef in Japan when he was approached by a customer who was a Peruvian businessman. "There was a big concentration of Japanese in Peru, and he invited me to come and open a restaurant with him," says Matsuhisa. Recalling his fascination with his father's world travels,

"I'm critical when the press comes out with stories about chefs at 22 or 23. That's not because of jealousy, don't get me wrong, but because I don't think it's good to have these 'Wunderkins.' Even if they have talent, they lack the techniques, and you need both to be a 'star' chef. These are the chefs about whom, ten years later, people ask, 'Where are they?'"

—ANDRÉ SOLTNER

Winning Moves: One Pastry Chef's Career

How does a long, successful career progress? Step by step, as evidenced by the career moves of pastry chef **Dieter Schorner** of Patisserie Cafe Didier (Washington, DC):

Age	Country	Position
14	Germany	Salted pretzels
17	Switzerland	Studied Swiss pastry; learned chocolates and confections
21	Germany	Worked in one of the country's finest pastry shops where he made 140 different types of chocolate
24	Sweden	Worked in the country's oldest pastry shop, which was the sole supplier to Sweden's royalty
25	Worldwide	Cooked on a Swedish-American cruise ship through the Caribbean and around the world, where he made ice carvings of bears, cats, eagles, and doves
27	England	After he was offered pastry jobs at both the Plaza-Athénée in Paris and the Savoy Hotel in London, he flipped a coin to make his decision to go to London, where he met his greatest mentor, executive chef Silvano Trompetto
32	Boston & Washington, DC	Worked with Sonesta Hotels in both locations, and opened a pastry shop at the Watergate

Worked as pastry chef in the following restaurants:

Age	Country	Position
32	New York	L'Étoile at the Sherry-Netherland Hotel
34		La Seine, started by the son of the founder of Tour d'Argent in Paris, where he was the only non-French employee in the kitchen
36		La Côte Basque, and would moonlight in the evenings as a pastry chef for Elysée, where he worked alongside Jacques Pépin
40		Le Perigord Park
42		Le Chantilly
45		Le Cirque
49		Café Fledermaus
50		Tavern on the Green
51	Washington, DC	Opened The Potomac
52		Opened Patisserie Cafe Didier

and knowing of Peru's abundance of fresh seafood, Matsuhisa agreed.

Emeril Lagasse recalls reading and conducting research in 1981 to find out "who was trying to make things happen in food," and hearing a lot about Ella and Dick Brennan. "A year later a friend told me that they were looking for a young American chef for their restaurant in New Orleans, Commander's Palace. Paul [Prudhomme] had been gone six or eight months and had opened K-Paul's. I spoke to Ella weekly or biweekly over about four months—about people, about philosophies and passions. Finally, she said she'd like for me to come down for a long weekend. As she walked me through the kitchen, she asked me, 'So, what do you think of all this great food?' I told her, 'It reminds me a lot of my mom's.' So, as Ella tells the story, it was in the first ten minutes that the connection started." Lagasse was named chef of Commander's Palace in 1982.

RUNNING A KITCHEN

The business of owning a restaurant will be addressed in Chapter 7. But chefs should always feel a *sense* of ownership, whether or not they actually have a piece of the business. After all, they are ultimately responsible for ensuring that the kitchen runs smoothly—from developing menus, to hiring and training the staff, to controlling food and labor costs. A chef must also manage the support systems that enable a kitchen to function, from ordering products and supplies and ensuring their quality, cost, and timely delivery; to contracting out the cleaning of the kitchen after hours to provide extra attention to floors, walls, stoves, ventilation systems, etc.; to making certain the kitchen adheres to all safety and sanitation requirements. Finally, a chef must coordinate with the owners and the management of the dining room, the "front of the house," to ensure that customers are served well.

A chef must implement management systems that will allow the restaurant to operate smoothly and successfully and to minimize mishaps. "But it's a give and take," points out Edward Brown. "When you take the time to look at your systems, you give up something somewhere else. Maybe you could have been a little more creative that day or invented a new dish, but instead you made yourself more money. The goal is to achieve a balance in your week or your month. Both are imperative."

Fresh Fruit Gyoza

LISSA DOUMANI
Terra
St. Helena, CA

"This recipe is special to me because the first job I took as a head pastry chef after leaving Spago was at 385 North and, as any chef will tell you, your first time out is really scary. Well, just about a month after I got there, 385 North hosted the second annual pastry competition in Los Angeles. The year before, Spago had won a couple of awards, so I was nervous, being the host restaurant and in a friendly competition with my friends at Spago, plus all the other top restaurants in Los Angeles. I made this dish to compete in the fruit dessert category and, luckily for my honor, I won! Thank goodness things went well, or I probably would have quit!"

. . . .

1 package gyoza skins

2 Bosc pears

1 cup sugar

2 Tblp. unsalted butter

2 medium prunes

1 cup armagnac

1 Tblp. cornstarch

1 cup water

. . . .

To set up
In a small saucepan place the prunes with the armagnac and let simmer until the prunes have plumped up and absorbed most of the armagnac. Set them aside to cool.

For the pears, core and peel them and then slice them into pieces about 1/15 of an inch thick. In a medium saute pan melt the butter and then add the pears and the sugar. Keep an eye on the pears, stirring often until they are a deep caramel color. Remove to a plate and let cool.

To assemble

Chop the prunes into medium small pieces—this is difficult since the prunes are sticky but just keep at it. Then also chop the pears up into about the same size pieces and mix the two together.

Now first mix together the cornstarch and the water to make a paste. Then separate the gyoza skins and lay them out on a clean surface. The package has about 50 skins and you will only be using between 18–20 so just wrap the rest up and freeze for later. Now on to each gyoza skin place a small teaspoon of the filling in the center. Then pick up the skin in one hand and with the other hand dip a finger into the cornstarch and run it around half of the gyoza skin edge, then fold the skin over making a half circle and pinch together. A tight seal is important so that the filling doesn't leak out. Repeat this process with the remaining gyoza skins. As you finish each one lay them out in a single layer.

To cook

You will need to make some clarified butter to saute the gyozas in. This is really easy. Just take a cube of unsalted butter and melt it in a saucepan and then set aside for a few minutes. When all the impurities have floated up to the top, use a spoon and skim them off.

In a medium saute pan that you have a lid for, put in 4 Tbsps. of the clarified butter and heat. Test the temperature with a corner of one of the gyoza it should just bubble when it touches the oil. Slip 8 of the gyozas into the pan and saute on a high flame until the bottoms are light brown; you will only brown one side of the gyoza. Then carefully add 2 Tblp. of water to the pan and cover immediately. (You have to be fast since this will steam and spatter.) Let the gyoza steam for a couple of minutes and then lift the lid and, if the tops of the gyoza are translucent, leave the lid on and saute for just a minute more to crisp on the bottom. Remove from the pan and place crisp side up on a plate that has 1/4 cup of orange cinnamon creme anglais sauce on it.

4 gyozas to an order.

Like the old yarn "It's easy to sculpt an elephant from a block of wood—simply carve away anything that doesn't look like an elephant," the secret to successful systems is changing or eliminating any systems which aren't successful. George Germon and Johanne Killeen made the radical decision to eliminate the sauté position altogether in their kitchen at Al Forno because of the "frenzies" it produced. That helped further define their style of cooking: "Now, everything is either roasted or grilled," Killeen says.

Al Forno, which makes everything from scratch to order, had to institute unique systems in its kitchen in order to be able to do so. For example, after deciding that "there's nothing like the taste of fresh ice cream, just as you turn off the motor," Germon and Killeen decided never to serve it any other way. They invested in multiple ice-cream makers so the restaurant could serve only made-to-order ice cream for dessert. Killeen hated the taste of tarts that had been baked and left to sit before serving, and so such desserts were also made to order. Mashed potatoes are hand-mashed to order: "Amber, the woman who mashes them, has forearms like Popeye." Even lamb, which in most restaurants is cooked off partially before dinner service, is cooked completely to order at Al Forno. "At home, we never cook off lamb and let it sit for hours. Why should we do that in our restaurant?" Al Forno's special high-heat ovens do allow the advantage of some shortening of cooking time. By now, the restaurant has the whole process down to a science: every dish has its own staging time, cooking time, and plating and delivery time. Perhaps not surprisingly, every cook also carries around his or her own timer.

Such precision doesn't come without a price: Al Forno's 20 cooks make for an enormous payroll. "But every person is absolutely necessary," Germon and Killeen insist. Do customers appreciate the difference? "They know that things taste better, but they don't necessarily know why."

Learning where and how to cut costs, without sacrificing quality, is something that has to be analyzed at the very smallest levels. "The cumulative results add up exponentially," says Edward Brown. "I started with limes. At the last restaurant I was with, I bought two cases of limes, every single day, and we used them all. When people see what's there, they use what's there. But one day, I decided to cut back a case a couple days a week. I never heard a word from the bartenders, nobody was ever out of limes, and it worked. A case of limes is $6, which saved us $12 a week, or $48 a month, or hundreds of dollars a year—just because I decided I could cut out two cases of limes a week. Then I looked at the lemons, then the oranges, then the snapper and the swordfish, and things that are in the $7–$8-a-pound range. When you look at every little thing—like a lime, or a bag of onions, or a case of celery—then by the time you get to the intensity of five pounds of beef or ten pounds of fish, you are so tight and so closely controlled that you are saving every penny that is possible."

How does Brown communicate his cost-cutting mind-set to his kitchen staff? "I let it be very apparent to people what I'm doing. You need to produce data and use it," he says. "I don't hide in my office and calculate food costs. I do it out front. People see that it's on my mind, so it's going to be on their minds. And if it's on their minds, then they're going to be my agents out there, doing what they can in their own small way."

Alfred Portale has also learned a thing or two about managing others since his early days as a cook. He notes, "The only way to teach people and to inspire them is through example. That's the very basis of the way I have approached training people in our kitchens. You want them to work super hard! You have to be right next to them working super hard. You can't *tell* people what to do or how to cut something or how to plate something—you have to *show* them, over and over again.

"I'm terrified of putting up something into the window that's not perfect, or dropping something onto the floor and not bending over to pick it up. That terrifies me. If I allow myself to do that then, as a perfectionist, as a professional, I'm finished. But worst of all is if somebody else sees me and says to himself, 'Look, the chef put up that terrible-looking thing' or 'If he doesn't care, why should I?' If you catch yourself cutting a corner or taking a shortcut or doing something that you know is wrong or trying to pass something off that isn't perfect, it's like an addiction. You've got to stop it immediately."

Taking good management a step further, Jimmy Schmidt and his META Restaurant Group (Detroit) are very involved with "Total Quality Management" (TQM), and have sent staff members to quality training seminars at the Ritz-Carlton, a recipient of the Malcolm Baldrige Award for exceptional quality. The restaurant staff even developed its own mission statement: "META

Restaurants will be known for consistency in providing the highest quality in facilities and products, and for friendly, efficient, personal service. We pledge to create an environment where each guest—internal and external—feels welcome, important, and genuinely appreciated. We will always exceed guests' expectations. The META Restaurant Group, in the pursuit of quality, is, and will continue to be, committed."

SETTING THE STANDARD

As the head of a kitchen, the chef sets its standards. His or her expectations about everything, from punctuality to cleanliness to precision, dictate standards to the rest of the kitchen. In addition to serving as a role model, some of this is done explicitly. One of the other most important roles of a chef is that of a teacher. Gordon Hamersley says, "You teach people to do exactly what, if you had time, you'd do yourself."

Emeril Lagasse meets with his staff daily for 30 minutes before lunch and dinner, and sometimes goes to great lengths to teach them about the ingredients used in the kitchen: "We talk about food, wine, the customer, and service. A couple weeks ago, I flew a whole palm tree in and, for three days, we did a seminar for the staff on how the palm tree is dissected and what parts of it make hearts of palm, then how the process is to cure it to make edible hearts of palm, and then actually serving the hearts of palm to the guest. Last week for two days we did seminars on about 15 types of exotic and wild mushroom varieties." He also mandates his staff's attendance at three wine classes a month.

Other chefs agree that hosting tastings for the kitchen staff is a way for everyone to learn. "Do tastings at the restaurant, whether it's olive oils or anchovies or whatever. That needs to be a continuing thing," says Bradley Ogden. "You should never be satisfied with what you've got—always try to reach for something better."

Chefs must learn how the ingredients they're working with should feel and smell and taste. Are the avocados at their peak? Is the fish still fresh? Is the cream that was good last night still good? They must also learn how to judge prepared and stored food, such as soup, to make sure it's still good the next day. If the taste is off, they must learn to analyze whether it is a result of one of the ingredients having gone bad or improper storage or some other factor, and take proper steps to correct the problem.

Jean-Georges Vongerichten observes that, "a lot of young people think that cooking is just art and painting. They forget that the main thing is flavor. We have a lot of young people that come in and want to do 'art,' and I say, 'If you want to skip your apprenticing, go downtown and open a gallery for somebody else. But if you are going to be a cook, you're going to have to learn how to season first.' " This includes teaching your cooks how to taste.

Alice Waters says that because so many people make decisions about how things happen at Chez Panisse, she spends time working with them to learn to really taste in a very critical way. "It's a matter of teaching cooks how to get the whole view of what's happening in the restaurant, how to see a menu, how to be critical about the ingredients we're using. Most people have taken shortcuts along the way and have not been exposed to such a range of flavors, tastes, and ingredients. A lot of places it's taken for granted that the ingredients worked with are of good quality, and many people probably haven't been the ones tasting five or ten different olive oils and asked to make a decision about why they like one over another."

A crucial part of the evolution of a cook involves developing the ability to taste. While this may seem basic, a surprising number of leading chefs know cooks who don't taste the food as they cook it. "I tell cooks they have no business being a cook if they're not willing to taste," says Susan Spicer. Joyce Goldstein agrees: "It's the difference between someone who's an artist with food and someone who's just intellectual with food. There are some chefs who, when you look at their menus, you know that they just play with ideas and put them together, and that they haven't eaten it."

Learning to taste analytically is quite different from tasting to enjoy. Anyone is able to identify whether they find the taste of a dish pleasing or not. The experienced cook can analyze the particular combinations of flavors—of both ingredients and seasonings—that make a dish "right." Jean-Georges Vongerichten believes "the most difficult thing in the business is to convey your tastes to some-

"Mr. [Joe] Baum is one of the best tasters I ever saw. What unbelievably talented taste he had and still has today. To please him was like having to please a king. I liked to work with him because he was really fussy—honest and fussy. He's one of the bosses that I enjoyed the best."
—ALBERT KUMIN

You have to think about food every single time you put something in your mouth. And it's not just particular foods like caviar, Burgundies, and Bordeaux. It's all food. We only pay a lot of attention to those things which eventually gain status. But every single food has more than one flavor. Even an apple is not appley; it has a dimension of a little bitter, a little citrus, and a little bit of this or that.

You learn to experience food. Most people cannot do that. They have this value system that certain foods are more valuable and other foods are less valuable. It's the same problem I had teaching art—people saw Western art as more valuable than primitive art. I had to say that it wasn't a class about form, but a class about understanding process—where art reflects status, function, ritual, class, identity, religious ties, historical context, scientific thinking. The same is true for food.

Many people cannot think about food. If I ask, "What is going on in this dish?," I hear, "What do you mean what's going on in this dish?" What I mean is what is the tomato doing? What is the onion doing? Where are the acids, the sugars, the flavors, the tones?

If I give people a chile (and I do this all the time in culinary classes) and ask them to tell me what it tastes like without telling me it's hot, after ten or 15 minutes, one guy will say, "I think licorice." Finally! We go from unsure to licorice, then to tobacco, then to plum, cherry, smoke.

You begin to recognize that no one's ever been taught. There isn't a palate class. For instance, if I asked students how many types of tastes there are in your mouth I'd bet 100 percent of them would say four. Basically, you get "sweet" and "salty" always. Then they'll say "bitter" and "sour." They never say bitter and sour first.

In Chinese there are five: there's also "hot." In Southeast Asia, there's also "aromatic." There's also "pungent"—something like fish paste which is not sour or bitter, but it's sour, bitter, sweet, and salty. Do they teach these things? No. So consequently, people don't use aromatics. They don't use pungents. They don't use hot. They learn to think that they are lower on the evolutionary scale of taste.

Don't forget—language is the psychological way of reinforcing the phenomenal object. It's basically organization in the phenomonological world. That's what language is. Listen to people speak.

I would like to teach graduate level composition. The way I teach is that I say there are these base tones, like garlic and smoky tones. We have mid-palate range, which are fruits and vegetables. We have high tones, which are lemon and chiles. These combined create chords.

We'd look at cuisine: Italian cuisine, French cuisine, Chinese cuisine. It is very biased and prejudiced that they make you make stocks for three or four days, and then they have you make curry by pulling a can off the shelf. This reinforces the idea that we have this great French tradition, and that the Indian tradition is really nothing—it's just really simple and not really worth anything. Do you actually make curry from scratch, from 25 different ingredients, and teach how it's made in [various regions of Asia], and that you can control acids, aromatics, and pungency?

Ethnic foods are like ethnic art, where people say, "Well, it's not as beautiful." And I say, 'Well, the form is not as finished; however, the intent is expression versus form." We discuss food at the same level as we discuss art. Are we creating finished form in order to have a certain vision, a quantitative vision, of the food experience, which cuts us off from the real physical and expressive experience in food?

We'd look at chords. We'd look at cultural chords. We learn in order to play well. Chords can be very complex. Then we throw in acids and create rhythm. People say "rhythm?" Well, yeah, how fast are the flavors? Can we slow them down or speed them up? But people don't get this. What I usually do is take a boom box and play a Guns-N-Roses tape. I say "this is what happens when you cook a recipe; these are all the notes. Now watch what happens with the equalizer system when I pull out the mid-range. You get all the notes playing, but it is distorted now. You get more bass and more treble proportional to the mid-range. It doesn't sound the same. Then watch what happens when I put up the treble and take the bass out. Food is a combination of chords and we control these chords by our bass notes."

To me Introductory 1A would be, "Okay, everybody, let's start describing"—because language is thought, and thought is language. There is too much preaching and not enough thinking. The processes are very important. It isn't really important that someone actually knows any recipes. It's more important that they actually understand the recipe. I mean, Beethoven did his last three symphonies when he was deaf. I can actually look at recipes—most good chefs can—and conceptualize all the players, and you can drop some in and take some out, but you understand food and the food experience and cooking as a process. That's what creates great cooks.

Rhubarb Pie

MARY SUE MILLIKEN
Border Grill
Santa Monica, CA

"Rhubarb has always been a favorite of mine. One of my earliest memories is of my mother, harried as housewives often were, handing me a small plastic glass of sugar and sending me out to the garden to eat rhubarb. Raw rhubarb is an acquired taste, but I love the ultra-sour and slightly bitter taste. This is an old-fashioned country pie at its best."

....

12 ounces pie dough

3 pounds rhubarb

1 1/2–2 cups granulated sugar to taste

3 tablespoons tapioca

2 cups streusel

....

Lightly butter a 10-inch pie plate.

On a generously floured board, roll dough to 1/8-inch thickness and line pie plate, leaving about 1/4-inch overhang. Pinch up excess dough to form an upright fluted edge. Chill about an hour.

Preheat oven to 350°F. To prebake, line dough with a sheet of parchment paper or aluminum foil and fill with weights, beans, or rice. Bake 25 minutes, remove paper and weights, and set aside. Prepare filling.

Clean rhubarb and cut across width in 1/2-inch slices. Combine with sugar in a large bowl. Let sit at room temperature 15 minutes. Sprinkle on tapioca, toss well, and let sit an additional 15 minutes.

Pour filling into warm, prebaked pie shell and sprinkle streusel over top. Bake until juices bubble, about 1 hour and 15 minutes. Set aside to cool on rack before serving.

8 to 10 servings

Reprinted with permission. © Mary Sue Milliken and Susan Feniger, *City Cuisine*, William Morrow and Company, Inc., 1989.

body else, to make sure they come out the same way. The women I've had in the kitchen season the way I want better than the men. I can't explain it. Many times, I take young people in the kitchen that want to learn, and the women pick it up right away. The guys get it, but it takes a month for some to season the way I season."

Alfred Portale also finds himself teaching his cooks how to taste. "We have a wild mushroom ravioli in a mushroom broth, with white truffle oil and chervil—it's marvelous. The mushroom broth is critical. It's different every day, and the cooks have to adjust it. They make a stock in the morning, and then the cook at night needs to taste it and make the adjustments. Maybe it needs an infusion of fresh mushrooms. Maybe it needs to be reduced a little bit. Maybe it's perfect. But you have to taste it and adjust it," he says. "If I come in at eight o'clock and I decide to plate a ravioli and I taste it and it's too light—there's no reason for that! The only time I get upset is when someone's done something he or she knows is wrong, and serves it anyway."

Because tasting and seasoning are more subjective than objective, it's difficult to teach through a set of rigid rules. "I really try not to be too dogmatic," says Judy Rodgers. "The food I do is hardly ever from recipes. The menu is written every day, and we nurse food along, and at six o'clock I taste it and maybe change it. What I try to teach people is 'I'm doing this because it makes the food taste good today. This is what I think tastes good, and I am the person whose palate you have to mimic.' I help my cooks try to glean that."

Rodgers writes the menus for Zuni Cafe along with explicit directions as to how she would like to see everything done, yet she still tries to encourage her cooks to develop and use their own intuition and judgment when it comes to cooking. "Occasionally I'll write something in a note which says, 'Do this, this, and this for the soup, and when you get it this far, look out the window and see what the weather is and decide what the soup wants to be,'" she says. "I mean decide if it wanted to be pureed, decide if the potatoes are so good that you don't want to break them down anymore, decide if it needs extra fat because of the weather. My cooks have been there with me for six years, tasting food nightly. They know what I want."

Edna Lewis agrees that it's important in cooking to leave room for inspiration. "It's a creative process," she says. "Things just hit

> "For me, having to follow a recipe is like putting me on a leash. I don't have the patience to do it."
>
> —TODD ENGLISH

you that you weren't even thinking about. You start cooking something, and the herbs you were going to put in will lead you to something else, and you end up with something tasting better than you would have thought."

There are other reasons to allow the freedom to make adjustments. Jimmy Schmidt points out that, "Sometimes people say, 'This is the way I always cook salmon—I don't know why it doesn't taste good now.' But it's impossible to have two pieces of salmon that are identical. Not every piece of fish will cook the same way—one piece will be lighter or heavier in texture, another piece will be cut thicker or thinner. The heat level in the pan will be different. The natural level of sodium within the fish will be different. You're dealing with an infinite number of variables. You must constantly think while you cook. It's like constantly running a computer program inside your head to account for all these different factors and how they'll affect your cooking."

One of the first aspects of seasoning a cook typically learns is how to salt food. If you can't season with salt, you can't move on to seasoning with saffron or any other herb or spice that's even more subtle or complex. Almost everyone has grown up eating salt, and it's a recognizable flavor. However, often the differences in taste among iodized, kosher, and sea salt need to be taught, and often chefs have their own preferences. "Even if someone's been cooking for five years, when you come to my kitchen you learn how to use salt the first day," says Gordon Hamersley. "When I went to work for Lydia [Shire], she taught me how to use salt the first day—and I was the sous chef! She taught me how to sprinkle it so that it evenly coats whatever you're salting."

There's even something to be learned about pepper. "As far as I'm concerned, you should only use pepper out of a peppermill," says Edward Brown. "Anything but freshly ground pepper tastes like dead, flat heat. What we want from pepper is not heat, it's flavor." Chefs also express different preferences for acidity, such as in their preferred ratio of vinegar to oil in a simple vinaigrette (perhaps ranging from 3:1 to 5:1) or in tasting a soup or a sauce and noting that "it needs a little lemon." At China Moon Cafe (San Francisco), Barbara Tropp emphasizes, "What we do here is about big flavors—acids, heat—so it's quite dramatic. What you're talking about here is taking chile and sugar and working them together so that the heat becomes very full flavored and very enlarged. Or you're working with citrus and salt so that the quality of the acid becomes vibrant rather than merely sharp." In pastry, there is also a range of preferences in the use of sweeteners, even in yeast. It is only by spending the time to taste critically that you will enhance your ability to discern increasingly subtle differences. In tasting you will also  come to recognize textures: when or whether they're right, and how a particular effect was created.

At the highest levels, the tasting process involves tasting empathetically, and learning to ask yourself: Is this the taste the chef is going after? Is this the taste the customer will enjoy? As Jimmy Schmidt points out, "How a dish tastes to a cook is different from how it tastes to a customer. Cooks don't sit down and eat a whole dish of food—we just take one little taste. The sauce may seem great on your finger or on a spoon but it may be very bland, for example, when paired with whatever it's saucing."

Learning taste distinctions through critical analysis and filing that knowledge away for future reference is one element of what is commonly referred to by leading chefs as "taste memory." Successful chefs have the ability to call up taste memories—to actually taste in their mind the exact flavor of something they tasted previously, even years ago—with the ease of punching buttons on a jukebox.

Tower describes the process of using inspiration in creating or re-creating a dish: "You must ask yourself, 'How can I do a modern version—without losing any of the things that made me love it in the first place, and without having ten slaves in the kitchen for four days?' Having tasted the best version, the real version, you work to be able to find your way back—through technique, through what's financially possible—to get the taste that you want to preserve."

Composing a dish is an advanced art. Jimmy Schmidt describes the ideal dish this way: "Being able to make a dish so that it changes and has a lot of components, so that as you're eating it you get different flavor combinations—[that] keeps a dish alive on the

CREATING A DISH

Galette de Crabe Le Bec-Fin

GEORGES PERRIER
Le Bec-Fin
Philadelphia, PA

"I wanted to create a dish with crab because on a trip to Maryland one year, I had a crabcake and found it heavy. When I came back to Philadelphia, using the technique of Jean Banchet's mousses (who I think is the king of mousses because of their lightness), I came up with a different texture and binding which gave me a perfect Galette de Crabe. Now I can taste this beautiful Maryland crab. Bon appetit!"

....

1 bunch scallions

1 lb. jumbo lump crabmeat

14 oz. peeled and deveined large shrimp

2 whole eggs

1 pt. heavy cream

2 T. Dijon mustard

1 T. Tabasco sauce

1 T. Worcestershire sauce

....

Cross cut the green part of the scallion 1/8" thick and sweat in 1 t. butter. Mix together with picked crabmeat. Set aside.

Put shrimp in very cold bowl of food processor. Process on high speed for 1 minute. Scrape down sides of the bowl. Add the eggs. Process on high speed until mixture is smooth and shiny (approximately 2 minutes). Scrape bowl again. Slowly add heavy cream while machine is running. Scrape bowl. Process one more time to make sure the cream is incorporated. Season with salt and pepper. Add mustard, Tabasco, Worcestershire; fold into crabmeat and scallions.

Saute 1/2 cup portions in oil in a non-stick pan over medium-high heat. Cook approximately 2 minutes on each side.

Makes 10 generous portions

palate. For example, we do crispy seared salmon triangles in a rimmed souffle with roasted shallot and charred ravioli, tossed in burnt butter with a saffron- and ginger-infused vegetable broth splashed on it, topped with fried scallions and ginger. In each bite, it's impossible to get the same amount of ravioli, fish, scallion, ginger, and broth—so you get different flavors throughout."

Nancy Silverton uses remarkably similar terms to describe her ideal dessert. "It's one that keeps your interest from the first bite through the last. It can start with temperature: as a really hot dessert cools, its texture changes, causing contrasts in textures."

In combining flavors and textures into a finished dish, perhaps one of the most important things you learn as a cook is what to leave out. While leading chefs have the maturity to use multiple ingredients more successfully, inexperienced cooks often make a dish too complex, out of eagerness to display everything they know about color, texture, and presentation on a single plate. An experienced chef knows which items don't belong, and what will bring harmony to the plate. Susan Spicer notes, "Sometimes people don't have the experience, or the taste memory. They're inexperienced at putting things together and get carried away with ingredients for ingredients' sake." Norman Van Aken describes the process of maturation for a chef as "learning when *not* to hit certain notes. I listen to a guy like [guitarist Eric] Clapton play, and I remember him playing with Cream [his early band] all over the guitar, hitting every note known to man. That's an appropriate metaphor for what I felt that I was doing as a young cook. That restlessness, that curiosity, is a big part of being a young artist. Now, I'm choosing the notes a lot more, as opposed to just playing all of them."

The secret sometimes lies in simplicity. Jimmy Schmidt describes another equally impressive dish which relies on fewer ingredients and techniques: "We prepare some of the local fish very simply. Their flavors are so subtle that we try to accentuate them rather than add a lot of other ingredients that would tend to mask them. We use whole butter, which is very sweet, for sautéing. The flour is seasoned flour with a touch of paprika, which has a sweet pepper flavor to it. It's done at very high temperatures, which is crucial

Jean-Georges Vongerichten "forces" his staff to eat at Jojo once a month: "So many people don't eat their own food. I never put a dish on the menu unless I eat it first."

Dry Poached Pear with Port and Cassis Ice Cream

JIMMY SCHMIDT

META *Restaurants*
Detroit, MI

"Growing up on a farm and having wonderful fresh fruit, especially pears, that matured to perfection after being picked from the tree, I tried to capture that perfect pear 'essence' in cooked form. Thus, the idea of poaching the pear in a dry medium that added no additional flavors, as well as allowed no flavors to escape, gave birth to this technique. When I enjoy Dry Poached Pear with Port and Cassis Ice Cream, it brings back memories of fall harvest with wonderful aromas of Thanksgiving in the air."

. . . .

1/2 bottle Beringer cabernet sauvignon port

1 cup sugar

3 tablespoons balsamic vinegar

1 3-pound box kosher salt

4 large Comice pears

2 tablespoons unsalted butter

1/2 cup dark brown sugar

2 cups cassis ice cream

4 sprigs mint

. . . .

because the butter starts to develop a little bit of nuttiness, and you're able to seal the fish and capture as much of the moisture as possible. It also gives it a crisp outside while the flesh is very, very tender." And even Nancy Silverton admits, "I also like desserts that are studded with something in every bite, but still simple."

Even within dishes, the flavors of basic components can be altered through the application of various cooking techniques.

In a medium-size saucepan, combine the port and sugar. Bring to a simmer over medium heat and cook until the liquid is reduced to 1 cup, about 15 minutes. Remove from heat and allow to cool to room temperature. Stir in the balsamic vinegar.

Preheat oven to 425°F.

Select a medium-size ovenproof pot large enough to later accommodate all four pears. Fill the pot with all of the salt and place in the oven for 1 hour to thoroughly heat. Remove the pot from oven. *Carefully* remove two-thirds of the salt to another pan. (Reminder: the salt is 425°F.!!) Position the pears on the remaining salt so that they do not touch each other. Completely bury pears in the salt you took out. Return the pot to the oven and cook until tender, about 15 minutes. Remove from the oven, and carefully remove the salt from around one pear; test tenderness by inserting a skewer, taking care not to puncture the skin. Remove the salt from around the remaining pears. Transfer to a plate. Carefully brush any remaining salt from the pears. Allow to cool.

Glazing the pears: Rub the 4 dry-poached pears with butter lightly to coat the skins. Then rub the skins with brown sugar, allowing the sugar to stick to the butter. Using tongs, hold the pear over an open burner or under the broiler to heat the sugar and caramelize it onto the skin of the pear. Allow to cool.

Spoon the sauce onto the serving plates. Position the pear in the center of the sauce. Scoop the ice cream and position next to the pear. Garnish with mint and serve.

Cooking notes

Cooked in this manner, the pear is seared by the salt, causing the juices to be trapped in the pear. The salt must be hot or the pear will be salty. For the same reason, do not allow the pear to cool in the salt. A properly cooked pear will have no taste of the salt.

Makes 4 servings

Mark Militello says, "One of the things I worked very hard on was developing flavors. I learned things from all different cultures, and I learned some great things from Mark Miller and Rick Bayless, who related how they developed some of their flavors within their cuisine—whether through roasting or toasting or whatever. If you're working with an onion, why just work with a plain onion?—do a roast. Or if it's a tomato, taste the effect of blistering the skin. With

Shirred Egg with White Truffles, New Potatoes, and Fresh Herbs

WAYNE NISH
March
New York, NY

"All of my childhood memories of food are of simple dishes with strong flavors. As a result, a clear preference in my work is to strive for such effect. I have included this recipe because I feel it represents some of my best work to date. It is simple, elegant, and delicious."

. . . .

1 stick of sweet butter

a pinch of kosher salt

4 or 5 Ruby Crescent potatoes, each the size of a fingernail, quartered

1 tablespoon extra-virgin olive oil

1 very fresh, extra large organic egg

a tiny pinch of kosher salt

1 teaspoon white truffle oil

1 tablespoon mixed fresh herbs (chives, chervil, parsley, tarragon, and basil)

1/4 ounce fresh white truffle from Italy

. . . .

Preheat an oven to 500°F.

On top of the stove, in a small saucepan, melt the butter, season with salt, and gently poach the quartered potatoes for a few minutes or until tender.

Meanwhile, in a cold, small steel blini pan (4 1/2" diameter) pour in the olive oil and swirl to cover the bottom. Pour out the excess.

Crack open the egg into the pan, season lightly with salt, and bake for 2 minutes or until just set.

Remove the egg to a small, round serving dish and garnish with the drained potatoes, truffle oil, and herbs.

Shave the white truffle over the dish in paper-thin slices and serve immediately.

Serves one

spices, you can toast them to bring out the oils. We've learned to do some very different things that way."

Preferences about flavors within dishes vary. Using desserts as an example, Nancy Silverton explains, "There are certain basic flavors—chocolate, coffee, lemon—that people either love or hate. The secret is to make a dessert for people who love that flavor." Charles Palmer agrees. "I'm a big believer in concentration of flavors, so that if something's chocolate, it should be all chocolate," he says. "If it's a chocolate torte, it should have layers of chocolate genoise and chocolate mousse, maybe covered in chocolate ganache and wrapped with chocolate and served with chocolate sauces and maybe light and dark chocolate twills. Once you have the base, the rest of it is just fooling around."

Beyond "hitting the right notes" in the creation of individual dishes, there is also a certain rhythm to a harmonious menu. "The most beautiful dinner is not where you finish one course and then get hungry again, but one which flows from one course to another," says Dieter Schorner. Joyce Goldstein adds, "I know when I've eaten a good meal. I was at Frontera Grill the other night and I had a wonderful meal. Why? Because these people understand what they're doing with their flavors. We had a variety of different chiles, but not all of them were hot. The flavors were 'round.' There was a contrast in the menu that Rick [Bayless] had put together for us— and you went on a ride through this wonderful meal. Everything was in its own balance. He understood his vocabulary, and he knew when to put the right words in the right places. It read like a sentence or a paragraph or a poem."

In time, as part of a process spanning many years, cooks may develop these advanced abilities which allow them to, in the words of Jasper White, "not just move the pans around over heat, but to impose their will on the food"—that is, to orchestrate exactly how the food they are cooking will look and smell and taste.

"You could make a list of all the capital sins why cooks should be shot: too many ingredients, discordant flavors, things that sound okay but really are flat, trendiness for the sake of trendiness, not understanding the real essence of the ingredients but using them like a Band-Aid . . ."
—JOYCE GOLDSTEIN

An experienced chef's greatness is often evidenced by his or her development of a "sixth sense" when it comes to cooking, and many of the chefs we interviewed alluded to this ability in some regard. Over time, they have developed the ability to cook at a more intuitive level, for lack of a better description. Susan Spicer describes how, as a chef, she's developed acute powers of sensory

EXTRA-SENSORY PERCEPTION

While walking by his cooks who were making tiramisu, Jeremiah Tower stuck a finger in the bowl and tasted it. "Stop!" he yelled. Once stabilized with whipped cream, the creation became Stars' Fantasy Cream, one of the restaurant's specialty desserts.

perception: "I've really developed my eyes so that I can look at something three feet away and say 'that needs rinsing off,' or 'that doesn't look fresh to me.' I know when someone puts something in a sauté pan and it doesn't make a noise that the pan wasn't hot enough. I listen when someone is chopping an onion and it's going 'crunch,' and I know without looking that that person needs to sharpen their knife. I listen when I'm making a sauce in a blender, and I know if the sauce has broken by the sound. I smell everything out of habit, to make sure it's right. This is what you have to do."

Jeremiah Tower recalls a friend in the perfume business who claimed she could "smell" fragrances in her head. He believes the same is true for chefs and tasting. "When you write a recipe, you can taste it in your mind," he says. Daniel Boulud agrees: "Many recipes are written by chefs before the dishes are ever made, because they're created in your mind. Your senses give you the combinations."

Patrick O'Connell insists, "I don't actually have to eat food anymore. I do eat and I do taste, but I swear I can review the taste of it—without actually tasting it—by the visual. I can tell the age of the person who made a dish, the number of years of experience they have in the kitchen and their IQ, and I can write you a short biography of them. A dish represents a distillation of a cook's entire being."

KEEPING IT FRESH

As the kitchen's "chief," there are no longer the immediate pressures of a raised voice to respond to, and a chef's greatest challenge lies in creating and acting upon self-imposed pressure to keep innovating. Lydia Shire says, "I'll be placing the food order and I'll find myself not looking for something interesting to bring in for specials. And right away I get a guilty feeling inside and I think, 'How can I expect Susie [Regis] to come in and get all excited over a special with me when I haven't done my part in going out and looking for something interesting to bring in here?' Of course I *like* all of this, but every once in a while you just need to push yourself."

The inspiration to experiment can come from various sources. Norman Van Aken says, "I remember getting jicama in at Sinclair's, and my dishwashers Carlos and Ray asked, 'What are you doing with that?' I asked them, 'What do you do with this thing?' Pretty soon they were peeling it and putting cayenne and lime juice on it, and eating it as happy as can be. So I tried it and said, 'Yeah, that's great!' Their attitude, unfortunately like that of a lot of people from other countries, was that their food was declasse—and I had to tell them that it wasn't. I might want to take part of the idea and create a bridge to something more familiar [to customers]. The term 'fusion,' to me, reflected my desire to harness both the rustic power of regional cuisine and the intellectual power of classical cuisine, and to put them together."

When experimenting, how can you tell when it's "right"? According to Joyce Goldstein, "When you think of really gifted cooks and how they play with ingredients, you know that at a certain point it was in balance for them. When you're tasting anything, it's like a seesaw—it's going up and down and up and down and finally you get in balance and, hopefully, you stop. That doesn't mean that all the tastes are even. Sometimes you want something to be lemony, maybe more lemony than lemons, because something is super rich and you want to cut it, or you want the lemon to be the star. But it's really in balance. Or sometimes you want sneaky heat—heat that people don't realize they've had until five minutes later. Not bludgeon-you-to-death heat, when all of a sudden you can't taste any other flavors because it's just hot. There's a balance to that as well."

The best chefs never remain static, but continue to evolve their styles and preferences. Often this involves a paring down of one's cuisine to its very essence. Jean-Louis Palladin uses the analogy of an artist. "Like a painter, a chef's style changes over time," he says. "The ingredients you use change. There's more simplicity, less sophistication. It's more pure, with no artifice." Norman Van Aken believes, "The death of any artist is to be afraid, to stop taking chances. [Bob] Dylan proved that. The really great ones continue to shatter the mold they make. Picasso was like that. I think that what will cause the good ones to go on will be the ability to continue to break their own molds, and to listen, to learn, and to move upon these influences in an interesting way."

"I love to see people who cook better than me. Michel Blanchet [of The Escoffier Room in Beverly Hills] makes an incredible dish of squab, red wine sauce, and mushrooms."

—JEAN BANCHET

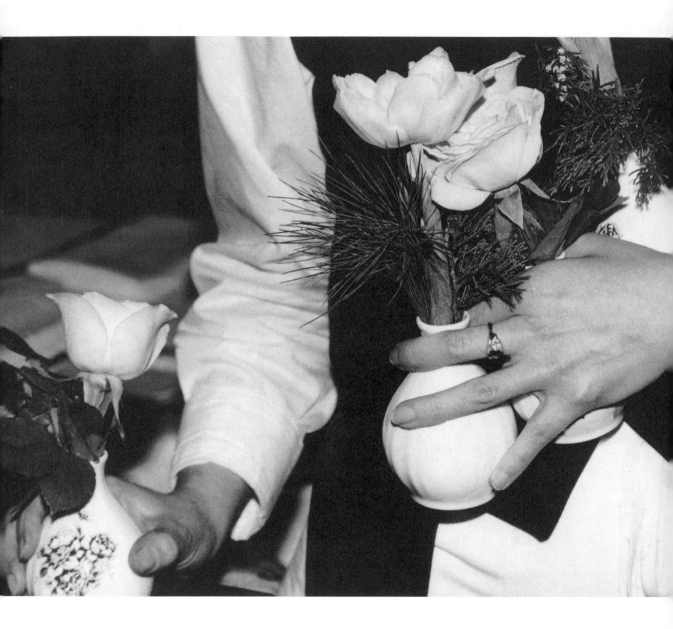

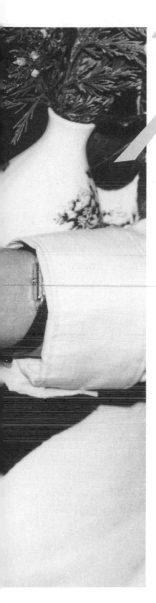

7

THE BUSINESS
OF COOKING

Operating
and
Running
a
Restaurant

*"Just do it. Do it your own way. Break all
the rules. And look for a niche—they're
still out there. The problem, it seems, is
that everybody is scrambling for the same
niche instead of being who they are."*

—PATRICK O'CONNELL

A restaurant is a living work of art—one which reflects everything the chef-owner thinks and feels about food and service. When a chef becomes a chef-restaurateur, his or her reputation rests not only on what is served on the plate, but on the very plate itself—not to mention the glasses, the flowers, the wait staff, the host, and every minute detail the customer, who is a guest of the restaurant for a few hours, notices and discusses the next day with co-workers.

Every word of criticism is taken personally because, at its best, one's restaurant is one's home. Nancy Silverton paraphrases London chef Marco White's sentiment as expressed in his cookbook *White Heat* on chefs' sensitivity to criticism: "If I came to your house for dinner late, criticized your furniture and your wife, and said your opinions were stupid, how would you feel?" Sometimes the "restaurant as home" analogy is even literally true: Silverton and husband Mark Peel live with their two children above their restaurant Campanile in Los Angeles, and Emeril Lagasse and his family live above Emeril's in New Orleans.

The primary difference lies in the bottom line, which is that running a restaurant is a business. "You can do anything you want, but the restaurant won't survive unless you can pay the bills at the end of the month," says Edward Brown. "It's all about controlling costs, managing people, and knowing how the process works. It's another whole career. But you have to be able to do both [as a chef-restaurateur]."

Leading chefs manage to stay gracious with their customers while tending to food costs, critics, and other mostly behind-the-scenes concerns in order to keep their restaurants successful. The business and management practices of leading chefs are like special effects in movies—they make the impossible seem effortless.

WHAT'S IT LIKE?

Depending on who you ask, running a restaurant can be made to sound easy, requiring only good common sense.

"Opening a restaurant is like throwing a dinner party," says Jeremiah Tower. "We all do dinner parties. You start at the front

Opening Lutèce: A Historical Perspective

André Soltner moved to New York City in 1961 to open Lutèce. "It was very, very difficult, for many reasons. Today, restaurants open and everybody goes to look because the media right away talks about it, so everybody goes to see. Then, it wasn't so. It was pretty quiet. Word got around by 'word of mouth,' so there was no explosion. Today, we are looked at as a classic restaurant. But then, we were looked at as very avant-garde. We opened with high prices. We didn't believe in anything frozen, anything canned, which was not so 34 years ago. Because of that we had much higher prices than our competition. When we opened, our prix fixe lunch was $8.50, and it was so much of a scandal in New York that we went down to $6.50. It was the talk of the city that there is a crazy guy who opens at $8.50." [In 1995, Lutèce's prix fixe lunch was $38.]

"We flew in fresh Dover sole. Nobody flew in fresh Dover sole, but every restaurant had Dover sole on the menu—it wasn't marked fresh or frozen. So we sold our sole for maybe $8, and some of our competition sold it for $4. We made less money than they did. Today, you try to sell frozen sole when everybody's educated enough to know the difference, and you go out of business.

"It was not easy. But we held on, and little by little, we had more business. The first two years, we were closer to bankruptcy than to success. But we held on, and it worked."

door, where guests come in. Is the light on? Is the carpet dirty? You go into the bathroom. Is there toilet paper? Is there soap? Is the soap dish clean? In the dining room, are there flowers? Are the glasses polished? Before you even get to the food or the wine, you take care of those things."

Patrick O'Connell finds Tower's analogy apt. "I think the feeling that I like best is a sense of walking into somebody's private space, or their home. I find that very touching. The more a restaurant can evoke that, the more trust I have in it and the more forgiving I am."

Tower admits that in order to be successful as a chef-restaurateur, "it has to be central to your life—you must be attuned to it all the time. I'm always on duty. I can walk into a restaurant and immediately tell which lightbulbs are out." And O'Connell

"I don't really think that there are a lot of secrets to this business. I don't think it's luck, and I don't think it's totally somebody's review that's going to make your restaurant. I think if you give people something really good, and if you really try to please them, and you try to make them feel happy . . . [Aureole] is all about making a restaurant that felt good and giving people food that was my food, but that was universally likable. The mistake a lot of people make is that they think a restaurant is going to operate on its own. If you have a restaurant that's as personal as this restaurant is, you have to be there all the time, and you have to make sure that people know that you're in, and that people know that you care."

CHARLES PALMER

A Day in the Life of a Chef-Owner

Jackie Shen of Jackie's (Chicago) says she sleeps about five hours a night:

3 A.M.	She comes into the restaurant with her black labrador retriever to set up specials and write out her order list
4 A.M.	The cook and dishwasher come in to clean up and Jackie catches 15 minutes of world news on TV
5 A.M.	Jackie places the orders for the restaurant
6 A.M.	She does pastry work, focusing on some of the more complex desserts
noon	Jackie cooks lunch
2 P.M.	She takes a one-hour break and walks her dog
3 P.M.	Jackie finishes pastry work, schedules the front of the house staff, and takes reservations
6 P.M.	She cooks dinner, working the fish station
10 P.M.	Jackie goes home

acknowledges, "It's hard. It's a balancing act to deal with banks, finances, payrolls, lawsuits, and still try to open your home every night and care about people. But it can be done."

How? "I think of every detail as being equally important," says O'Connell. "How are you going to enjoy the food if the lighting is off or the server is dumb or the flowers are dead? The whole experience has to be conscious, so the chef needs to emerge as the controlling influence from the kitchen and produce the entire production, keeping it all at the same level."

Managing so many intricate details requires that a chef-restaurateur juggles many different roles and responsibilities. Joyce

Goldstein says, "You need people skills, management skills, and artistic skills. I wear 17 different hats." After working 16 hours a day doing everything from transcribing recipes to running staff meetings, "I might not have touched a mushroom. I feel guilty all the time, but I'm too valuable to peel onions."

Anne Rosenzweig concurs. "While many aspire to owning a restaurant, most don't have any business experience or any idea of how hard it really is," she says. "You become a businessperson first, dealing with bankers, accountants, bookkeepers, lawyers. You're also responsible for the front of the restaurant—training, dressing, feeding the wait staff. You have to develop your wine list, and be responsible for tasting and buying wines. You have to take care of everything. Young chefs don't have a clue—they don't understand that the focus is taken away from the kitchen."

Despite the challenges, chefs find many rewards in having a place of their own, from having an opportunity to take advantage of multiple talents to being their own boss and having relatively more control over their schedules. "Opening your own place is the best route to success," says Elizabeth Terry. "I've always wanted to succeed and to please, and I've never been good at taking orders."

"Your life and your career are two different things, but real success—not necessarily happiness—comes from fusing the two."
—Jeremiah Tower

KNOWING WHEN IT'S TIME

Deciding when it's time to open a restaurant is sometimes a matter of personal comfort. For some chefs, having one's own restaurant by a certain age is a long-term goal. Gaining experience, a reputation, and perhaps even potential investors gives them the means to begin to realize this goal. Daniel Boulud recalls, "My goal was to have my own business by the time I reached 40. I didn't have the money myself to open my own restaurant, so I definitely had to rely on hard work in order to become attractive for someone to invest in."

For other chefs, deciding to open a place of their own is practically a foregone conclusion. Chris Schlesinger had worked in various kitchens before becoming sous chef at Boston's Park Plaza Hotel, where he was relieved to be fired after six months. Schlesinger knew he couldn't keep working places where he didn't care about the food. "It wasn't so much 'Gee, I can't wait till I have my own restaurant so I can do my own thing.' I just knew I wasn't going to tolerate working for other people—that was the main thing," he says. "I didn't have a choice."

Pasta-in-the-Pink
with Red-Pepper Purée

GEORGE GERMON AND JOHANNE KILLEEN
Al Forno
Providence, Rhode Island

"Shortly before we opened Al Forno in January 1980, we were hesitant and anxious. In an attempt to avoid facing the inevitable opening, the new responsibilities, and our mounting anxieties, we started thumbing through old issues of Gourmet magazine. In an article about Italy, we found a photograph that changed the course of our lives. We saw chiaroscuro, a casserole of what looked like baked pasta. The lighting was dim, the background smoky and mysterious. The only clear color in the photo was a flash of red that was probably tomato. The top of the casserole looked crusty and charred as if licked by the flames of a wood-fired oven. Our imaginations raced as we started conjuring up what the pasta tasted like. The image was so enticing that we could almost smell the aroma from the steam curling above it.

"We decided on the spot to change the format of our menu. That pasta was the kind of food we wanted to serve in our restaurant. That photograph evoked for us the new restaurant's possibilities. We began experimenting with baked pastas, and adapted the flavors and textures that were familiar to us from our travels in Italy."

For the most publicly successful chefs, who have garnered rave reviews for their employers, the decision is sometimes rooted in wanting to profit directly from the reputations they developed through their talent and hard work. Before he opened his first restaurant, Jean-Georges Vongerichten, who had earned the hotel restaurant Lafayette (NYC) four stars, says he twice offered the

4 red bell peppers, charred and peeled

1/2 cup chopped canned tomatoes in heavy puree

2 cups heavy cream

1/2 cup freshly grated Pecorino Romano (1 1/2 ounces)

1/2 cup coarsely shredded fontina (1 1/2 ounces)

2 tablespoons ricotta

1 1/2 teaspoons kosher salt

1 pound imported conchiglie rigate (pasta shells)

4 tablespoons (1/2 stick) unsalted butter

. . . .

1. Preheat the oven to 500 degrees.

2. Bring 5 quarts of salted water to a boil in a stockpot.

3. Halve the peppers, remove the seeds, and puree them in a blender. You should have about 1 cup of puree.

4. In a large bowl, combine all the ingredients except the pasta shells and butter.

5. Parboil the pasta for 4 minutes. Drain and add to the ingredients in the bowl, tossing to combine.

6. Divide the pasta mixture among 6 to 8 individual, shallow, ceramic gratin dishes (1 1/2- to 2-cup capacity). Dot with the butter and bake until bubbly and brown on top, about 7 to 10 minutes.

Serves 6 to 8 as an appetizer

Variation

For a nice variation, add 2 Italian hot or sweet sausages that have been parboiled for 8 minutes, their skins removed, and coarsely chopped.

Lafayette to "do like Le Cirque and separate the restaurant from the hotel" by giving the hotel 10 percent of the restaurant's gross for rent. The hotel demurred, and Vongerichten left to launch his bistro Jojo.

Charlie Trotter personifies the fact that there's no single answer that's right for everyone. Before opening his own restaurant, Trotter

Whole Roast Artichoke with Aioli

LYDIA SHIRE
Biba and Pignoli
Boston, MA

"These artichokes are the best! We have used them at Biba whole or in part—maybe cut a different way, but cooked with the same ingredients. My greatest 'food friend' from Rhode Island, Bob Fortunati, taught me how to cook this dish—it was his mother's recipe. I've sat with Bob for hours as he told me about how his family cured their own hams and olives, and made their own vinegars, and so on. Thank you, Bob!"

....

1 1/2 cups capers

1 1/2 cups parsley

1 1/2 cups garlic

1 1/2 cups anchovies

salt and pepper, to taste

3 cups olive oil

1 cup water

12 artichokes

....

Blend the capers, parsley, garlic, anchovies, salt, and pepper in a food processor. (Do not over process.) Bring the olive oil to a boil and add the caper mixture. Bring the water to a boil, and add the caper/olive oil mixture. Place the artichokes in a baking pan just big enough to hold them. Pour the mixture over the artichokes. Cover with foil. Place in the oven and baste every 15 minutes so the caper/olive oil mixture goes down into the opening leaves. Bake one hour until tender.

Serve with a little of the basting liquid and a spoonful of basic garlic aioli.

had only three years of cooking experience, in more than 40 different restaurants, and had never been a chef or even a sous chef. "I'd never held any position higher than a line cook," Trotter admits. "On the one hand I thought, 'Should I spend another year cooking? Should I go to New York and cook?' You always can say, 'I need more knowledge. Do I know enough about pastry? Do I know enough about butchering? Do I know enough about this or that?' And the answer is always 'No, no, no.' But, on the other hand, do I know enough to make it go? And based on some of the [notable] restaurants that I was spending two days or two weeks in, saying, 'This is a monstrosity. I know I can do better than this,' I decided maybe I should go for it.' "

You begin to prepare for the experience of opening your own restaurant the first day you step into a kitchen. An entire cooking career, whether three years or 13 or even 30, spent carefully observing and learning everything your employers have to teach is the best preparation for setting off on your own.

You might actively seek additional exposure to other aspects of the restaurant business, namely, in the front of the house. Jasper White, after having been sous chef at the restaurant at the Copley Plaza Hotel, spent a year running the Harvard Bookstore Cafe on Newbury Street—as its general manager, not its chef, "I didn't like it, but learned as much as I could. I kind of taught myself and really paid attention to the table service, running the business, processing credit cards. Because at this point I had a goal, which was to have my own restaurant. I knew at some point to grab that year, and that's where I grabbed it."

To expand his knowledge, Chris Schlesinger formed a restaurant study group with others, including his eventual partner Cary Wheaton, to figure out what would be involved in opening a restaurant. When the group actually found a space available in Cambridge's Inman Square and it was time to take the next step, Schlesinger says, "Everybody but Cary and me dropped out. Cary and I had no inten-

tion of really doing it—none at all. But we did it." The space eventually became the site of the East Coast Grill.

Despite the traditional notion that in real estate the most important factors are "location, location, location," Charlie Trotter set about looking for an out-of-the-mainstream site, inspired by New York City brownstone restaurants like Lutèce and La Tulipe. He recalls, "I liked the fact that they were very discreet and had no signage, in a neighborhood with dwellings on either side. I found [the site of Charlie Trotter's] after looking at about 40 sites, from liquor storefronts to office building spaces. We have a residence on either side of us." Similarly, when Todd English was looking to open Olives, he says he knew Charlestown (just outside Boston) was a risk, but that he wanted to be in a neighborhood. "I remembered all the Ma-and-Pa joints off the beaten path from my travels in Italy," he says. Olives also became a destination restaurant.

Zarela Martinez looked at 150 restaurant sites in Manhattan before selecting the current site of Zarela, which she said cost her an estimated $200,000, including legal fees. She signed the deal in four days and opened the restaurant with less than $20,000 in working capital within ten days. "The restaurant was there, and I just put up ribbons and brought in arts and crafts from home to decorate," giving the restaurant its notably festive ambiance.

Restaurant design can make a great difference. "Wolfgang [Puck] wouldn't be Wolfgang without Barbara [Lazaroff]," says Nancy Silverton of Puck's interior designer wife. Silverton and husband Mark Peel were the first pastry chef and chef, respectively, of the original Spago in Los Angeles. "The initial plans were for a pizza place with sawdust on the floor and red checkered tablecloths. Barbara added the design element, and made it about more than just food. Now, when you walk into Spago, you're walking into Wolfgang and Barbara's home," Silverton says.

Lydia Shire's aesthetic tastes are reflected in more than just the food at Biba (Boston): "I interviewed six architects, and when I decided on [noted New York restaurant designer] Adam Tihany, I kind of told him the things that were important to me, and he just went from there. I knew I didn't want any black in this restaurant, and that I wanted lots of curves. I knew I wanted Kilim rugs. I took him to my house and I showed him the Kilim rugs that I have at home that I love. In the end, he let me pick out certain fabrics, and I

Quail Saltimbocca

MICHAEL FOLEY

Printer's Row
Chicago, IL

*"This was one of my first specials from Printer's Row in 1981.
Cooked correctly, either from the grill in the summer or the sauté in
the winter, it brings back lots of memories of me opening my first
restaurant, standing alone and cooking on the line nightly with the
strain of operating as an entrepreneur weighing heavy
on my 'pan,' so to speak."*

Bone two five–six-ounce quail. Try to bone them without piercing the
skin. Stuff them with a mixture of rice that has been cooked with
thyme-seasoned chicken stock and half red wine. Cook the rice with
the normal ratio of half liquid to solid. (I prefer to use basmati whole-
grain rice for a little more rustic flavor.) Follow carefully the instructions for cooking the rice, as it will take more liquid.

After stuffing the quail, wrap it with a very thin piece of prosciutto.
Be certain to place a small piece of fresh sage in between the quail and
prosciutto before stringing the bird. Tie the quail with two ties so the
prosciutto is on strong.

Add a little olive oil to a small sauté pan. When mildly hot, brown
the birds on all sides, starting with the legs first, doing the breast and
back last. Add a little of the quail or stock you make from fresh bones.
Cook gently in the oven for about five to seven minutes. The rice
should be hot inside but the bird still lightly pink, or it will be dry.

The olive oil should be absorbed by the bird. Add a little more
stock to the pan and swirl in a little butter. Add more sage if you
desire. Adjust the seasoning with lemon, salt, and pepper.

Serve with buttered spinach, zucchini, or another green vegetable
sauté.

Serve with a simple potato cake, placing the quail over the
spinach, with the cake underneath. Spoon the juices around.

Excellent with a Rhone Style Red, Barolo, or Full-Bodied Chenin
Blanc

picked out the tiles on the walls. I actually designed the whole wood-burning oven area—I drew it on paper and I knew that I wanted it round. It was a good match. I don't take any credit for the design here; I only take credit for giving Adam the direction he needed."

Not everyone is in a position to hire an architect or designer. The East Coast Grill "was just what we wanted to do. It was driven by how much money we had," says Chris Schlesinger. In his case, this proved to be fortuitous. "We were fortunate because what we wanted to do jibed with where the market was headed. We opened a couple of years before the grill trend really exploded, before the casualization [of restaurant decor and prices], before the health concerns. We were there and established when they all hit. We were in the right place at the right time."

PREPARING THE MENU

While Charlie Trotter was having preparatory work by architects and designers done on his restaurant in Chicago, he began to cater dinner parties in people's homes, once or twice a week for eight months, where he tested the recipes he was developing for Charlie Trotter's menu. "One dinner led to another. There would always be a couple at the party who'd say, 'Oh, we owe people a dinner, this is perfect, would you come in two weeks and do a dinner?' I charged money, but just enough to cover the costs, and maybe a little more. I stayed very active doing that, and I was able to actually fine-tune many of the dishes that made it to the opening menus."

Trotter's catering business had additional benefits. He adds, "What I didn't know at the time was that the parties were also serving the purpose of forming a small groundswell of intimates. So when I finally opened, there were some 400 people who had experienced my food, and were privy to this restaurant. A lot of clients had been willing to let me step up before the meal and say, 'I'm going to open this restaurant on the North Side, and have a location, and I haven't picked out the name yet, but I have several ideas—what do you think?' They felt like they were part of it. I didn't understand the importance of that then."

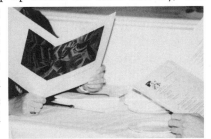

The hardest part of developing their opening menu for Terra, according to Lissa Doumani and Hiroyoshi Sone, was figuring out what constituted their cuisine. "It's very hard when you've been at a restaurant that's as well known as Spago—you assume that what you've been doing is Spago cuisine. You forget that it's yours, because you made it up, and it happened that you did it at Spago. If you do it outside of Spago and continue to do something in the same light, it's still your food. If you try to drop all of your past to find out who you are, you're going to be put away or become psychotic from it. Still, it took a while to get to that comfortable place where we weren't worried about 'whose' food we were doing."

Many chefs have developed specialties on their menus which have particular strategic advantages, such as memorability. Frequently, the first things customers are served when they sit down in a dining room are water—and a basket of bread. "No one in the city was baking their own bread when Emeril's opened," says Emeril Lagasse, which allowed him to develop this specialty. Lydia Shire features naan bread baked to order in Biba's tandoori oven, as well as a couple of other types of freshly baked breads. She explains, "I've always loved Indian food, especially in London I love their breads. One thing I wanted was a great bread basket. I always thought that some of the bread you get in restaurants is so matter-of-fact. I really wanted to have the best bread basket in Boston."

Despite growing concerns about cholesterol, Jean Joho features two cheese carts at Everest (Chicago) and finds that 80 percent of his customers order cheese after their meal. "I've always loved cheese," says Joho, who has become known for spotlighting American cheeses. Georges Perrier adds, "I think the first course that you serve, the appetizer, is also very important, because I think it is what the customer is going to remember. And because it comes last, people tend to remember desserts. I have worked very hard on that, and I have four full-time cooks in pastry, and four apprentices, sometimes. I'm not ashamed to say that I think we have the best dessert cart in the country, and maybe in the world."

"Focus on what you do best. If you do only one thing well, be the best at it."
—Victor Gielisse

A RECIPE FOR SUCCESS

A chef-restaurateur learns quickly that the success of a restaurant lies in much more than its food. Charlie Trotter says the most important lesson he learned from the time he spent in Europe was "that it's *not* just food. Food is an equal part of a little formula that encompasses ambiance, service, and a wine program. Food is only one of the four parts, and no one of those parts is greater than the other parts. In Europe, I saw the attention paid to all these little things and I realized there was so much more."

According to Emeril Lagasse, "When the customer calls to make a reservation, or pulls up to the valet—that's when the whole process starts. We work at that, we talk about that, we study that, and we have training sessions about that. We try to know just about every customer when they walk through the door. I have 'commandments' that must be followed in order to work in the front of the house here, including 'name recognition,' where an effort is made to greet customers by name; 'gang service,' where all entrees are served at the same time, like a ballet; and 'in-house marketing,' where we try to get personal—but not too personal—with our customers. Even waiters will drop customers notes. We even have an in-house computer system which allows us, when Mr. Kohlmeyer comes in to have his Beefeater martini, to have it there waiting for him before he even sits down.

"If it's raining outside, the valet knows instantly that the umbrella box and three 'Emeril's' umbrellas have to be out for use in escorting customers to and from their cars. We also have a special mat for the front door so that clients can wipe their shoes clean. They're greeted by name. They're escorted to their table. Somebody has to be at their table within 30 seconds of their being seated. We even have service signals on the table so that others know whether their cocktail order has been taken. It's a very, very detailed process from the moment the guest pulls up to the valet to the time the guest leaves and the valet or the front door says goodnight—hopefully by name."

The ambiance of a restaurant, from its design to the background music played, sets the stage, and is a critical part of a restaurant. Jean Joho believes that while food is certainly important, "the reason people go to a restaurant is to enjoy themselves. It's not a church. You must make people feel welcome, relax, and enjoy the experience. Your goal is to get the customer to come back."

The secret, according to Georges Perrier, is that "everybody wants to be recognized and important. When their reception at a restaurant is good, people feel good: 'Oh, they want me here!' That should be a restaurant's number one prerogative."

Does making customers feel welcome always involve giving them exactly what they want? The issue of how far a chef-restaurateur will go to please a customer is an intensely personal one.

"My whole life—well, the last 45 years of it—I gave my blood for the customers," says André Soltner. It goes without saying that some chef-restaurateurs believe strongly that satisfying customers is what being in this business is all about. "[César] Ritz said 80 years ago, 'The customer is king,' " says Soltner. "And that still has to apply to our work, if you're in the restaurant business."

Michel Richard agrees. "You must learn to please customers. You have to love them, you have to respect them," he says. "I have more respect for customers than they have for themselves. I don't try to impress them. I want them to enjoy, to discover new things. They have no idea how much we try to extend our hearts, how much we try to give to them."

Hiroyoshi Sone and Lissa Doumani credit their experience at Spago with teaching them the importance of always pleasing the customer. "Wolfgang [Puck] will do anything for a customer," says Sone. Doumani adds, "There's a customer at Spago who always wanted Beef Wellington, and he did that for him. There was another customer who had to have Häagen-Dazs ice cream, coconut haystack cookies, and Tab. At Terra, you can have anything you want, as long as we have the ingredients. Certainly the most important thing for the 1990s is giving customers what they want."

Emeril Lagasse believes it is critical for chef-restaurateurs to really pay attention to customer needs. "We constantly have our ear to the ground for what the customer wants, and what the customer's expectations are," he says. "That's most of the problem with other restaurants—they don't do that." Because it provides insights into what his customers are thinking, Janos Wilder believes that a negative letter from a customer is actually a favor. "I'll pull their orders from that night, I'll speak with the waiter and the cook," says Wilder. "Then I'll call a staff meeting and make sure everyone is giving a sincere effort."

Many chefs count on customer requests as a way of making sure they keep innovating. Jasper White says, "I

Dieter Schorner remembers the time at La Côte Basque when Salvador Dali came in for dinner five nights in a single week. "He would order a whole plate of fried parsley for his entree. Yes, it tastes fantastic—but five days in a row for dinner? And he ordered the same thing for dessert every night: broiled grapefruit with honey." By comparison, Aristole Onassis's tastes seem less exotic: "For lunch, he would always request minestrone soup and steak tartar, with vanilla ice cream and concentrated apricot purée for dessert."

Patrick O'Connell on Customer Service

We have a mood indicator at the Inn at Little Washington: every customer is given a mood rating when they walk in the door, from one to ten. The waiter needs to assess the mood of the party. This forces him not to treat them as a deuce [table of two] or a four-top [table of four], but to see them as human beings whose moods (whether they have anything to do with what we're doing or not) will ultimately affect the enjoyment of the experience. So it's the waiter's business whether they had a flat tire on the way or a marital dispute or anything. It also empowers him to change it, and that's the game.

So if it's below seven, it must be brought up to a nine by the dessert dupe [the kitchen's copy of the order]. Then if it's below six, it's put up on the blackboard by the kitchen: "Table 22, 5." And everybody who walks by that table lavishes warm vibrations, energy, and smiles, and makes every effort to turn it around. And it happens every single night. The first thing that everyone is instructed to do in our place is that whenever there is a problem or a complaint, smile. Give the person the complete reassurance that you've handled 1000 things 1000 times worse, and this is a piece of cake and no problem at all.

Because this mood indicator comes into the kitchen, the whole kitchen staff is alerted, and it's a real team effort on their part to bring somebody up or to change the experience. So they're part of the game, too. If need be, everything would be rushed to the critical or problem table, or some little extra thing would be sent. We use the phrase "pushing them over the edge," doing that extra thing, which is actually so easy, and it's so effortless—really, it's just caring. Usually I find that as soon as the cranky guest realizes that it actually matters to the staff whether or not they have a good time, it's crucial that they do. The customer turns around. Right away, it's a new experience for them that somebody cares.

Elisabeth Kübler-Ross—a fascinating woman—wrote a book called *The Five Stages of Death and Dying*. She realized that it is an experience which has identifiable, universal phases to it that everyone goes through, and that knowing them and chronicling them is helpful to people because it gives them a handle on the whole thing. So, I did it with "the five stages of dining," breaking the experience down into five distinct phases.

"The Five Stages of Dining"

1. *Anticipation.* To a great restaurant, this can begin two years or longer in advance, and people have little, yellow, faded clippings in their purse that they've carried around. They've always wanted to come. If nothing else, it starts in the car on the way there. They begin to think about what they might eat.

listen to what people want, and I believe in making people happy. Over the years I've had many requests for vegetable plates, so about three years ago I put it on the menu, and it stays on the menu—just so that people don't have to feel awkward if that's what they want. It's there for them." White has also made an effort to balance lighter dishes with heavier ones, after hearing concerns from his customers. "Still, as a special occasion restaurant, I don't feel a need

2. *Trepidation:* Then they hit the door. They open the door; the anticipation collides with what I call trepidation: kind of a primitive terror that the experience won't live up to their expectations or that reality has intervened with the fantasy. Or that they should have worn the black dress instead of the red one. Or that the maitre d' would be rude. It will evoke what I call "restaurant bruises" from the 90 million horrendous, awful experiences that they've had in other restaurants. And this is a very delicate kind of phase. At each phase, the waiter has a counter phase that he flips into to deal with this, so that we're in control.

3. *Inspection:* This is on the part of the diner. This happens after the second sip of the cocktail. They're in their seat and they still haven't looked around and eyed the room because they are too intimidated or too uptight. Only when they are given a drink are they really there. It's like an Irish wake, where the body of the person is brought out to prove that the person is dead. People aren't really where they are until they really experience it. So they are not conscious of being there, and they don't allow themselves to experience anything until maybe the second sip of the drink. Then you see them checking out the room. At the same time, if they see a flaw—a chipped glass, a dead flower—then they take a little nosedive down.

4. *Fulfillment or Ecstasy or Animal Satisfaction:* This doesn't take place until three-fourths of the way through the main course. They won't allow themselves to consider the experience a success until they have gotten to that place in the main course. Prior to that you'll hear them say, "Everything's been great—so far. Delicious—so far. But you haven't delivered yet, Sucker." They must be observed as experiencing a complete state of ecstasy at that point. At our establishment, they must use a superlative such as "fantastic," "wonderful," "incredible" or "amazing." I train the staff that "fine" means "awful." Do you think that somebody's going to pay $125 for a meal that's "okay," "very good," or "fine"? Absolutely not. This is supposed to be a superlative experience. If they don't use a superlative, then something's wrong. So get them something else. Do something. Move in. Don't accept "very good."

5. *Evaluation:* This begins when the check is picked up, the bottom line is examined, and the wife usually whispers, "How much was it?" and the husband says, "$236" and they smile. It was either worth it, or it wasn't worth it. And that evaluation continues for days later at the office when people say, "How was it? How much did it cost?"

As soon as you have one person on staff who is not plugged in, it doesn't work. You have to create a kind of energy field. I think that they expect people in the country [The Inn at Little Washington is an hour and a half from DC, with no signs] to be sweet and innocent and kind and helpful and all of that. But I think it would be even more dramatic in a city, like New York, to have all warm, wonderful people who are genuine in providing such service."

to address everyday needs," says White. "I still use ingredients like veal stock, butter, and foie gras."

If a customer at Stars asks for anything, staff members are not allowed to say "no." Jeremiah Tower has a log book at Stars (San Francisco) with information on the specific preferences of his regular customers. "Every time two particular customers come in, waiting at their table are open packs of Pall Mall and Lucky Strike ciga-

Stuffed Breast of Capon

JEAN BANCHET

formerly of Ciboulette
Atlanta, GA

"When I opened my first restaurant (Le Francais) in Wheeling, Illinois in 1973, I had to have chicken on the menu. Being tired of seeing and eating roasted chicken, barbecued chicken, grilled chicken, etc., etc., I came up with this new chicken dish which became very popular, very fast. It still is a favorite on many menus."

....

2 2 1/2-lb fresh capons

4 leeks (julienne cut)

2 pieces fresh ginger

1 quart of whipping cream

1 quart of chicken stock

2 eggs

4 slices of truffles

rettes, with an open matchbook." Tower speaks with admiration of the level of service of some of the great hotels of Europe. "At the Hassler in Rome, I could have called up the concierge at midnight and said 'I need a pair of rabbits,' and he would have said, 'Yes, of course, sir.' Not 'It'll take 24 hours' or 'Oh my God, call back in the morning!' He would have just said, 'Yes'," enthuses Tower. "Just say 'yes.' Then figure it out. Don't tell the customer your problems; they're simply not interested."

Does this mean Tower thinks the customer is always right? Not at all. "The customer is usually hardly ever right," he says. "I hate them for not trusting the restaurant. They should know why they're there." However, Tower has found his customers to be much more trusting over time. "At Chez Panisse, there was no choice on the menu. I was always going out to the dining room, and if I knew customers very well, I'd say, 'Isn't it about time you trusted me a little bit?' Sometimes I'd just go out and [making the motion of spearing

2 tablespoons chopped shallots

juice of 1/2 lemon

4 oz of fresh butter

2 cups of dry white wine

. . . .

Remove breasts from capons, with skin. Put aside. Bone and skin legs, put the meat through a grinder. With the two whole eggs put the ground meat into a food processor to make the mousse, adding 1/2 a quart of cream and salt and pepper to taste. Stuff chicken breasts with the mousse and wrap in plastic wrap. Set aside.

Saute the shallots, adding the white wine and ginger. Reduce all the way and add the chicken stock. Bring to boil, add the capon breasts, cover saucepan, and cook slowly for about 15 minutes. Remove breasts. Add leeks to stock and reduce to syrup. Add the rest of the cream, reduce by 1/3, and add the lemon juice and fresh butter. Keep hot. Slice the capon breasts on plates and pour the sauce around the slices. Put sliced truffles on top of each breast.

Decorate plate with watercress on lemon.

Serves 4

food with a fork and moving it toward someone's mouth] say, 'Try it. Just try it. If you don't like it, I'll buy you dinner.' And they would try the veal kidneys. They'd never had *wonderful* veal kidneys before. And then they'd try the duck confit, the goat cheese, the mascarpone, the buffalo mozzarella, the walnut oil. In 1973 or 1974, no one had ever seen these ingredients before, and they didn't want to eat them. Americans are very, very conservative about food. But now, they're coming to trust a well-known restaurant or chef more, and they'll try it."

Alice Waters agrees. "I would like to persuade them to try things they might not eat otherwise, and I feel like I'm pretty persuasive. I like to think that we're helping them to moderate what they're eating, and showing them that you don't have to eat a 12-ounce T-bone steak—you can enjoy just a couple of ounces of meat cooked quickly on the grill," she says. "But in case I'm not persuasive, I try to accommodate them. If I have the time, I'll really go to an extreme."

Pasta from Hell

CHRIS SCHLESINGER

East Coast Grill and The Blue Room
Cambridge, MA

"Constantly challenged by my fire-eating customers to create hotter and hotter food, I decided to put a stop to it once and for all by developing a dish that would satisfy their desires and quiet their demands. A dish so hot that there was no hotter; so hot that never again would I have to take a ribbing from the heat freaks. This is it. Your heat source here is the Scotch Bonnet chile pepper, widely accepted as the hottest commercially cultivated chile pepper in the world. Many of my customers think this dish is just a bit too much, Kitchen Out of Control. But a handful of others, with sweat coming off the tops of their heads, eyes as big as saucers, bathed in satanic ecstasy, tell me that it's the best thing I've ever created. The truth lies somewhere in the middle, and in fact the heat of this dish can be controlled by using far fewer peppers without impairing the flavor of the dish. But . . . every once in a while, when the really hard case sits down and insists on something that has a 'real kick' to it, whip the full-bore Pasta from Hell on him. We're talking culinary respect here."

Several chef-restaurateurs have made efforts, sometimes out of frustration, to educate their customers. Raji Jallepalli recalls, "When we first opened the restaurant, I used to have an impossible time getting people to eat medium-rare pork—they would send it back. I used to educate the waiters to tell them that 'The chef feels that the flavor is at a maximum the way it is. I want you to try it, and if you don't like it, we'll give you whatever you want.' Little by little, I changed their minds about these things."

2 tablespoons olive oil

1 yellow onion, diced small

1 red bell pepper, diced small

2 bananas, sliced

1/4 cup pineapple juice

Juice of 3 oranges

4 tablespoons lime juice (about 2 limes)

1/4 cup chopped cilantro

3 to 4 tablespoons finely chopped fresh red or green hot chile peppers (Scotch Bonnet or Habañero are best) or 4 to 6 ounces Inner Beauty Hot Sauce

About 1/4 cup grated Parmesan cheese

2 teaspoons unsalted butter

1 pound fettuccine

Salt and freshly cracked black pepper to taste

. . . .

1. In a large saucepan, heat the oil and sauté the onion and red pepper in it, over medium heat, for about 4 minutes.

2. Add the bananas and pineapple and orange juices. Simmer over medium heat for 5 minutes, until the bananas are soft.

3. Remove from the heat, add the lime juice, cilantro, chile peppers or Inner Beauty sauce, and 3 tablespoons of the Parmesan cheese, and mix well.

Serves 4 as an appetizer

Michael Foley believes that being too far ahead of the market is just as bad as being too far behind it. "At one point, the only place I could forward my cause was through my restaurant, which worked a little bit against me. Every time people would see me, they'd think, 'Oh my God—here he comes again!' It was a bad thing, because they got a negative opinion of what I thought was something very positive. I wanted them to eat more grains! I would do cooking classes on these things, and it got to the point where I was forcing my opinions on people, because they weren't ready," he says. "You have to teach to a 'teachable moment.' The people we were talking to were not listening. They didn't want to listen. They wanted to go out to the next fashionable joint. *Now* is probably the 'teachable moment' in the mainstream."

Every chef must set his or her own limits in terms of striking a balance between the dual, and sometimes conflicting, roles of restaurateur and chef. While the restaurateur thinks that pleasing customers goes hand-in-hand with running a successful business and making money, the chef who feels a need to make a statement through the food that is served also feels the need to draw the line somewhere.

"I don't believe the customer is always right," says Johanne Killeen. "We try to make as many accommodations as possible. If we can make concessions and still make something really good, then we do it. But if somebody wants to eliminate ingredients from our dishes to the point that we think 'This is not our cooking, this is not going to be good,' we just don't do it." Do customers ever leave? "Occasionally. As gently as we try to present this, some customers feel that it's not the way it should be, but it's a rare, rare thing." George Germon is even more emphatic. "People who go out should be going to experience what this particular restaurant does, and not alter it," he says. "If a person has dietary restrictions and other considerations, and wants to get out of the house, he should eat at home and go to the movies."

The one area chef-restaurateurs are in agreement that the customer is always *wrong* is customers' too-frequent practice of failing to cancel—or, worse yet, failing to show up for—their scheduled, and even confirmed, reservations. Nancy Silverton says, "We don't try to overbook the restaurant, but last Saturday we had 80 no-shows—and those were for reservations that had been confirmed by phone that day! So we do have to take this into account." Lydia Shire fumes, "We had 40 no-shows tonight. That's so rude! I'm sure those people, if it were done to them in their businesses, would be furious."

THE POWER OF THE PRESS

If chefs have pet topics, this is definitely one of them. They can go on and on about critics, probably for as long as critics can go on and on about restaurants.

Admittedly, sometimes their comments have to do with their awe at their benefitting from the power of the press. Patrick O'Connell recalls, "Within weeks after we opened the restaurant, a gentleman diner asked to see me and introduced himself as a critic from the second biggest newspaper in Washington, which was then the  Evening-Star. It was the neck-and-neck rival of the *Washington Post*. He said, 'I never do this, but I would like to introduce myself. I need to ask you if you really want me to write a review of your place.' I said, 'You know, it's taken us many years to get the door open, and we'd be quite delighted if you would like to say something about our existence.' He said, 'No, I have to ask this because what I'm going to say is going to change your life. You may have to hire someone just to answer the telephone after they read what I'm going to say, because I'm going to tell the truth: This is absolutely fantastic!' The idea of hiring somebody to answer the telephone was humorous because during the day, I answered at the stove on a long cord and took reservations, and at night Reinhardt [Lynch, O'Connell's partner] answered it from the front desk as he seated people." The adoring review—and dozens that followed—put The Inn at Little Washington on the map.

The majority of chef-restaurateurs' concerns, however, have to do with the flip side—the potentially destructive power of a single reviewer's negative, or even lukewarm, opinion of their restaurant. "Nobody has 'made it' in this business," points out Raji Jallepalli. "You're subjecting yourself daily to critique from both consumers and the media."

In addition to having the power to potentially make or break a restaurant with a single review, critics are seen as having influence over certain chefs' efforts in the kitchen. Edward Brown sees other chefs doing complex dishes with 15 ingredients in their attempts to please the press. "That way, they can not like seven ingredients on the plate and still be left with eight that they do like. They're afraid to be simple, and don't have the courage to put three things on a plate and let them stand on their own."

Daniel Boulud articulates what he believes makes the difference between good and bad critics: "I think once you know the chef—

Anne Rosenzweig recalls that Arcadia (New York City) was reviewed after being open only six weeks. "It was a two-star review that read like a three-star review." All plans of having Arcadia remain a "nice, neighborhood restaurant" were dashed: "It was two years before things slowed down at all."

what the chef's spirit is, what makes him happy and what business he's trying to attract—it's a good critique. But when you just have a checklist. . ."

It's precisely this attitude that bothers Mark Miller. "Food critics are worried about the same old check-off list: 'The lobster wasn't overcooked, and the plate was nice, and we got seated on time, and they had a good wine list. Oh, I think I'll give it three stars.' It's like, how pretty can the toilet paper get?" says Miller. "Food critics are quantitative—what it costs, what it looks like. Real criticism is an ability to perceive more acutely a particular phenomenon by having knowledge beyond the ordinary. The critics don't respect us, and are not creating respect for us as professionals. We really don't have anyone who writes about food the way that people write about drama or opera or dance. It's not taken seriously."

As a point of example, he says, "When reviewing modern dance performances, good dance critics don't write about the way people were dressed or what they paid for their ticket or how long the performance took. They write about the ability of the choreography to be in relation, or in counterpoint, to the music, how well the dancers performed, and the important significance of this dance in the history of dance. They try to educate the public about a particular form. They don't say that this was worth going to or how much it was worth. They educate you that if you should go to this dance, these are some of the things that should help you to understand what you are seeing.

"Similarly, great food has to be understood not by what it looks like initially, not by what it tastes like, not by what you paid for it. You have to understand it in terms of the human experience of food. Most critics don't understand the history of a particular chef—what he's done, where he's gone, what he's trying to do with his food. You never hear about this in food criticism," Miller says. "I think that if critics are going to write about restaurants, they should write about the totality of the restaurant experience. This includes how long the restaurant has been in operation. Is it fair to review a restaurant in the first month, just because your newspaper wants to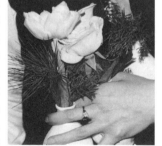

get it out first? Well, is it fair to go down to an artist's studio and start reviewing the paintings he had before the show? Do you go to the theatre previews and then start writing a review? This is what the food critics are doing, basically. But chefs and restaurateurs are afraid of the press. They don't want to say anything that's going to challenge anybody."

Understanding the power of the press has led leading chef-restaurateurs to develop ways of trying to manage it. Patrick O'Connell says, "We do an exercise with our wait staff. They have to each take a well-known critic—from *The Washington Post*, *The New York Times*, *New York*, or elsewhere—and they have to write two reviews in the style of that critic: one on our restaurant, and one on another restaurant. It has to mimic that style, and in doing that, they get into the head of the reviewer. It's terribly instructive. They get into the vocabulary. They also see what a difficult job it is, encapsulating that experience so concisely.

"All the critics have different prejudices, from one extreme to another. So-and-so hates this, so-and-so loves this, whatever. Just be attuned to it, be alert to it. And as somebody said, 'They have a lot to do with our success. It's their job to remain anonymous, and it's our job to know who the hell they are.' And there's nothing wrong with that. That's an intelligent sort of business, to be able to sniff a critic. So I have all my staff trained to the extent that if they sniff a critic, they let me know right away. They write a 'C' on the check, and that means it's a critical table. So I call my staff over and check it out."

Throughout more than 30 years in the restaurant business, André Soltner seems to have developed a healthy philosophy concerning the press. "I never wanted to be number one, because there really is no number one," he says. "We were in the Zagat guide for five or six years as number one. Three years ago, we were number three. We're number six today. The press called me and said, 'How do you feel?' I said, 'I feel great! Look, 30 years ago, I was number one. Ten years ago, I was number one. Eight years ago, I was number one. Thirty years, and I'm number three! You don't think that's good?' The dream of most is to be in the top ten—and I'm number six after 30 years! I can cope with that. I can take it because I never thought I was number one."

El Presidio Pan-Fried Chicken

JANOS WILDER

Janos
Tucson, AZ

"We were sitting around the picnic table one spring Sunday afternoon quite a few years ago, wondering what to cook for dinner. We really wanted hamburgers, but they were too high in cholesterol, particularly when made plump and juicy the way we like them. My wife Rebecca suggested making patties from chicken and seasoning them with chile and lime. We did, and they were great. Some years later, when a cook was stumped for a lunch special, I remembered our home barbecue, tweaked the recipe a bit with tomato, cilantro, and cheddar, breaded the patties and pan-fried them (no low-cholesterol treat, these morsels) and served them with calabacitas con queso, black beans, salsa fresca, and tomato beurre blanc sauce. They were an instant hit. Several years after that I was to appear on Live with Regis and Kathie Lee. At the last minute they selected El Presidio Pan-Fried Chicken for me to make with Regis. He ended up making quite a mess of himself in the process, and we had a terrific time on the show. The dish has now become a staple whenever we serve lunch."

(This dish is very much a blending of French techniques and Southwestern ingredients. Essentially a French mousse, but with chilies, cilantro, and cheddar providing the flavors of Tucson. I like to serve it with salsa fresca and black beans.)

. . . .

8 boneless and skinless chicken breasts

3 egg whites

2 Anaheim chilies roasted, peeled, seeded, and finely diced

1 1/2 cups grated cheddar cheese

3 tomatoes peeled, seeded, and small diced

6 scallions, finely diced

1 1/2 tbsp. finely chopped fresh garlic

3 tbsp. roughly chopped fresh cilantro

3/4 cup heavy cream

salt and pepper to taste

. . . .

Breading

. . . .

3 cups flour

1 1/2 cups milk

3 eggs

4 cups coarse dry breadcrumbs

. . . .

1. Cut breasts into chunks and quickly process in a food processor along with the egg whites. Do not puree; chicken should be fairly coarse.

2. Fold in chilies, cheese, tomato, scallions, garlic, cilantro, and cream. Season with salt and pepper.

3. Shape mixture into round patties about 1/2 inch thick.

4. Set out individual containers of flour, milk, and breadcrumbs. Dust with flour, then dip in milk, then coat with breadcrumbs, handling carefully so that croquettes maintain their shape.

5. Preheat oven to 350 degrees.

6. Heat 1/2 inch oil or shortening in a sauté pan. Add croquettes and fry until golden brown, turning once. Finish in oven for seven minutes.

Yield: 8 servings

ADVERTISING

If the media attention generated by newspaper and magazine reviews for the restaurant is insufficient or a review is not forthcoming, restaurateurs can attempt to stimulate additional interest through paid advertising. Large-scale advertising is often prohibitively expensive for a single location restaurant. Rick Bayless notes, "In Chicago, Lettuce Entertain You and Levy [both Chicago-based corporations with multiple restaurants] have so much money that they keep us [the independents] on our toes." That's exactly why a number of fellow "couple owners" around Chicago, including Charlie and Lynn Trotter, have cooperated with Bayless and his wife Deanne on joint advertising and promotions. Bayless also notes that the independents have an edge over their larger competitors in offering a personal presence in their restaurants. "We're always here, and we talk with our customers, which helps to create loyalty," he says.

Jimmy Schmidt's META Restaurants, on the other hand, can take advantage of economies of scale in its advertising by marketing all of the restaurants as a group. Schmidt describes a recent advertising theme: "One of the ads has a picture of lettuce in the field, with a headline that reads, 'In five hours, this will be a salad.' Another ad reads, 'Most restaurants call week-old fish "fresh." Most restaurants aren't run by Jimmy Schmidt.' We basically just promote the things that we do well, and what our standards are. We don't have time—nor does the customer really want to listen—when they're sitting in the restaurant. I want them to come in relaxed. Those who understand it will appreciate it; those that don't will still have a good meal."

PROMOTION

When business declined one winter for the first time ever, Rick Bayless responded by creating a newsletter to send out to a mailing list of his restaurants' 2000 customers. "It allows us to talk directly to our customers, and to let them know what we're all about," he says.

Janos Wilder sent announcements of the opening of Janos in Tucson to rented mailing lists of doctors and lawyers as well as members of local country clubs and museum societies. He also publishes a newsletter two or three times a year with information on the restaurant and special events. In addition, he has a response

card on each guest check so that customers can indicate particular areas of interest, such as catering services or wine-maker dinners. Customized information on the topic indicated is mailed to the customer within 24 hours. In addition, a computerized database is maintained with this information so that Wilder can keep costs low by sending specialized mailings only to customers who have previously indicated an interest in the topic.

Raji Jallepalli has a list of customers to whom she faxes the menus for special dinners she prepares on Sundays. "I also bring in 15 people at a time into the kitchen for cooking workshops like Toasting and Tempering of Spices; Creamless Sauces; Versatile Uses of Lentils; Fusion Beurre Blanc; Emulsions, Extractions, and Extensions; and Coulis Techniques, and everyone is served a three-course meal after the workshops." Jallepalli also organizes special dinners to introduce new items to the menu at her restaurant, and holds bimonthly wine tastings.

It behooves chef-restaurateurs to wear the hat of marketer to keep their restaurants in the public eye, and to keep themselves and their clientele excited. Charlie Trotter sent letters to his best customers about his trip with Emeril Lagasse and their wives to France to visit leading restaurants and vineyards. In the mailing, he promised an extraordinary dinner two days after their return, incorporating dishes and wines inspired by their travels. (They faxed recipes and instructions to the Chicago staff on a daily basis during the trip.) "It's also a fun way for us to go and see these things, and do a dinner when we get back," Trotter says.

Leading chefs find themselves inundated with requests to participate in special events benefitting both good causes and, ostensibly, their own visibility through the resulting publicity. "A big part of being a chef is doing benefits—for cancer societies, cystic fibrosis, Meals on Wheels, S.O.S.," says Gary Danko. "It's a very interesting culture we live in now because this whole cooking thing has just sort of catapulted into these huge events for food and wine, and socializing is a big part of it."

Such out-of-restaurant demands can have chefs spending much of their time away from their restaurants promoting them, at bene-

"Food writers, when an event is
for them, expect you to go. But
if they come to the restaurant
and you are away, they say you
are an 'absentee chef.' So my
decision, which I made more
than 20 years ago, is:
Restaurant first, all the rest second—and only if the restaurant
doesn't have to suffer."

—ANDRÉ SOLTNER

fits and other publicity events and meetings. Michel Richard described a recent week in his life as: "Monday in Vancouver, Wednesday and Thursday in New York City, Saturday in Santa Fe, Sunday morning in New York, and Sunday evening in Washington, DC."

Participation can be not only time-consuming, but expensive, with some chefs estimating their out-of-pocket expenses in the thousands or tens of thousands of dollars—or more—a year. One chef who doesn't plan to participate, however, is Patrick O'Connell, for reasons other than the time and other expense involved. "I, for one, will never do those collective dinners for 250 people, where you go into a strange kitchen and you make one of seven or eight or nine dishes, and you have no control whatsoever, and it goes out and you have no concept of how it's being present-ed," he says. "It's not what I do."

Still, many leading chefs appreciate the opportunity to get together with their peers—to compare notes on business, and to share ideas on food. "I enjoy the camaraderie, and learning what's happening outside my own kitchen," says Susan Spicer.

EVOLUTION OF A RESTAURANT

A restaurant should never be static and unchanging; rather, it is a dynamic entity that continues to change and evolve over time. "We've all seen a lot of 'hot' restaurants that eventually fall into mediocrity," says Jimmy Schmidt. "They may not be doing anything differently than they did at their beginning, but they haven't evolved. If you and your staff aren't evolving, then your restaurant isn't evolving."

Lissa Doumani likens owning a restaurant to being a parent. "In many ways, that's what it feels like to us. When we come back from being out of town, we drive by the restaurant to make sure that all the lights are off and it didn't burn down. You worry about it. You watch it grow. You look for your customers to say that it's better than it was the last time, because you want to know that you're growing."

Chefs need a vision to get their restaurants off the ground and to guide their necessary evolution. Their evolving vision is what keeps them fresh, educates their staff and inspires their customers to keep coming back. Beyond that, Patrick O'Connell says, "I think it's important for the chef to make a connection with the guest in one form or another, not necessarily working the tables for compliments, but perhaps by putting a line on the menu expressing what they hope to do with the food, or what their inspiration is and where they're coming from. Or a thought for the day on a menu that changes frequently. Humor, I think, is a missing ingredient. I think there needs to be more fun and more humor—not forced, but natural humor—in terms of the dining room experience."

O'Connell believes we've yet to see the ultimate potential of the restaurant business actualize. "This business affords the opportunity to draw on every single talent that you have, but it's not viewed that way yet. It's viewed as more of a technical expertise or a trade, instead of the art form that it is," says O'Connell. "Nobody's pushing the outer limits, in terms of what it's really all about."

8

TRAVEL, EATING, AND READING

Learning Something New Every Day

"Whatever you invest in yourself right now will come back to you a zillion times later. But you have to be willing to invest. You have to start spending your money on cookbooks and going to the best restaurants and traveling, for example, instead of blowing it on music CDs. I see too many cooks who stop thinking about food when their eight hours are done."

—LYDIA SHIRE

The best chefs, like the best restaurants, continue to evolve and grow. Nothing is stagnant; everything changes, either for the better or for the worse. If chefs are to change for the better, then their influences must be positive. There are three items that can provide nourishment and energy for positive change: the air you breathe, the food you eat, and the ideas you ponder. Travel can literally impart a breath of fresh air, as well as help give rise to a new perspective. Johanne Killeen and George Germon describe their experiences while traveling through Italy "like eating food for the first time." Eating new and different foods can nourish the spirit as well as the body. And reading can provide "food for thought," imparting new ideas or giving new depth to old ideas. Taken together, the combination of these influences can expand your real understanding of food.

Leading chefs never stop learning about food. This is the most important theme that our conversations drove home. They are always seeking out opportunities to learn more about food and to expand the way they think about food. Food becomes the lens through which they often see, experience, think about, and talk about the world. (Many even "pepper" their conversations with culinary terms—such as talking about putting things "on the back burner," letting ideas "simmer," etc.) Beyond the classroom and the kitchen, working chefs can find ample opportunities to increase their knowledge, primarily through travel, eating, and reading.

Chefs travel for vacation, but also to absorb culture and food. Their destination may be dictated by their desire to go to the source of a particular style of food. Eating out on their nights off is another way chefs keep up on what their colleagues are doing. On a Sunday or Monday night (chefs' most frequent nights off) you'll often find a chef "researching" a friend or colleague's restaurant over dinner. Many chefs have extensive cookbook collections of literally hundreds or even thousands of books, which they turn to for information or inspiration. Food rarely leaves their thoughts.

"I like to ski, and in the summer I play tennis. I may be doing something completely different [from cooking]. But I don't forget cooking during this time," admits André Soltner. "I think all the time about what I can do different, what I can do better. So I do that when I am on the ski lift, I do that when I sleep."

It's hard to describe the exact ways in which this knowledge manifests itself; the benefits accrue to the chef in a much more holistic manner than they do in any single, identifiable way, such as in improving technique or seasoning. Somehow, everything a chef has ever tasted, smelled, touched, seen, heard, read, or otherwise experienced is translated through the chef's hands and finds its way onto a plate. The greater these experiences, in both quality and quantity, the more the chef is able to bring to the kitchen. Aspiring chefs shouldn't stint on seeking out such experiences. Rather, you should view spending on travel, eating, and reading as an investment in yourself, your education, and your personal and professional development.

Jeremiah Tower observes that too many young Americans are raised on fast food, TV, and pop music. "It's frightening—they grow up with absolutely no other cultural heritage. They've never even wandered around the United States, let alone been to Europe. They know absolutely nothing about the richness of experience—to have had some sort of experience that blew their mind, whether it was sliced tomatoes in Italy or having a plate of mussels on the ocean in Capri or whatever it is that just triggers them. This is a problem for an industry which relies on people's senses and the richness of their personalities. It's hard to do that on a corn dog."

Seeking out such experiences can be futile, however, if you're not awake to all the new impressions these experiences can bring. First, you must change yourself by changing your attitude toward the world, opening yourself to all the positive impressions it may bring. If you eat every meal at McDonald's on your first trip to Paris, you're not likely to grow and evolve. On the other hand, trying unfamiliar foods can help you grow. If you find a new food unpleasant, you can make a game out of trying to like it. For that matter, take a fresh taste of your favorite foods and try to dislike them. When you try to consciously understand the allure and distaste of various foods and experiences to you, real understanding follows.

"Travel is key. You have to travel. You have to get bombarded. You have to put yourself into a new food context. You have to challenge that you know anything at all. You have to let go. Go to India. Go to Thailand. Go to China. Push yourself out there."

—MARK MILLER

Travel has the potential to make the biggest impact on a person because of its all-encompassing nature. When you find yourself on

WHY TRAVEL?

Pollo en Escabeche
(Pickled Chicken Salad in Aromatic Spices)

MARK MILLER
Red Sage
Washington, DC

"This is a dish that I created for the Coyote Cafe (Santa Fe) that represents the Spanish influences on Southwestern cuisine. Whenever I eat this dish it reminds me of my adventures on horseback in Spain in 1980. I travelled across the Andalusian countryside for ten days, passing through the white hill towns in the hot summer sun. The countryside was carpeted with sunflowers and dotted with black bulls. We would leave very early each morning while it was still cool out and ride until noon when the sun was at its peak. The days would reach into the low 100s.

"For lunch we would stop for two hours to rest the horses in the shade and take a meal in the old country inns that were stone cooled. On the sideboards there were cold dishes in refreshing sauces like this chicken in escabeche. These Spanish dishes were the prototype for all ceviches in the new world. We usually had pheasant or chicken and it was always served in brown terracotta dishes with crusty country bread and cool, refreshing wine on old wooden tables. I spent ten days on horseback from Arcos de la Frontera in central Spain to the beaches of the Atlantic The best way to experience a country is to ride through it!"

Most Americans think of pickles as a vegetable garnish for sandwiches or burgers, but pickling in a spicy, aromatic brine (*"en escabeche"* in Spanish) was another essential method of preserving meat, fish, seafood, and vegetables in the days before refrigeration and canning. The pickling brine always contains salt as well as an acid in the form of vinegar or citrus juice, which chemically "cooks" and preserves the ingredients. The technique has been used for centuries, especially in the Mediterranean region. You often see this method of "cooking" used in the wonderful *tapas* dishes of Spain. The Spanish in turn brought this technique to the New World—one example of this transfer of culinary ideas is Latin American seafood ceviches. Ceviches use citrus juice to pickle fish and shellfish; citrus fruit was introduced in the Americas by the Spanish.

This recipe makes a very refreshing salad for a hot summer day, and an ideal picnic or buffet item. It's important to make sure that the vegetables don't get overcooked in the pickling brine, or they run the risk of becoming too soggy. Note that the chicken should be marinated overnight. The pickled vegetables can be made up to one week ahead.

Marinade

....

2 teaspoons black peppercorns

1/2 teaspoon allspice berries

1/2 teaspoon cloves

1/2 teaspoon cumin seeds

4 teaspoons dried Mexican oregano

24 cloves roasted garlic, minced to a paste

1 teaspoon salt

2 tablespoons rice wine vinegar

2 boneless, skinless chicken breasts, about 8 ounces each

....

Pickling Liquid

....

2 quarts (8 cups) rice wine vinegar

1 quart (4 cups) water

8 serrano chiles, thinly sliced into rings, with seeds

1 teaspoon dried thyme

2 teaspoons fennel seeds

1 tablespoon coriander seeds

1 teaspoon allspice berries

1 tablespoon star anise

1 cinnamon stick

2 cloves

1 cup sugar

1 cup packed fresh cilantro leaves

....

(Continued on next page)

Vegetables

....

2 red bell peppers, seeded and cut into 1/4-inch rings

2 yellow bell peppers, seeded and cut into 1/4-inch rings

2 poblano chiles, seeded and cut into 1/4-inch rings

6 cloves garlic, peeled

salt to taste

8 ounces mixed baby greens, such as arugula, mizuna, frisée, mustard greens, red leaf lettuce (about 8 cups)

12 fresh cilantro sprigs

....

To prepare the marinade, grind the pepper, allspice, cloves, cumin, and oregano in a spice grinder or blender to a fine powder. Transfer to a mixing bowl, add the garlic, salt, and vinegar, and mix well.

Rub the chicken breasts with the marinade, cover with plastic wrap, and let sit overnight in the refrigerator.

To prepare the pickling liquid, place the vinegar, water, herbs, spices, and sugar in a saucepan and bring to a simmer. Reduce the liquid over medium-high heat by one-third. Remove from the heat, add the cilantro, and let steep for 20 minutes. Strain into a clean pan and return to a simmer.

Cook the vegetables in the pickling liquid until cooked, about 8 to 10 minutes. Transfer to a mixing bowl when cooked, cover with some of the pickling liquid, and allow to cool.

Meanwhile, preheat the oven to 325 degrees. Season the marinated chicken with salt, place on a baking sheet or in an ovenproof dish, and roast for about 8 to 10 minutes, until cooked through. Let cool and cut into thin strips.

To serve, place a bed of baby greens on each serving plate. Top with the pickled vegetables and arrange the sliced chicken at the side of the vegetables, on top of the greens.

Garnish with the cilantro sprigs.

Yield: 4 servings

street corners in other countries with unfamiliar languages and dialects and currencies, not to mention new sights and sounds and even new smells, it's almost impossible not to look at everything in a new way. Your immersion in a new and different environment causes you to rethink everything you might take for granted at home—from apparel to customs to food.

Sure, you're saying, travel sounds great—for those who've already hit the lottery. However, Mark Miller has little sympathy for aspiring chefs who claim they can't afford to travel anywhere. "You can get a charter flight for $398. If you did without a pair of sneakers, which cost $150, and a Walkman, you'd probably have the trip paid for. You can go to Costa Rica today for a dollar a day. You can go to Chile and live for a month on $300 or $400," he argues. "I still travel extensively. I go to a new country every year, and am out of the country five to ten times a year, constantly challenging my palate." Nor does he have any sympathy for those who shy away from travel because of potential risks. "People worry, 'If I travel, I'm going to get sick.' Well, I've had hepatitis twice. I've had dysentery several times. Life is dangerous. But you need to embrace it."

When chefs travel, they take special delight in absorbing the food and the culture of their destinations. The countries they choose to visit may be dictated by their desire to sample particular styles of food. Italy and, of course, France are both popular destinations for this reason. Many chefs love food first, and everything else second—and tend to plan their days accordingly. Susan Regis says she and Lydia Shire are ideal travel companions: "We love to do the same thing—shop and eat. That's it. Forget about the Sistine Chapel."

In his own early days as a cook, Patrick O'Connell would close his small restaurant every January in order to travel. "We'd go to the greatest restaurants in the world, and we'd spend every cent we had experiencing them," he recalls. "Sometimes we would have a letter of introduction, sometimes we wouldn't. It was [food writer] Bill Rice who wrote our first letters of introduction, to Paul Bocuse, Alain Chapel, and other chefs [in France], and they welcomed us and took us to the market and invited us to eat with their families. It blew us away that they were attuned to the purity of our motives."

"It definitely helps, whether you go to France, or to California. It's nice to just kind of stir up your mind and see new food and see new ideas."

—Debra Ponzek

Winter Vegetable Couscous with Ras El Hanout

GORDON HAMERSLEY

Hamersley's Bistro
Boston, MA

"I'll never forget the first time I ate a couscous in Paris. I went with a friend who lived there and he told me all about the North African influence in French cooking. We sat in this tiny place filled with the unfamiliar smells and demolished this platter of couscous, vegetables, and lamb. The next day I went to the North African market to buy the spice mixture Ras El Hanout to bring back with me to America. The customs man checked it out with interest, too! Ever since, I've always included North African flavors in my conception of bistro cooking."

. . . .

4 tbl. olive oil for cooking the vegetables

3 Portobello mushrooms—cleaned and sliced

1 red onion—peeled and quartered

1 pint Brussels sprouts

1 celery root—peeled and cut into large chunks

2 purple-top turnips—peeled and quartered

6 large chunks rutabaga—peeled

2 leeks–cleaned and sliced

1 medium cauliflower separated into chunks

1 tsp. thyme and marjoram mixed

3 c. vegetable stock

5 c. couscous

1 tbl. Ras El Hanout

10 parsley leaves for garnish

salt and cracked pepper to taste

. . . .

In a pot large enough to hold the stew easily, heat the olive oil until hot but not smoking. Add the vegetables and herbs; stew them covered until they are about half cooked. Add 3 cups of vegetable stock and continue cooking until the vegetables are cooked. They should be just tender. Season with salt and pepper. At the end of the cooking the flavors of the vegetables should have blended together well, but each one should hold together and be distinct.

Meanwhile cook the couscous

Wash the couscous with water and add the ras el hanout and salt to taste. Try one or two teaspoons to start and see how it goes. Do not overpower the dish but add enough to get the taste and add character to the dish. Let it stand for about 20 minutes and then rub the couscous through your hands, separating the grains as you go.

To make the vegetable vinaigrette

Take 2 cups of vegetable stock and reduce it over medium heat by 3/4. Add 2 tbl. lemon juice and let cool. Add 1 tsp. dijon mustard and then whisk in 5 tbl. olive oil. Season with salt and pepper and reserve.

When ready to serve, make a well in the vegetable stew and put the couscous in the middle. Add 1 cup of vegetable stock to the pan and cover. Cook over medium heat on the stove until the couscous is heated through and the vegetables are hot.

To serve

Slide the vegetables and couscous out onto a warm platter and garnish with the parsley leaves. Serve the vinaigrette on the side.

WHAT'S THE BIG DEAL ABOUT FRANCE, ANYWAY?

France has historically been a destination which inspires rhapsodies among many aspiring chefs. Gordon Hamersley says, "I knew I'd never be at peace with myself until I'd cooked in France." He and his wife Fiona, Hamersley's maitre d', subsequently spent 18 months traveling through France. "I wanted to live and breathe French food, not just French kitchens. So we ate and drank as much as possible, and traveled around the countryside and worked in various stops along the way. It taught me more about the French and the way they approach their food than just working in a three-star restaurant would have."

While traveling in France after graduating from The Culinary Institute of America, Charles Palmer recalls, "I saw a much greater respect for food. After lunch, people would ask, 'What's for dinner?'" A family he stayed with had a seven-year-old son. When Palmer asked the boy who the President of France was, he didn't know. But when Palmer asked him who the greatest chef in France was, the answer came without hesitation: "Paul Bocuse."

Susanna Foo also ate her way through France. On a 1984 trip, she skipped breakfast and lunch and spent every night for nearly two weeks eating dinner in three-star restaurants. "I realized how refined, dedicated, and proud French chefs are," she says.

Chris Schlesinger argues that it's important that aspiring chefs travel wherever their desires take them. "Do whatever you want to do. Choose a place or a country based on whatever draws you there—the art, the people, a woman you met who lives there. You can learn about the food of that place. If you're 18 and you've never been away from home and feel like going to Hawaii, go to Hawaii for a couple years. Or if you've always wanted to learn Italian, go to Italy," he advises. "Personalize your 'route' according to whatever you're into. It's not a matter of sitting down and analyzing 'what's best for my career'—that's putting the cart before the horse. It's a matter of saying, 'This is what I want to do, so I'm going to go do this.' A lot of times you'll incorporate that into wherever you end up. What it's about is having some sort of feeling and desire."

Rick Bayless followed his own passions to Mexico. "I'd always been interested in Mexican cooking, and I had the background to be able to do quite a bit of it, but I hadn't studied it in any kind of formal way," he recalls. "We worked hard for a couple of years, saved up all our money, put everything in storage, and just headed off. That was a very formative time in my life. We went to every state in Mexico. We cooked in both homes and restaurants. I'm very interested in street cooking and marketplace cooking, and so we really talked to people. That's a great place to learn, because they do all the cooking right in front of you. They'll tell you, 'I'm going to make my sausage in the morning. If you want to stop by, I'll show you how.' "

It was Anne Rosenzweig's love and study of ethnomusicology which led her to spend a year living in West Africa, Nepal, and Kenya. "I was welcomed into the community by being taught how to cook," she recalls. "Everything involved food—it was part of the religion. Most of the cultures were fairly poor, but the food was always delicious, made with only the simplest ingredients. I learned it takes real ability to make the simplest things taste wonderful." The influence on her as a chef was strong, but subtle. "People often ask me, 'What can I find on Arcadia's menu that was similar to what you ate in Liberia?' " says Rosenzweig. "I have to admit that flying termites didn't quite make it on my menu."

Bradley Ogden took his first trip to Europe in 1985, as a guest of the Spanish government, with Alice Waters, Mark Miller, Lydia Shire, Ruth Reichl (now restaurant reviewer for *The New York Times*), and Colman Andrews (author of *Catalan Cuisine*). Ogden recalls being impressed with the incredible markets, which he found "so clean. Each stall was hand tiled." His memories of the trip were vivid and lasting: "I recall going into this one little shop with Alice and Ruth in Barcelona, down this little alley. When you walked in, the only thing you could hear was this crackling noise. It turned out to be fresh roasted hazelnuts and almonds—there were two great big huge vats out of this olive wood-burning oven, and all you could smell was this incredible aroma throughout the store."

Jean-Georges Vongerichten spent time traveling through Asia while working in Bangkok, visiting Vietnam, Cambodia, Laos, and Malaysia. He subsequently opened restaurants in Singapore, Hong Kong, Japan, Portugal, Geneva, London, and Boston—his first stop in the United States. "I came for a weekend in New York. I went to the

"Travel for six to eight weeks. Go to the Greek Islands. Go to northern Italy, go to the south of France. Spend two weeks in every area and really observe the culture. If you then happen to run into somebody that says, 'Hey, I could use some help in the kitchen,' you've already established some grounds."
—VICTOR GIELISSE

fish market, and other places I'd heard so much about. I went to Balducci's and I saw all the stuff and said, 'Wow! This is great!' I said, 'That's it. This is where I want to be.' I fit in right away."

LEARNING THROUGH TRAVEL

Allen Susser found the change from cooking food to "living" food transformational. "I think there's some rich culture in food that gives you a sense of 'being' in cooking," he says. "There's so much within each culture, and how they treat food. You really have to see where food comes from, and the depth of the cultural beginnings to really understand food and get a great flavor for the food, to get it worked into your system. You have to live food, if you really want to be a chef."

Susan Regis agrees. "How can you make fresh pasta without knowing the roots of where it came from and how they do it, really? Travel brings an anthropological perspective. The food comes to mean more to you as a cook, and somehow that gets translated to the plate," says Regis. "While I'd never been to Italy before I met Lydia [Shire], now I've been three times. Travel is so crucial."

Bradley Ogden believes travel plays an important role in developing a palate. "If somebody tells you, 'Oh, I had the greatest French bread outside of Paris . . .', you're able to have a basis of comparison to say, 'That wasn't the greatest French bread. I've had really great French bread right here in San Francisco from Acme Bread.' "

Cindy Pawlcyn encourages chefs to travel and eat all over America so that they can hone their palates. "How many people have eaten lobster in Maine or stone crab claws in Florida? How many have tasted the difference between barbecue in Kansas City versus Texas? You're born with a palate, but you need to develop and perfect it. You need to taste food, get it in your memory, and be able to draw on that taste memory when you next prepare something similar. And you need to learn to develop distinctions between similar things, to be able to taste the differences between a New Zealand lamb and a Napa Valley lamb, and learn how to use the products differently."

His New Orleans travel led Edward Brown to develop an appreciation of different ingredients, even Worcestershire sauce. "It's a totally misconceived item in the United States," says Brown. "It's a

Spaghetti Alla Carbonara

JOYCE GOLDSTEIN

Square One
San Francisco, CA

"Given our new 'cholesterol consciousness,' this is not the ideal pasta to eat every day, but it is my favorite. I spent the better part of a year in Rome eating this in innumerable trattorie, trying to find the best version. Now I eat it a few times a year and still find it delicious. It is difficult to get the perfect texture, and provides a constant challenge for the cook to not scramble the eggs or overcrisp the pancetta. But it is worth the effort."

....

3/4–1 pound pancetta, cut in 1/4-inch thick slices

1 pound spaghetti

4 eggs

8–10 tablespoons grated Parmesan cheese or part pecorino and part Parmesan cheese

1 tablespoon freshly ground black pepper

2 tablespoons butter

2 tablespoons olive oil

....

Cut pancetta into 1/4-inch-wide pieces.

Bring a large kettle of water to a boil. Drop in 1 tablespoon salt and drop in the pasta.

Combine the eggs, cheese, and black pepper in a large serving bowl. Keep near the stove or atop warming shelf.

While the pasta is cooking, heat butter and oil in large sauté pan and add the diced pancetta. Cook, stirring occasionally, until bubbles appear in the pan. The pancetta will be cooked but not crisp. When the pasta is al dente, drain well and add to the bowl with the eggs and add the pancetta and most of the drippings. Toss very quickly to combine. The sauce should be a thick liquid. Serve at once. Pass additional cheese and pepper if desired.

wonderful, sophisticated thing. It's not a crappy little condiment to be taken for granted, like yellow mustard—it's the salted broth extracted from cooking tamarind seeds."

Travel abroad taught Alice Waters—and a legion of chefs who subsequently followed her lead—something about standards of freshness. "I really can't say enough about my first visit to France. I think that experience of tasting lots of different things, seeing how other cultures eat, how they do things, the way people shop, made such a difference," she says. "People were still cooking from their back gardens or from the farmers' market [in the 1960s], and I didn't know what it was that made that food so good. It took me a long time to figure out that that's what it was. It just tasted fantastic; you know, it was just a chicken, just a lettuce salad, but there was something about it. And then you'd start to put two and two together and it wasn't just a chicken—it was a chicken that was eating all the scraps from the backyard and was running around back there. It wasn't just salad—it was lettuce that they'd grown or they'd just gotten from the market.

"It was a real revelation to find what 'fresh' means. It means 'alive.' Even in salad, there's a life to a lettuce that is that day; every day it's kept in the refrigerator, it changes, it loses its life, it starts to get old. It's very different from when you go out there and pick it and eat it. France led me back to the garden."

Barbara Tropp recalls learning similar standards of freshness when she spent two years living with Chinese families in Taiwan in the late 1970s. "We shopped the market twice a day. Before I went to class, I shopped the market with the old man who headed our household—he was the gourmand—and the servant woman, and then after lunch we would again shop for dinner. I was part of an intriguing, very old-fashioned family where the husband was from Yangchow and there was an older wife who was from Beijing and a younger wife who was from Shanghai, so among the three of them they hit the epicurean epicenters of China. These were people who had grown up in imperial China with those standards of eating— they were all from well-off families—so that we shopped as if it was still the early 19th century. There were no refrigerators. You never bought a fish that wasn't alive. You never bought a vegetable that was more than eight hours out of the ground. All of what I later came to experience as so-called 'California cooking' to me was just everyday Chinese cooking as it had been done."

The effect of travel on Patrick O'Connell was no less than transformational. "After spending a year traveling, I had a whole different sense of the restaurant business, particularly in France. Food became art. I saw people crowded outside pastry shop windows, enraptured by the visual [elements]," he says. "So often I think that people aren't aiming high enough in the field, or they're imitating the imitators, instead of going to the source and always looking to the best."

O'Connell's own early "search for the best" led him to experience culinary nirvana. "I had many peak food experiences. Marrakesh, for one. It was a breaking-through of all the piles of sand bags that our culture puts on you (mostly about sensuality, I think) in regard to food and its primal connection. It's very much blocked in middle-class suburban households. I think a peak food experience requires you to be a little out of control, so I would often find myself eating couscous in a tent or something in Marrakesh and experiencing something I had never experienced before. And the same in Paris, in Vietnamese restaurants or in little bistros, having brand-new sensations that I didn't dream existed."

Bradley Ogden's "greatest trip in the world" was an eating binge in New York City with noted restauranteur Joe Baum when Baum was working as a consultant to Ogden's Kansas City restaurant. "We went to 40 places in two days," he recalls, rattling off a long list which included Balducci's, Dean & DeLuca, The Four Seasons, and Windows on the World. Particularly memorable was a dinner at The Coach House during a power blackout: "The restaurant was lit by candlelight, and all the cooking was done table side by the owner himself. There was just a table of four of us in the entire restaurant, including me and Joe Baum. I still remember everything, every detail: the black bean soup, the pepper steak, the crispy duck, and an incredible, incredible huckleberry tart for dessert, thickened with a blueberry and honey puree. I can still taste it. Those two days comprised the most enlightening experience."

Judy Rodgers first heard about Chez Panisse in Paris during her junior year of college abroad, and went to meet Alice Waters when she returned home in 1976: "She was the only person I knew in America who had any sense that 'A raspberry is not a raspberry is not a raspberry— you've got to get good ones!' "

Orchid's Tangy Cool Noodles

BARBARA TROPP

China Moon Cafe
San Francisco, CA

"I learned to taste food—and also to become cheerfully obsessed by it—during two years in Taipei in the early 1970s, when I was a graduate student in Chinese poetry living in the very traditional homes of families from northern and central China. When I returned to the United States to continue graduate study, my chin hung down to my knees, so much did I miss the terrific food I'd eaten daily in Taiwan. To assuage my spirit, I taught myself to cook the food I'd loved, drawing on books, Chinese friends and the fabulous taste memories I'd brought home.

"This Peking-style cold noodle dish was the first of my "creations." I mixed it up in the sink because I didn't have a bowl big enough! In Chinese fashion, I named it after myself, "Precious Orchid" being my very lyric Chinese name. In some ways, I think this first dish is probably the best dish I've ever made, so full it is of my love for Taiwan and the Chinese people who embraced me."

. . . .

1 lb. very thin (1/16-inch) fresh or frozen Chinese egg noodles

. . . .

© Barbara Tropp; adapted from *The Modern Art of Chinese Cooking*,
1982, William Morrow.

TRAVEL'S INFLUENCE ON CHEFS' FOOD

Some chefs' travel is literally translated to their plates, through specific dishes on their restaurants' menus. Edward Brown's travels through the country hills of Italy inspired a dish which Brown calls a "bean soup pancake." "I had been traveling through Florence, and I was taken to a country restaurant up in the hills of Chianti. The owner of the restaurant suggested an appetizer he described as a crispy *ribolita*, or bean soup, which was outstanding. I thought it

Seasonings
....

3 1/2 Tbl. Japanese sesame oil

3 1/2 Tbl. black soy sauce

1 1/2 Tbl. balsamic vinegar

2 Tbl. sugar

2 tsp. kosher salt

1/2–1 Tbl. hot chili oil

1/4 cup green and white scallion rings, plus extra to garnish

....

1. Defrost noodles, if frozen. Fluff noodles well to separate the strands.

2. Cook the noodles in ample boiling water until al dente, swishing occasionally with chopsticks, about 2 to 3 minutes for fresh noodles. Drain, rush under cold running water to chill, then drain well.

3. Combine the seasonings in a large bowl. Add the drained cold noodles and toss well with your fingers to coat and separate each strand. Add the scallion rings and toss to mix. Taste, and adjust with a dash more sugar, if needed, to bring forth the heat.

4. Serve in bowls of a complementary color, garnished with a sprinkling of scallion.

For do-ahead cooks, seal and refrigerate the finished noodles for a day or even two before serving at room temperature. The flavors only enlarge as the noodles sit.

Serves 6 to 8

---

was a great idea, but just the *base* of an idea. [When I returned home] I made it into a meat appetizer by using some braised veal shanks. To enhance that, we added marrow to the plate, garnishing the marrow with sea salt, and served it with a reduced red wine and veal stock sauce."

Observing new techniques and presentations can be as inspiring as the food itself. "When I travel, I look for pans that will make me think of a new dish that I want to make," says Lydia Shire. "For instance, I never forgot a little quail grill with a spit they brought to our table to turn quails on at a restaurant in Montreal. I went and had them made [for Biba]. They were outrageously expensive, but [in this business] you can't just sit and rest on your laurels. You've got to ask, 'What did I do this week that's special?' Travel can help by inspiring new ideas."

Jasper White contrasts what he gets out of traveling with how he sees it influencing his good friend Shire. White says, "When I travel and I taste something, I say, 'This is so good that it can't be duplicated on the other side of the ocean.' But with Lydia, it doesn't frighten her. She's driven to create a version that's better than anything anyone's ever tasted. It's a matter of personality. She's comfortable doing that, and I wouldn't be. So I don't try. I just feel comfortable with a little bit, here and there. I spent a month in China and everyone thought I would make everything Chinese when I came back. I do have a spring roll on my menu now, but it's all seafood inside—the classic combination of flounder and crab—and there's no julienne anything. That's as far as I go." Similarly, Mark Miller points out, "Design is about looking at something and understanding what someone else has created, and bringing that into one's own work: taking moo shu pork, for example, and translating it into a Southwest mode."

White also believes it's important for aspiring cooks to have the experience of tasting food at its source. "Chinese food—you cannot explain how good it is until you go to China. You can't taste it here; you have to go there to taste it," he says. "I believe the same thing is true of Italian food and French food. You really have to taste it there to truly understand it. I don't think it travels. I become introspective about food, and the traveling almost reinforces that introspectiveness. When I come back I say, 'I just want to be unique' and my way of being unique is to do uniquely New England food, using the ingredients that are here. I've matured. I'm not a young chef anymore. I've put in 20 years now, and I know what I like. And I keep growing, and learning, but in a different way."

EATING YOUR HEART OUT

With the shrinking of our 'global village,' you don't need to leave the United States in order to experience the foods of other countries. Nor do you need to cross the ocean to make a pilgrimage to a

Omelette with Bacon
and Croutons

JUDY RODGERS
Zuni Cafe
San Francisco, CA

*"I spent a lucky year in France with the Troisgros family in 1973.
Some of my fondest memories are of homey suppers I shared with
Madeleine Troisgros Serraille (la soeur) and her family, while the
famous frères were stirring up sorrel sauce back at the restaurant
where I lived. She often made a huge, satisfying omelette for dinner
and this was one of my favorites."*

Cut 4 slices of bacon into 1/2 inch-wide bands and set aside.

Tear some stale Tuscan-style bread into mouthful-sized wads, toss
with virgin olive oil whisked with a little bit of Dijon mustard and season with sea salt. Toast until just golden on the edges, but tender in the
middle. Toss with lots of freshly cracked pepper.

Crack 9 very fresh eggs into a deep bowl and beat with a whisk
about 30 strokes. Add 9 tiny pinches of salt and beat a few more
strokes. Do not overbeat; the eggs do not need to be perfectly homoge-
neous.

Heat a large, steel omelette pan and render the bacon until it is just
beginning to color. Add approximately 1–1/2 tablespoons unsalted butter and raise the heat. When the butter is just starting to foam, whisk
the eggs once and pour over. I prefer my omelettes rolled, so I slide the
cooked egg to the far edge of the pan as I go. When about 1/2 of the
eggs are set, drop in the warm toasted croutons, and continue sliding
the cooked eggs forward, enveloping the croutons as you go. The bacon
will end up dispersed throughout the omelette, rather than bunched up
in the middle. Once the omelette is completely "rolled" tip the pan
forward to brown the eggs slightly. Tip onto a warm platter, and serve
instantly. Madeleine would always serve a salad of dandelions or other
bitter greens afterward, to be eaten on the same plate to mix with the
remains of the omelette.

for 4 people

Jasper White once worked with a husband and wife team in Seattle whose passion for food was contagious. "It's not like before there were famous chefs there weren't great chefs. This was a great classic chef from the old school—he knew the book inside out, and knew these wonderful dishes, stuff that would blow your mind. You would never see this today, it's so old-fashioned: Roast Pheasants with Sauerkraut and Champagne. He'd cook the sauerkraut with apples and ham hocks, and then roast the pheasants. On a big platter, he'd put the sauerkraut out with the pheasants all around it, and put a bottle of champagne in the middle with the wire top off. The sauerkraut heated the champagne, the cork flew out, and an eruption of champagne doused all the food. Then he'd cut up the pheasants and you'd eat the sauerkraut and the pheasants with the rest of the champagne."

culinary mecca. You can find some of the world's greatest French food in the United States-based restaurants of the French chefs interviewed for this book. You'll also find some of the best Mexican food prepared by native Mexicans and even non-natives who've opened Mexican restaurants in the United States after extensive research and travel.

"Some of the Thai food at Bangkok Cuisine [an inexpensive Boston restaurant] is not that much different from what I ate in Bangkok. And it will cost you about $10,000 less [than flying to Bangkok]," points out Lydia Shire. "If you don't have the money to travel, for a lot less you can buy good books and go to the best restaurants, and you're almost there."

Although he's never traveled to Japan, Edward Brown has found eating Japanese food in the United States and speaking with sushi chefs an education in itself. "I've come to admire the Japanese respect for food. There are more rules for making sushi than in Escoffier, to the level of which direction you actually slice the fish," says Brown.

By eating out on their nights off, chefs keep up with what their colleagues are doing in other restaurants, as well as remind themselves what it's like to be a customer. For the most part, when chefs eat out, they are driven to unlock the secrets of everything they eat. Sometimes, though, it's hard to enjoy a meal rather than critique it, because their perfectionistic mental checklists are always running.

"I try to relax when I go out to eat," admits Jimmy Schmidt. "I look at the overall experience. The dining experience is beyond just food—it's how the food plays on the plate, how it plays in the room, the aromas, and everything else that's happening are crucial to that whole experience. I look for what kind of pleasure it gives me. I may come across a new techniques or a different flavor, or a different combination, but I first look at it as a consumer. Then I break it down and say, 'Well, how did they do that? How did they get that flavor?' I like to see other people's food, not to get ideas that I take back, but to stimulate some other idea that falls within my range of cooking. That's the fun part. If you're a painter and you go out and see Stellas, that doesn't mean you go back and paint Stellas—you go back and do something else in your own range."

While it's almost clichéd for American chefs to get inspiration from traveling through Europe, some European chefs have likewise traveled through the United States. After leaving his job in the

1980s, Jean Joho took three weeks off to travel to New York, Los Angeles, and San Francisco. "While I was working, everybody had been talking about 'nouvelle American' cuisine, and I had no idea what they meant. I wanted to find out what they were talking about," admits Joho. "I ate at almost every major restaurant." He also spent a week in the kitchens of Chinois on Main and Stars, a professional courtesy often extended to chefs visiting from other cities. Joho advises, "When you go out to eat, see what you enjoy eating. You can change your style later on, but this gives you a direction for developing your own style of food."

A single meal can mark a critical turning point. Wayne Nish was in the printing business when he went to Switzerland on his honeymoon in 1980, and found himself at Fredy Girardet's restaurant. "It opened my eyes. I had a nine-course dégustation, and I was just flabbergasted. I had no idea that anybody was doing stuff like that. I'd never seen lobster out of the shell, and I was eating fresh foie gras and black truffles for the first time. The flavors were scintillating. It left me speechless," he admits. "I remember my wife looking at me from across the table before I could even say it, and she said, 'You should be doing this.' I didn't possess the arrogance. I thought there was no way I could be doing this." Because of his business involvements, it took Nish three years before he finally made it to cooking school, after which he's never looked back.

Many of the chefs we interviewed could recount in minute detail entire meals they had eaten many years previously. Visiting Michelin-starred restaurants in France by himself, Charles Palmer found he was able to pay much more attention to the food. Palmer claims he can still recall "absolutely everything" about his restaurant visits, including lunch by himself on the terrace at Alain Chapel, starting with the house specialty Champagne cocktail: "Champagne with peach purée and cassis. I remember having little  fried fish from the region as a first course. I had rolled, marinated salmon with salad wrapped inside it, like a roulade. I still remember the saddle of rabbit with caramelized garlic and beans, which, at the time, I thought was kind of strange. I was by myself, so the captain spent a lot of time speaking with me," Palmer recalls. "When I men-

Two lists of the world's top 10 "fancy" restaurants and the top 10 "casual" restaurants were compiled by food writer Patricia Wells and published in the International Herald-Tribune *in October 1994. Here are her picks:*

Fancy: 1) Joël Robuchon, Paris; 2) Restaurant Fredy Girardet, Crissier, Switzerland; 3) Lai Ching Heen, Hong Kong; 4) Le Louis XV (Alain Ducasse), Monte Carlo; 5) Osteria da Fiore, Venice; 6) Jiro, Tokyo; 7) Guy Savoy, Paris; 8) Taillevent, Paris; 9) Restaurant Daniel, New York City; 10) Da Cesare, Albaretto della Torre, Italy.

Casual: 1) Al Forno, Providence, Rhode Island; 2) La Tupina, Bordeaux; 3) Frontera Grill, Chicago; 4) City Chiu Chow Restaurant, Hong Kong; 5) Ca l'Isidre, Barcelona; 6) The Seafood Restaurant, Cornwall, England; 7) Checchino dal 1887, Rome; 8) Cibrèo, Florence; 9) Viridiana, Madrid; 10) Le Caméléon, Paris.

tioned to him that I was working at Georges Blanc, they sent me about six desserts. At the time they were doing these little paired soufflés: one was chocolate and one was raspberry. I tried every dessert on the cart. The one I remember best was a pear napoleon: caramelized roasted pears layered between puff pastry, with a pear zabaglione or crème anglaise. Very simple, but just incredible tasting." I remember that. I can still remember tasting that."

Jeremiah Tower described the memorable experience of eating a simple yet delicious white bean soup at Georges Blanc's namesake restaurant in France several years before. "I was amazed and thought, 'My God! How did he make that?' It was such an amazing thing. And then I realized it was half white-bean purée, but they were new crop dried white beans, or fresh white beans, which are extremely difficult to get here, and half crème fraîche, with a teaspoon of chopped black truffles sprinkled on top. You don't need to do much more than that. By tasting it, you could probably go back to your own kitchen and try it three or four times and probably get it. But it took me a while to figure out the quality of the crème fraîche and the new white beans, instead of the stuff we tend to get here, which I think is the second- or third-year rubbish that they export."

Aside from learning about food, learning about service and presentation is key for chefs. Tower recalls taking members of his staff to the Crillon in Paris for breakfast—at $60 per person—as a "seminar" in service excellence. "Breakfast at the Crillon is a legend. We'd spend two hours analyzing everything about the service at the table, down to how the butter is put on the plate. Once they'd stayed at the Crillon or the Ritz it all became clear, all my yelling and screaming and demanding suddenly made the point."

Tower is still befuddled over one aspect of the service he received one night at the Hassler in Rome. "We'd arrived, we were exhausted, and we asked the legendary concierge where we should eat. Once we got to the restaurant he'd recommended, I didn't like the look of it, so we ate at another restaurant close by. When we came back, there was a different concierge at the desk. As we walked in, he said, 'Good afternoon, Mr. Tower' and asked me how I'd enjoyed not the restaurant the concierge had recommended, but the one we'd actually eaten at! My general manager was blown away, and he asked, 'How did they do that?' and I said, 'Oh, I'll explain it later,' thinking 'How *did* they do that?' "

Eating out offers aspiring chefs the opportunity to meet people who share their passion for food. Years ago, Zarela Martinez and her mother decided to go on a culinary expedition to New Orleans. Their first stop was a local cooking school where, Martinez recalls with disdain, they made peanut soup out of canned chicken stock and peanut butter. She and her mother decided to instead eat at every great restaurant in the city and then try to duplicate what they'd eaten. The two were seated at K-Paul's near where chef Paul Prudhomme was cooking, and Martinez's mother urged her to speak with him. "I told him about our experience at the cooking school, and he made me an offer," Martinez recalls. "He said he'd teach me Cajun food if I would teach him how to make Mexican food." Martinez and Prudhomme spent three or four days cooking together, becoming fast friends.

Even shopping for food and speaking with people in the markets can be educational. I enjoy wandering through farmers' markets, like the one at Union Square in Manhattan, and even little out-of-the-way specialty stores selling produce, spices, meats, and often unusual ingredients. Stopping by a meat market for flank steak and asking a question about the tripe that was prominently displayed, I was given an impromptu recipe for tripe from the Italian butcher who claimed it was one of his favorite dishes. When I was living in Boston, I used to love shopping in Chinatown and an Asian supermarket called Ming's, particularly after being taken on a tour by a coworker who knew a lot about Asian ingredients. Visiting in-laws in the middle of Illinois, I've even stumbled across little ethnic shops selling exotic cheeses and rices, as well as their own freshly baked breads. A little exploration—wherever you live—can yield new culinary discoveries.

Charlie Trotter recalls, "The first weekend I moved to San Francisco, I read the *San Francisco Chronicle* and it said 'Sunday morning tour of Chinatown conducted by Barbara Tropp.' So after I'd been in the city four days, I went on a tour of Chinatown with Barbara Tropp. Right off the bat I had this unbelievable point of reference, and I was set for the next year and a half. I knew exactly where to go to get duck feet, I knew exactly where to go to get water chestnuts, I knew exactly where to go to get greens, bamboo shoots, lemon grass, fish, and squid. It was perfect. It set the tone."

These excursions can also provide inspiration. Debra Ponzek recharges by just wandering through Balducci's or Grace's Market in

"Almost everything I do is associated with food. I'm always thinking about food. I was driving down a country road in Sonoma the other week, and I thought I saw morels growing by the side of the road. I thought it was the neatest thing. I turned around, went back and got out of the car, but found they weren't morels. My girlfriend thought, 'Are you nuts?' I guess I am obsessed with food, maybe at times too much to an extreme."

—CHARLES PALMER

Manhattan. "I'll be browsing and see something and find myself saying, 'Oh, I forgot I could get those mushrooms now.' It stirs up ideas."

READING: FOOD FOR THOUGHT

Wayne Nish remembers first meeting Craig Claiborne at a dinner party: "For me, it was like getting an audience with the pope. He was my number one idol in food. He was not a chef, he was not a restaurateur, he was a journalist but, as such, he brought the world to me."

Reading offers chefs a way to make sure they are not cooking in a vacuum, but rather that they are informed about what has taken place in the past and inspired by what is being created in the present as detailed in cookbooks, books about food, and magazines. "As you try to figure out what direction you're moving in as a chef, it's helpful to read to discover what your colleagues are doing and what directions they're moving in," says Jean Joho. "Young professionals definitely have to buy books and magazines and do all they can to keep learning about food." I found that since I never attended cooking school, I relied particularly heavily on books to supplement my on-the-job learning about food. Reading offered me a portable, convenient, and relatively low-cost way to learn.

The chefs we interviewed were not dispassionate about this topic. According to Alfred Portale, "It is singly the most important aspect of this career: reading, and studying, and being influenced. If you don't read, you're illiterate. You can't possibly succeed in this business unless you are well read and well prepared and you read everything. I used to just study constantly, constantly—reading, rereading, testing, thinking about it, contemplating, talking about it, experimenting."

Reading can broaden the repertoire of any aspiring chef. "In any place you're working, you're following through on pretty much one identifiable style of the chef you're working for, which by no means is the only way to do something," says Allen Susser. "By reading, you're seeing other techniques, other ways of doing things, other  ways of adding different nuances to what you have, and the how's and why's. Reading cookbooks and reading industry and consumer magazines is really important."

While cooking at Chez Panisse, Judy Rodgers spent a summer house-sitting for Lindsey Shere [the pastry chef], who had an extraordinary cooking library.

"Basically I went home every night from work and read a cookbook in order to learn, because I was definitely in over my head." Rodgers admits.

Many chefs went through periods of intensive reading during their early days in the business, representing almost a 'rite of passage' into the realm of becoming a serious professional. Norman Van Aken admits, "One of the cornerstone changes for me in my life was having someone say to me, 'Why don't you read cookbooks?' I had always considered myself well-read, and so I asked, 'Like who?' He said, 'Like Beard—why don't you read James Beard?' And after work I went to a bookstore and picked up James Beard's *The Theory and Practice of Good Cooking*. I found it was a whole new way of looking at food, and it blew me away. It started to affect the way I was cooking at work, and I started spending all my money on cookbooks."

In his own early days as a cook, Charlie Trotter read incessantly about food and wine. "Everything I could get my hands on—every cookbook, every food history book. In San Francisco, I lived in a studio apartment with no furniture. I slept on the floor in a sleeping bag. For a year and a half, all I had was a light and maybe 200 books and kitchen stuff." he recalls. "I really felt like there were so many people out there that seemed to know so much stuff, and I asked myself, 'How do I learn this stuff? What do I do? How do I get this information?' I learned you've just got to read and think about it."

Mark Militello recalls going through a stage "where I just couldn't get enough knowledge. I would give my wife a kiss and turn over in bed and grab two or three of my new books. When you're younger, you're much more experimental—you're kind of searching. But I still read constantly."

Anne Rosenzweig recalls that she would spend ten hours a day in the kitchen, and then go home and read books. "That was my academic training, that you always had to read. I think that helped speed up the process for me," she says. "I would come up with questions, and the next day I'd go into work to ask the chef, who was enamored of the fact that I was so studious. He'd order the ingredients I'd asked about, and then we'd work with it."

You can even discover a mentor through reading. Raji Jallepalli found a mentor in Jean-Louis Palladin through reading his cookbook: "I happened to see his cookbook, and found it one of the very rare, special cookbooks which inspired me a lot. Ordinarily, I don't

"Cooking's not a secular thing. I've learned more about the history of the world because of my interest in cooking than I ever did in school. When I was writing Big Flavors of the Hot Sun, I learned about different lands, even the history of the Roman Empire, by researching the spice routes."
—CHRIS SCHLESINGER

Chefs' Top 20
Recommended Books and/or Authors

- Escoffier's *Le Guide Culinaire: The Complete Guide to the Art of Modern Cookery*. The first translation into English by H. L. Crackwell and R. J. Kaufman of *Le Guide Culinaire* in its entirety, published by Van Nostrand Reinhold. *"When we were young chefs, we were almost forced by our chef to read Escoffier. To me, it's the basics. We should not forget these things. The danger is with trends, that the young chefs can follow the trends without knowing the classics. And when the trend changes, they are stuck. You need this basic training, and then you can do anything you wish."*—ANDRÉ SOLTNER

- *Larousse Gastronomique: The New American Edition of the World's Greatest Culinary Encyclopedia*, edited by Jenifer Harvey Lang. New York: Crown Publishers. *"[When first entering the profession], every night I would read heavy-duty stuff like* Larousse. *I would just read and read and read and try to understand what it meant. When you don't know about food, you look at something like* Larousse *and think that it's pretty bizarre that people thought about food like this."* —CHARLES PALMER

- Julia Child's *Mastering the Art of French Cooking*, Simone Beck and Louisette Bertholle. New York: Alfred Knopf, 1962.

- Irma S. Rombauer and Marion Rombauer Becker's *The Joy of Cooking*. Carmel, IN: Bobbs-Merrill Company, Inc.

- Elizabeth David's *Elizabeth David Classics*. New York: Alfred Knopf, 1980.

- *James Beard's American Cookery*. Boston: Little, Brown, 1980. *"Oh, I love James—just to read. One of my favorite books of his has one chapter about Thanksgiving, and another about Christmas. He tells about his childhood and why his mother liked crab and not lobster, and her plum pudding recipe. I mean, I could read that over and over and over and over."*—LYDIA SHIRE

- Alice Waters' *Chez Panisse Menu Cookbook*. New York: Random House, 1982.

- *Paula Wolfert's World of Food*. New York: HarperCollins, 1994.

- Richard Olney's *Simple French Food*. New York: Macmillan, 1974, or *French Menu Cookbook*. David R. Godine, Publisher, 1970.

- Craig Claiborne's *The New York Times Cookbook*. New York: HarperCollins, 1990. *"That was my bible when I grew up."*—MARK MILLER

- Ali-Bab, *Etudes Culinaire*, Flammarion, 1928. *"The best book ever written."*—MICHEL RICHARD

- Paul Bocuse's *Regional French Cooking*. New York: Random House, 1977.

- *The New Professional Chef*. The Culinary Institute of America. New York: Van Nostrand Reinhold, 1992. *"Unbelievable."* —EDWARD BROWN

- Madeline Kamman's *The Making of a Cook*. New York: Macmillan, 1980 and *In Madeleine's Kitchen: A Personal Interpretation of the Modern French Cuisine*. New York: Macmillan, 1992.

- Fernand Point's *Ma Gastronomie*, Paris: Flammarion, 1969. *"It has really no recipes in it, but has a lot of sayings and quotes. He's very fanatical about butter and about life, and about throwing people out of his restaurants when they lit up cigarettes. This was in the '50s that he did all this stuff. He was the man who trained Bocuse, the Troisgros brothers, Alain Chapel—they all came from Point. Almost all the great chefs of France came from Point. He's very inspiring and old-fashioned and funny. It's a wonderful book. It's probably out of print, so if you see it, grab it."*—JASPER WHITE

- Time-Life Books' *Food of the World* (1968–70) and *American Cooking* (1970–71) series.

- Harold McGee's *On Food and Cooking: The Science and Lore of the Kitchen*. New York: Collier Books, 1984.

- Georges Blanc's *The Natural Cuisine of G. Blanc* and *Ma Cuisine des Saisons*. Stewart Tabori Chang, 1987.

- *Simply French: Patricia Wells Presents the Cuisine of Joël Robuchon* by Patricia Wells and Joël Robuchon. New York: William Morrow & Company, 1991.

- *The Auberge of the Flowering Hearth* by Roy Andre De Grouts, The Ecco Press, 1992. *"I think everyone should have to read Auberge of the Flowering Hearth the moment that they say they're interested in a culinary career because it identifies the concept and the potential of a mystical, spiritual experience happening in relation to the dining experience."*—PATRICK O'CONNELL

Larry Forgione says. "If you wanted to pursue what I pursued, I would recommend Waverly Root's Gastronomy in America, Evan Jones' book on American cooking, Beard's book on American cooking, the Time-Life series of regional American cookbooks (the old one, not the new one), the old White House cookbook, any of Mary Margaret McBride's cookbooks, and any books that you can get your hands on that were printed before World War II that were compilations, like the Junior League cookbooks. That's how I got to know a lot about regional American cooking, through those types of books."

read cookbooks and pick up the phone and call the chefs. But for some reason, the book was too magical, so I left a message for him," she recalls. "He called back, and I congratulated him on the book. He asked me what I did for a living, and I explained that I was a chef doing fusion cooking. He was impressed and said he'd come to Memphis. A couple of weeks later, I did a special dinner for him. He said I needed to be exposed, and invited me to come to his kitchen. I spent about a week there, and it was very helpful. It helped me to pick up some of the classical techniques, stocks, and plate presentations."

Larry Forgione recalls his treasured friendship with James Beard, who had an incredible library, as being a critical learning experience. In addition to reading Beard's books, "I would go up and sit and talk with him. He was himself a living encyclopedia. That's how I got all this information about the way things were and the way things should be. Other things, about the way foods grow, you don't find in cookbooks. You have to go and spend time in the farmers' market, or go and visit someone's farm. You don't have to go *work* on a farm for six months; you just have to understand the concepts behind it."

Jasper White credits Evan Jones' *American Cooking*—"a history of American food, with recipes"—with kindling his own interest in American cooking. "You have to remember 1976. I just got out of The Culinary Institute of America. [It] didn't have the American Bounty restaurant then; it was the diner and The Escoffier Room. There was nothing in between. So you'd aspire to learn French classics—that was the vision every chef had, and it wasn't that long ago. Everything's changed now, but back then it was all French. I bought Jones' book because of my interest in history, and read it and got a great sense of tradition and heritage in American food, that I never got from The Culinary Institute of America, which might as well have been The Culinary Institute of France. I didn't go off on a binge, right away, but it grew inside me. That book kind of simmered on my shelf for years, and I'd pick it up from time to time. The recipes were fairly good, nothing real great, but the dishes were great: baked beans and Brunswick stew and chowders and all the great traditional American dishes. That book was one of the great ones."

Norman Van Aken describes the process he uses to get inspiration from his books: "I'll get pork tenderloin in the kitchen and

wonder, 'How am I going to cook this tonight?' And I would have seven books out in front of me, flipping through them thinking, 'Pork tenderloin, pork tenderloin—oh, pork *chops*, I'd better read this.' I'll be in a Thai book, a French book, and an Italian book all at the same time. So I start cross-referencing all this material very, very eclectically, and informing myself of what to do."

Daniel Boulud skims cookbooks, but doesn't read recipes: "A title might inspire the combination of two ingredients," he says. Alfred Portale agrees. "It's not really a literal thing where you look up a recipe and say 'Oh, I'll try that.' That almost never happens," he says. "Usually I read the index, in the back. Somehow, that starts to spark things. If I have 40 percent of the plate, or I have an idea, but I need the rest of the garnishes, then it might get a little more specific. But again, it's only an idea. I almost never take a recipe out of a cookbook."

Looking at pictures of visual presentations of food can help you begin to develop an aesthetic sense. "The more pictures you look at, the better," says Cindy Pawlcyn. "In time, you'll begin to develop a sense of what you like and don't like." Patrick O'Connell admits, "Because I'm such a visual person, all the early issues of *Gourmet* were very, very helpful. The mood was evoked—not the food itself, but the mood. The fantastic photography [by Ronnie Jacques, one of their renowned photographers] captured and said so much to me, that I can look at a picture, and everything starts clicking, clicking, clicking away," he says. "But my mind moves too fast now to read cookbooks any longer. So if I do, I just flip the pages very quickly, and scan the ingredients."

Many leading chefs have developed extensive personal libraries consisting of hundreds and even thousands of cookbooks and books about food, which they turn to for both information and inspiration. "I have well over 600 cookbooks at home. I can't say I've read every one of them, but I've read more than 400 of them, cover to cover," says Jasper White. "Many books and all books have served as an inspiration to me. I think the repetition of reading many books and seeing certain ingredients together time and time again has been a great teacher to me."

"I'm mad about Italian food. I have a book by Carol Field called Celebrating Italy. *They celebrate anything, but what I found was they celebrated lard! A day of celebration of lard?! I couldn't have agreed with her more! They also put pepper in their bread, weaving it through the dough, and they put cracklins in bread. Italians are mad for pork, and so are Southerners. A lot of Italian cooking is really like Southern cooking."*

—EDNA LEWIS

*Allen Susser is working with
other Miami-area chefs like
Norman Van Aken and Robin
Haas, in conjunction with The
American Institute of Wine and
Food, to establish a culinary
library for local cooks to "gain
access to a greater depth of culinary knowledge."*

The same chefs, however, lament young cooks' lack of interest in reading about food and cooking, aside from glancing at an occasional magazine. "No one wants to borrow books anymore," observes Susan Feniger. Barbara Tropp also notes, "What kid coming out of cooking school reads? No one! I know I sound like an old fart, but people with backgrounds like Anne's [Rosenzweig] and Alice's [Waters] and Joyce's [Goldstein] and Jeremiah's [Tower] and Mark's [Miller]—all of us were people who began to love cooking by reading, and who have a very philosophical bent to our cuisine."

To encourage his staff to read, Patrick O'Connell allowed each staff member to pick a favorite book, and also created a small library. What books does he recommend to his staff? "I think particularly when you're starting out, it's essential to use books that you totally trust to give you excellent results. Certainly, anything Craig Claiborne does is thoroughly tested and worked out. He even has a 'recommended cookbook library' in his autobiography (*Craig Claiborne's A Feast Made for Laughter: A Memoir with Recipes*; Holt, Rinehart and Winston, 1982), which I think is very helpful."

Part of growing as a cook involves opening yourself up to new worlds, new experiences, and new conceptions of what food can be. This may include savoring a meal in one of the world's best restaurants, if your previous culinary experiences are more humble. Or it might involve coming to appreciate the rich history and sublime flavors of a modest ethnic dish, simply cooked and seasoned, if you've had the privilege of being overexposed to expensive Western foods. Or it might be an unexpected combination of ingredients, discovered in a rare cookbook, which you would not have run across in a general cooking magazine, if that was your only food literature source. Travel, eating, and reading can provide the all-important sparks leading to new illuminations.

Selected Chef-Authors' Books

Bayless, Rick and Deanne G. Bayless. *Authentic Mexican: Regional Cooking from the Heart of Mexico*. William Morrow and Company, Inc., 1987.

Boulud, Daniel. *Cooking with Daniel Boulud*. Random House, 1993.

Gielisse, Victor. *Cuisine Actuelle*. Taylor Publishing Company, 1992.

Goldstein, Joyce. *Back to Square One: Old-World Food in a New-World Kitchen*. William Morrow and Company, Inc., 1992.

Killeen, Johanne and George Germon, *Cucina Simpatica: Robust Trattoria Cooking from Al Forno*. HarperCollins, 1991.

Lagasse, Emeril and Jesse Tirsch. *Emeril's New New Orleans Cooking*. William Morrow and Company, Inc., 1993.

Lewis, Edna. *In Pursuit of Flavor*. Alfred A. Knopf, 1988.

Martinez, Zarela. *Food From My Heart: Cuisines of Mexico Remembered and Reimagined*. Macmillan, 1992.

Miller, Mark. *Coyote Cafe: Foods from the Great Southwest*. Ten Speed Press, 1989.

Milliken, Mary Sue and Susan Feniger. *City Cuisine*. William Morrow and Company, Inc., 1989.

Milliken, Mary Sue and Susan Feniger. *Mesa Mexicana: Bold Flavors from the Border, Coastal Mexico, and Beyond*. William Morrow and Company, Inc., 1994.

Ogden, Bradley. *Bradley Ogden's Breakfast, Lunch & Dinner: Savory American Fare for Contemporary Cooks*. Random House, 1991.

Palladin, Jean-Louis. *Jean-Louis—Cooking with the Seasons*. Thomasson-Grant, 1989.

Pawlcyn, Cindy. *Fog City Diner Cookbook*. Ten Speed Press, 1993.

Peel, Mark and Nancy Silverton. *Mark Peel & Nancy Silverton At Home: Two Chefs Cook for Family & Friends*. Warner Books, 1994.

Richard, Michel. *Michel Richard's Home Cooking with a French Accent*. William Morrow & Company, Inc., 1993

Rosenzweig, Anne. *The Arcadia Seasonal Mural and Cookbook*. Harry Abrams, 1986.

Schlesinger, Chris and John Willoughby. *The Thrill of the Grill: Techniques, Recipes and Down Home Barbecue*. William Morrow and Company, Inc. 1990.

Schmidt, Jimmy. *Cooking For All Seasons*. Macmillan, 1991.

(Continued on next page)

Susser, Allen. *Allen Susser's New World Cuisine*. Doubleday, 1995.

Tower, Jeremiah. *Jeremiah Tower's New American Classics*. HarperCollins, 1986.

Tropp, Barbara. *China Moon Cookbook*. Workman Publishing, 1992.

Trotter, Charlie. *Charlie's Trotter's*. Ten Speed Press, 1994.

Van Aken, Norman. *Norman Van Aken's Feast of Sunlight: The Sumptuous Cuisine of Key West's Master Chef*. Ballantine Books, 1988

Vongerichten, Jean-Georges. *Simple Cuisine: The Easy, New Approach to Four-Star Cooking*. Prentice Hall Press, 1990.

Waters, Alice. *The Chez Panisse Menu Cookbook*. Random House, 1982.

White, Jasper. *Jasper White's Cooking From New England: More Than Three Hundred Traditional and Contemporary Recipes*. HarperCollins, 1993.

Wilder, Janos. *Janos: Recipes & Tales from a Southwest Restaurant*. Ten Speed Press, 1989.

Other Recommended Reading

Daria, Irene. *Lutèce: A Day in the Life of America's Greatest Restaurant*. Random House, 1993.

Franey, Pierre, with Richard Flaste and Bryan Miller. *A Chef's Tale: A Memoir of Food, France and America*. Alfred A. Knopf, 1994.

Mariani, John. *America Eats Out: An Illustrated History of Restaurants, Taverns, Coffee Shops, Speakeasies, and Other Establishments That Have Fed Us for 350 Years*. William Morrow and Company, 1991.

Mariani, John, with Alex Von Bidder. *The Four Seasons: A History of America's Premier Restaurant*. Crown Publishers, Inc., 1994.

Studley, Helen. *Life of a Restaurant: Tales and Recipes from La Colombe d'Or*. Crown Publishers, Inc., 1994.

If you can't find a particular culinary book through your local bookstore, two mail order resources include Kitchen Arts & Letters in New York City at (212) 876-5550, and Books for Cooks at (800) 355-CHEF.

Crème Brûlée Napoleon with Hazelnut

MICHEL RICHARD
Citrus
Los Angeles, CA

"When I was 16, on vacation in Spain, I was madly in love with a
local young maiden. We went on a date, to a restaurant, and we ate
a Crème Catalane, which was a kind of crème brûlée with anise flavor. After that, I had my first kiss. In the United States, we prefer the
vanilla to the anise, and I added the crunch to the crème brûlée, with
my pastry background, to constitute a napoleon. Both the silky texture of the cream with the crispy and crunchy texture of the thousand
leaves complement each other very well. When I bite into the Cake of
Love, it reminds me of the Catalan adventure. Today, the Crème
Brûlée Napoleon with Hazelnut still remains my favorite dessert as
the Crème D'Amour."

This is the most popular dessert at Citrus. Its success does not come
as a total surprise to me, for it is the ultimate napoleon. Made without
flour, its Crème Brûlée filling is lighter and more refined than the
Pastry Cream classically used. Studded with chopped caramelized
hazelnuts, its phyllo dough layers are even crispier and crunchier than
the puff pastry traditionally sandwiching the creamy interior. Unlike
puff pastry, phyllo dough doesn't shrink. I've used a Caramel Sauce
here, but the vanilla base of the filling lends itself to any flavoring or
fruit accompaniment. This spectacular dessert offers an advantage to
the home cook as well in that it does not require a Grande Diplome
de Patisserie to execute. Though its multiple components may make
it appear complicated, steps are simple to achieve. Everything except
assembling the layers can be completed in advance.

© 1993 by Michel Richard and Judy Zeidler. *Michel Richard's Home Cooking with a French
Accent.* William Morrow and Company, Inc.

(Continued on next page)

Crème Brûlée, Caramel Sauce, and hazelnut sugar mixture can be prepared two days in advance and refrigerated. Phyllo dough squares can be baked at any time during the day dessert is to be served. Assemble napoleons just before presenting.

....

1 cup hazelnuts

3/4 cup sugar

8 sheets phyllo dough, defrosted overnight in refrigerator, if frozen

1/2 cup (1 stick) unsalted butter, melted

About 1/2 cup powdered sugar

....

For hazelnuts, preheat oven to 350°F. Place hazelnuts on small baking sheet and toast until brown, about 15 minutes. Rub nuts in sieve or towel to husk. Grind nuts coarsely with sugar in food processor, pulsing on/off. (Can be prepared ahead, transferred to airtight container, and set aside at room temperature.)

For pastry, preheat oven to 300°F. Line 2 large baking sheets with parchment paper. Remove phylo from package and unroll. Remove 1 sheet and cover remaining phylo with plastic and damp towel. Brush sheet with melted butter and sprinkle generously with hazelnut-sugar mixture. Top with second sheet of phylo, pressing to seal. Brush with butter and sprinkle with nut mixture. Repeat with third and fourth sheet.

Using ruler as guide, trim edges with knife or pastry wheel to form 12x16-inch rectangle. Cut pastry into 3 strips lengthwise and four strips crosswise, forming twelve 4-inch squares. Transfer squares to prepared baking sheets in single layer using large spatula. Bake 10 minutes or until brown.

Make and bake 12 additional 4-inch squares using 4 sheets of phylo and remaining butter and nut mixture. Rewrap remaining phyloo and refrigerate or freeze for another use.

Preheat broiler. Place as many phylo squares as will fit under broiler at one time on baking sheet. Sieve powdered sugar generously over squares and broil several inches below heat source until golden brown, about 1 minute, watching carefully. Transfer to racks in single layer. Repeat with remaining squares. (Can be prepared ahead.)

To serve, divide Crème Brûlée among 16 pastry squares, nut-side-up, spreading evenly. Make 8 napoleons by stacking 2 Crème Brûlée-filled squares and topping with 1 unfilled square, nut-side-up. Place napoleons in center of 8 large plates. Reheat Caramel Sauce and ladle around napoleons. Serve immediately.

Technique tips

Filo dough is less brittle and likely to tear if it has not been frozen. Though harder to find, unfrozen filo dough can often be purchased at a Middle Eastern market.

When working with filo dough, keep unused pieces wrapped in plastic and covered with damp towel so they don't dry out.

Tip

Prepare half of filo squares using half of filo dough, melted butter, and nut mixture and bake. Prepare second half of filo squares with remaining ingredients while first half is baking.

8 servings

Créme Brûlée

....

1/2 cup milk

2 cups heavy cream

1/2 cup sugar

1 or 2 vanilla beans, slit lengthwise

9 room-temperature egg yolks, blended with fork

....

Place milk, cream, and sugar in heavy, medium saucepan. Scrape seeds from vanilla beans into milk mixture. Add beans and bring to boil over medium-high heat. Remove from heat and let beans steep for at least 1 hour or until mixture cools to room temperature. Discard beans (or wash, dry, and reserve for another use).

(Continued on next page)

Preheat oven to 300°F. Place 9x13-inch baking dish in larger baking pan. Pour enough water into larger pan to come 3/4 of the way up sides of baking dish. Remove baking dish and place baking pan with water in oven to preheat.

Whisk egg yolks into cooled custard mixture. Strain through fine sieve into baking dish. Place dish in baking pan with water and bake until custard is set and knife inserted into center comes out dry, about 45 minutes to 1 hour. Remove baking dish from water bath. Cool, then cover and refrigerate until 15 minutes before assembling napoleons. (Can be prepared 2 days ahead.)

Technique tip

Adjust heat so water in water bath does not go above gentle simmer. If water boils, custard can curdle.

Makes about 2 cups

Caramel Sauce

....

1 1/2 cups sugar

Water

1 1/4 cups heavy cream

....

Place sugar in heavy medium saucepan. Cover with water and cook over low heat until sugar dissolves, swirling pan occasionally. Increase heat and boil until sugar caramelizes and turns a deep mahogany brown, watching carefully so mixture doesn't burn. Stand back to avoid splatter and gradually pour in cream. Simmer sauce, stirring occasionally, until caramel dissolves and sauce is smooth and thick, about 3 minutes. Cool, then cover and refrigerate. (Can be prepared 2 days ahead.)

To serve, stir over medium heat until melted and warm, thinning with additional cream or milk as desired.

Variation
Sauce can also be served cold. Thin with additional cream or milk.

Makes about 1 3/4 cups

9

PERSEVERING IN THE FACE OF REALITY

*Through
Bad
Times
and
Good*

*"When you make as many mistakes
as I've made, then you'll know as
much as I know."*

—Jacques Torres

As a beginning cook, almost every mistake I made—from forgetting a pan of nuts that went from roasting to smoking in the oven, to nearly slicing off the very tip of my finger on a meat slicer—caused me to question whether I was really cut out for this profession. I thought then that what made a great chef great was having never made a mistake. I wasn't alone.

Jackie Shen recalls crying constantly for the first six weeks she worked as an apprentice. "No one had ever yelled at me before," she says. "It was a real ego-deflator. I felt like a piece of dust. I thought I must be too dumb and couldn't hack it." Wayne Nish remembers, "One guy I worked for screamed at me so much I knew exactly how many fillings he had."

But mistakes are par for the course for a cook. "Perfection is not a word for this world," maintains Jean Joho. "It does not exist. Everybody makes mistakes. Anyone who says he never makes a mistake is a liar."

Even master chefs make an occasional masterful mistake, indeed, sometimes about the very cooks they are criticizing. "Jean Troisgros, one of our greatest chefs in France, and a wonderful guy, had Bernard Loiseau as an apprentice 15 or 20 years ago. And Troisgros said to Loiseau's father, 'He's never going to make it,'" recounts André Soltner. "Today Bernard Loiseau has a three-star restaurant [La Côte d'Or in Saulieu] in France."

While the country's leading chefs possess the gift of being able to make the difficult seem effortless, this is a result of their years of experience—which includes making many, many mistakes. What led to their success was "persevering in the face of reality" or triumphing over such difficulties, setbacks, or even out-and-out failures. Rather than being debilitating, to leading chefs these experiences represented just another (albeit painful) way for them to learn.

"Adverse situations are the best teachers. Learning by mistakes is one of the most profitable ways to do it—painful, but profitable—because you learn really quickly. You have to. You'll either learn how to do it or you won't be there," says Jimmy Schmidt. "There are many times when I questioned what the hell I was doing, why I was even in this business, because of the long hours, the relentlessness, the thankless jobs. But you have to have perseverance. No great gains occur by doing simple, easy things. It necessitates long, regular, steady, meticulous growth. Life isn't a 100-yard dash. It's a long-distance race."

Larry Forgione believes, "You should always look at every experience, even the negative ones, as building this wealth of information. Just step out into the world and go forward."

When today's leading chefs were just starting out in their careers, they made their share of silly mistakes. Susan Regis recalls her embarrassment at not having the kitchen lingo down in her first cooking job at Seasons at the Bostonian Hotel. "I thought 'rare squab' was some kind of extinct bird," she remembers.

Rick Katz found hotels a safe haven for learning by doing, because their volume made it easier for them to absorb a beginner's mistakes than a small, independently owned restaurant could. Katz had a memorable first day on the job as a pastry assistant at a Sheraton hotel. "I misread a recipe and instead of adding four *ounces* of salt to what I was making, I added four *pounds*. They were very nice about it, telling me to just go requisition some more salt. Another time I was trying to make a buttercream, and it kept breaking, until I realized the problem was that I was putting too much into the mixer," he recalls. "But it took me three months and 100 pounds of butter to find that out."

He learned other lessons much more quickly. While at Stars, Katz recalls that Jeremiah Tower, whom he characterized as "the most brilliant person I've ever worked for," tasted every single thing that went out of the kitchen. "He was an absolute stickler for freshness," says Katz. "One day I rewhipped the flavored butter without tasting it, and the chef walked by and he tasted it. He immediately flipped the entire tray of butter upside down in our open kitchen and walked away. He'd made his point—and I never forgot it."

Bradley Ogden dropped out of The Culinary Institute of America after 12 months, going to work as a chef at a Holiday Inn. He remembers, "I was supposed to be making meatballs. I tried making them three times, and I couldn't get them to hold together into a ball shape. Finally, I asked someone who pointed out that

Chocolate Meringue Cookies

RICK KATZ

Bentonwood Bakery and Cafe
Newton Centre, MA

"When I was growing up, my mother made meringues with chocolate chips. We called them 'white cookies' and ate them still warm and soft in the middle. Now, I'd be embarrassed to serve a soft meringue—I guess I've gained and lost. In any case, I'm always thankful for the wonderful treats of my childhood. I still enjoy them."

The unsweetened chocolate cuts the sweetness of the meringue.

....

6 oz. unsweetened chocolate

8 oz. bittersweet chocolate

1 cup egg whites

1/2 tsp. salt

1/2 tsp. cream of tartar

1 1/2 cups sugar

....

Put unsweetened chocolate in food processor and pulse until finely chopped.

Chop bittersweet chocolate into 1/4" cubes.

Preheat oven to 200°F.

Whip the whites on medium speed of electric mixer till frothy. Add salt and cream of tartar. Whip until soft peaks. Add 1 cup sugar slowly in 5 additions, beating 2 minutes between each addition. Once meringue is stiff and shiny, add remaining 1/2 cup sugar and both chocolates and mix thoroughly by hand with rubber spatula.

Drop spoonfuls onto parchment-lined baking sheet and bake approximately 2 1/2 hours.

In an airtight container, these cookies keep for several days.

meatballs were supposed to be formed when the meat was raw, not after it had already been cooked!"

When Ogden decided to return to The Culinary Institute of America four years later to complete his degree, it meant borrowing money from his in-laws and living in a self-described hole-in-the-wall apartment with his pregnant wife and child. It also meant working full-time while he finished his second year. "Being older and more mature made me extremely motivated," he admits. Upon graduation, he received the award given to the graduating student voted by professors as being most likely to succeed, not to mention numerous job offers.

On the drive out to the job he had accepted in Kansas City, Ogden had many of his treasured possessions, which were being moved, stolen in St. Louis. But he finally arrived, and moved his family into their home before his scheduled start date of September 15. He recalls that the night before he was to start, "A major flood hit Kansas City, wiping out the restaurant."

A philosophical Ogden admits, "Actually, it worked to my advantage. They gave me a job at another restaurant, paying me a good salary, working 40 hours a week—which was the first time in my life I'd ever worked only 40 hours a week. During that time, I got to work with all the corporate people, and work on all the opening menus and develop the dishes for the reopening in January."

Others' early jobs weren't always such a bed of roses. In one of the first kitchens where Anne Rosenzweig worked, she was hired by a chef who thought women didn't have the stamina for kitchen work. "He thought he would upset me so much that in two or three days I would leave in tears," she recalls. She, however, saw it as a challenge. "I thought it was kind of silly. Having done field work at 19 and living on my own in a mud hut in Africa, some guy telling me I couldn't do something didn't mean a thing."

Coworkers sometimes had their own unique ways of welcoming cooks to a new kitchen. Mary Sue Milliken recalls that on her third day at a particular job, a coworker offered her a sea urchin to try and, not wanting to seem unadventurous, she popped it into her mouth. "It was horrible—it hadn't even been washed, let alone cooked, and it was incredibly gritty," she remembers. "The guy was fired soon thereafter, for other reasons."

Diversity in the Kitchen

In 1992, 60 percent of the employees in the restaurant industry were women, and almost 30 percent of all cooking school students were women. About 12 percent of those employed in the restaurant industry were African-Americans, and a similar percentage were of Hispanic origin.

As the women chefs interviewed for this book exemplify, women are represented at the very forefront of cooking in this country. But women's place at other levels of the profession has gone through a real evolution. Women were not admitted to The Culinary Institute of America until 1970, whereas they now comprise about 25 percent of the Institute's incoming students (and more than half of the students in its Baking and Pastry Arts program).

As is true in every other type of organization in America, women are likely to find certain employers and lines of work within the profession more accepting than others. In particular, pastry work is associated with a somewhat less-pressured pace. As Rick Katz points out, "It's not as hectic as working the line because, in general, baking isn't tied to the service of a restaurant." Pastry chefs are typically the first cooks at work and often the first to leave at night, and have somewhat more predictable hours than line cooks. In addition, the work itself tends to offer pastry chefs more independence. Says Nancy Silverton, "I always liked having a small part of the kitchen that I could control myself."

The restaurant business does not lend itself well to flexible work policies, which might ease parental pressures for either men or women. As women still bear the majority of the responsibility for child rearing in most American families, however, this issue is likely to be of particular concern to them. A cook needs to cook when the restaurant's customers want to eat—period—whether that means breakfast at 7 A.M. or post-theatre dinner at 11 P.M. The new International Association of Women Chefs and Restaurateurs (see Appendix C), spearheaded by Barbara Tropp, was formed in 1993 to address issues of concern to women in the profession.

Murphy's Law often rules the day, especially on days when the stakes are particularly high. Replacing Charles Palmer as chef of the Waccabuc Country Club, Todd English made careful preparations for his first lunch serving the club's 'grand dames.' While the food was being served, English had to nurse both a cut finger and jangled

Nationally known black chefs beyond Edna Lewis and Patrick Clark are difficult to identify, although this is also changing. More African-Americans appear to be entering the profession, and are in fact being encouraged to do so by organizations such as The Culinary Institute of America's Black Culinarian Alumni Chapter, founded by Jason Wallace and Alex Askew. While their historical lack of representation at the higher levels of the profession is clear, their hesitancy to enter the profession has been lessening. It's only recently that the "chef-as-celebrity" phenomenon has brought acclaim to the profession. In years past, blacks might have become cooks because they had few other options open to them.

Edna Lewis comments, "I have noticed that there are a lot of blacks [who] are going to cooking school, male and female. And they get tucked away at the Marriotts. You never hear or see the daylight of them because they are not well known to chefs in the restaurants. In that way, you don't know how many black chefs there are. People who get recognition are people [who] work in restaurants. They are visible and, if the food is good, people find out who the chef is. But in hotels it's so impersonal and you have so many thousands of people to cook for I don't think you have a chance to be known."

Some of the most difficult kitchens in the United States for minorities and women to break into and advance in have been those with a very traditional French attitude. However, a sign of our changing times echoes in the conviction of French-born chef Jean-Louis Palladin that "a mixed kitchen is important to me. You need to have a mix. I have four women and three blacks in my kitchen." Norman Van Aken adds, "One of the interesting things that I've found is that it makes no difference if they're men or women or whatever—either they're tough as nails, or they're not."

Chefs are beginning to recognize the value of diversity and the creative energy that comes from having people of many different backgrounds working together. Cultural diversity brings obvious benefits to a kitchen, in terms of work habits, techniques, familiarity with various ingredients and even styles of cooking, which has the potential to help everyone learn more.

"The influences I always draw back on include a guy who worked in a gas station who was one of those rare mechanics who could fix anything. Every day he would cook lunch for us, and I was always intrigued with his style of cooking. The things that he would cook would be phenomenal. And another was a guy named Whitney Dean, who was a black-hat chef that I worked with at the University Club. He was from Barbados, and had a French background. I got a lot from both of them, coming from two different points of view. I count them as my two biggest influences, besides my dad."

—GEORGE GERMON

nerves upon learning that he was 15 lunches short. "We ended up figuring something out—you always do," he says, adding, "But maybe that's why I serve so much food at Olives."

Trying to meet customers' requests—at all hours—sometimes thwarted chefs' own perfectionistic standards. Dieter Schorner was

Schenkli: A Swiss Carnival Delight

DIETER SCHORNER

Patisserie Cafe Didier
Washington, DC

"Schenkli reminds me of my carefree youth where as a student in Basel, Switzerland, I, together with some friends, would go to the Carnival, which happens to be the biggest in all of Switzerland. Usually before going to the Carnival, we would first gather at a friend's house where we would wine and dine with Schenkli. Where Schenkli, wine, laughter, and conversation abound, the world never looks rosier."

. . . .

4 eggs

200 g sugar

200 g milk

zest of 2 lemons

5 g baking soda

100 g butter

750 g all-purpose flour

5 g baking powder

. . . .

1. Cream eggs and sugar. Add zest of lemons. Dissolve baking soda in milk and add soft butter. Add flour and baking powder. Do not overwork.

2. Roll logs the thickness of a finger. Cut in 1 1/2-inch slices and fry in hot vegetable oil to hazelnut brown color. Drain excess oil by placing it on a grill or paper towel. If desired, sprinkle with a little cinnamon sugar and sift with confectioners' sugar. One glass of wine and you are in heaven!

the pastry chef at La Côte Basque when a customer came in one night asking for a soufflé at 11:30 P.M. "I had some mixture left [for a soufflé], but if it sits too long, the air goes out of [the beaten mixture]. Since it was so late, the soufflé fell flat like a pancake the moment it was placed in front of the customer," he recalls.

Schorner said that instead of reprimanding him, the chef, who liked him, decided to have some fun. "When the manager on duty came back all upset to find out what had happened, the chef told him, 'Well, usually we have a pump in the kitchen to blow air into the soufflé, and the pump broke.' The manager shouted, 'Chef, I've told you, whatever you need, you get! Go out tomorrow and fix the pump!' "

It's hard to be inspired to excel when you can't stand the products you must work with. When Jean-Georges Vongerichten first traveled to Thailand to work, he found he hated many of the ingredients he tried. "The first time I tasted coriander, it tasted like soap," he says. "I thought it was inedible. I couldn't touch anything because everything was too spicy for me."

Susanna Foo had a similar experience. She was once asked to prepare a special dinner for 40 at a company's request, by preparing dishes made with its liqueur. She found that the recipes, which were French, all called for butter and cream. Foo believes that the resulting meal did not represent her best work, and she regrets having done it. "I don't feel comfortable using butter and cream. It's not Chinese. When cooking fish, we'd use oil to grill the fish and then put sauce on. To make fish with cream is very strange to me. When you follow a recipe, you adjust it a little bit to your taste. You can't do this if you can't tell if it tastes right or not."

Vongerichten, who later opened the successful Thai-inspired restaurant Vong (NYC), also faced cross-cultural problems trying to manage other cooks as a consulting chef in Thailand. "Nothing was working," he recalls. "I was the only European in a restaurant with 50 employees and the cooks wouldn't listen to me. Someone finally had to explain to me that because the chef there was Thai, he was

"I hate people who say, 'I'm not a cook, I'm a chef.' First of all, if you can't cook, you'd better not be a chef. The funniest thing happened—one night, an older woman customer said to me, 'Oh, are you the cook?' And I said, 'Yes, I'm the cook.' And some other customers said, 'Oh, no, he's the chef!' If it's a title you're looking for, you're in the wrong business."

—CHARLES PALMER

Salmon Congee

SUSANNA FOO

Susanna Foo
Philadelphia, PA

"Congee is a soup whose basic ingredient is rice, and it is a favorite breakfast dish in China, especially in the south. There are almost as many versions of congee as there are cities in China, with everyone offering a preferred version. Rice congee is often embellished with shredded chicken, seafood, beef, or fish. My husband's family enjoys their breakfast congee with eggs, sausages, or picked mushrooms, while my family prepares congee with sweet potatoes, pumpkin, or mung beans. Texture can also vary. My grandmother, for example, insisted that the rice in congee should be firm, with each grain separate. If the cook was distracted and the rice became mushy, my grandmother would be quite upset. However, other people prefer a softer rice, with the liquid and solids blended together. When I was a child, rice congee was offered with scallion pancakes, or a dish of stir-fried vegetables and meat. I realized early on that congee offered a large canvas for culinary experimentation. Starting with basic congee, I added and subtracted ingredients until I came up with Salmon Congee. It's served as a soup course in my restaurant, but it can be a main dish at home—soup-and-fish-in-a-bowl—that would need nothing more than another light course to make a complete meal. The salmon in this congee is thinly sliced and then marinated. It's gently cooked when hot soup is ladled over it. I find this the best way to prevent overcooked fish."

Prepare the congee in a pot that's both deep and heavy. A sturdy soup pot will prevent the soup from boiling over and the rice from sticking.

1/4 pound fillet of salmon, thinly sliced

1/4 cup vodka

1 tablespoon soy sauce

5 tablespoons olive oil

1 tablespoon grated gingerroot

3 shallots, minced

1 stalk celery, finely chopped

1 jalapeno pepper, cored and seeded, finely chopped

1/2 cup rice

1/4 pound shrimp, peeled and deveined, finely chopped

8 cups fish stock or chicken broth, homemade or canned

1 tablespoon rice wine vinegar

Salt and freshly ground pepper to taste

1/4 cup chopped coriander or basil leaves

Place salmon in a shallow dish. Combine vodka, soy sauce, and 2 tablespoons of olive oil. Mix, and pour over salmon. Toss salmon gently in marinade and refrigerate for at least 1 hour.

In a large, heavy, soup pot heat remainder of oil. Add gingerroot, shallots, celery, and jalapeno pepper. Sauté, stirring, for 3 minutes.

Add rice and shrimp to vegetable mixture. Stir, and add stock or broth. Bring liquid to a boil. Reduce heat until liquid just simmers, and cover. Cook, stirring occasionally to make sure that rice does not stick to the bottom of the pot. Remove from heat when rice is tender, about 1 hour and 15 minutes.

Stir rice wine vinegar into Congee and season to taste.

Divide salmon with marinade in 6 to 8 soup bowls. Ladle hot Congee over salmon and garnish with coriander or basil leaves.

Serves 6 to 8

losing face and that I had to talk to the chef to have things done through him. But I didn't find this out for six months."

Given their hard work and frequent frustrations, sometimes chefs simply burn out. Alice Waters thinks that this seems to happen around the seven-year mark for most cooks. "It's very difficult to tell somebody that you can see that their focus is different from other people's in the kitchen and that they're not 100 percent here but clearly thinking about other things," she says. "It's important that they go off and see what it's like to work in other circumstances and to find out what their real passions are. I try to encourage people to move on and change. I'm a big believer in the sabbatical program. In an informal way, it does happen here. After seven or eight years, I just say, 'Get out of here, and go take a trip for six months, and see what you think when you get back.' Very often people come back and they're a lot better and it's great to have them return."

Some of the lessons that can only be learned over the years include trusting your gut instinct. Nancy Silverton and husband Mark Peel moved to New York City with the mission of revamping Maxwell's Plum, but left less than a year later. Silverton says, "It didn't work out, but we don't regret it. We learned that no matter how much money, press, and prestige is at stake, you must be in an environment that makes you happy." In fact, it was after this failed experience that the couple decided to take some time off to travel to Italy which in turn inspired them to later open Campanile in Los Angeles.

Sometimes setbacks strike when they're least expected. Norman Van Aken recalls refusing to cook Bisquick shrimp at a restaurant where he was working. "I got fired," he admits. As chef of David Keh's restaurant Cafe Marimba (NYC), Zarela Martinez spent her days in the kitchen and her evenings working the door. She helped it become successful, and decided to celebrate by taking a six-week trip to Mexico, during which she was fired. The restaurant took a nosedive from there until she went back as executive chef to restore it to its old luster.

Restaurant reviews also caused their share of ups and downs. Martinez recalls getting reviewed by Bryan Miller in *The New York Times* when she was chef of Cafe Marimba, and the huge letdown of receiving only one star. "I cried for three days. Then I sat down and wrote him a four-page letter about how I believed that the more talent you had, the greater the responsibility that accompanied it." In the letter, Martinez detailed the responsibility that she felt—and took—in sitting down with her waiters on a daily basis to explain each dish and each ingredient. She eventually won a two-star review from Miller—and an assurance that her letter would be published in Miller's forthcoming book on restaurant reviewing.

The mere thought of being reviewed can be, well, *unsettling*. Wayne Nish had just become the chef of La Colombe d'Or (NYC) when Bryan Miller walked in one night with an elderly couple. "By this time, I had already cooked for Miller [at The Quilted Giraffe and The Casual Quilted Giraffe] maybe 16, 18 times, on separate occasions. I had been a senior member at The Quilted Giraffe, I was well trusted, and was even allowed to make up my own stuff spontaneously for him during the review process." How did this excellent preparation prepare Nish for being reviewed once he was himself the chef? "I recognized him, and I went in the kitchen and threw up," Nish admits.

Miller returned for subsequent visits, tasting everything on the menu and even a few specials. Nish knew his review was imminent. "I figured if I was lucky, I'd get a good two-star review and I'd be really happy," he says. So it came as a total surprise to open the paper and find that Miller had given La Colombe d'Or not two, but *three* stars. "I hadn't even been in the business for five years, and it was the first time a nonwhite-tablecloth restaurant had been given three stars at the time."

How did Nish respond to receiving such an unprecedented, positive review? "I went into the kitchen to show the newspaper to the guys. The pressure was off, the relief came, and I turned around and threw up again."

Some chefs fairly credit a review with providing feedback that, while hard to accept, can point to areas which need improvement. Janos Wilder, who makes a practice of calling his staff together to discuss the contents of certain reviews, says that [former *New York Times*

"There's so much that can go wrong in a restaurant, and yet the standard we're judged by is 'perfection.' "
—GORDON HAMERSLEY

Voodoo Beer Steamed Shrimp with a West Indian Cocktail Salsa

NORMAN VAN AKEN
Miami Shores, FL

"Bisquick recipes faded fast after those early 'daze' in Key West. The influence of islands south beckoned and changed my cooking dramatically. Here's my take on a simple dish perfect for the informal gathering of pals. Put a little salsa music on, too! With Tito or Celia going on in the background, you'll think the perspiration may be coming from their energy as much as it will be from the Scotch Bonnet peppers in my West Indian dipping salsa. It's New World—hot, hot, hot!"

. . . .

1 tablespoon fennel seeds

1 tablespoon whole black peppercorns

1 tablespoon allspice berries

1 tablespoon mustard seeds

1 teaspoon cloves

2 tablespoons olive oil

1 medium red onion, peeled, and roughly chopped

1 head garlic, cut in half cross-wise

2–3 jalapeno chilies, stem discarded, and chopped up roughly, seeds and all

2 bay leaves

peel of one orange, all white pith scraped away

32 large, fresh, shell-on shrimp

3 (12 ounce) bottles of "Blackened Voodoo Beer" (or other)

. . . .

1. Heat a large pot and add the fennel seeds, peppercorns, allspice berries, mustard seeds, and cloves. Allow them to toast by themselves and become fragrant for about 30 seconds.

2. Now add the olive oil. Allow the oil to warm and add the onions, garlic, chilies, bay leaves, orange peel, and spices. Stir completely. When the vegetables begin to get deeply glazed add the beer and bring to a

boil. Now add the shrimp and return to a boil. Immediately lift a shrimp out at this point and check to see if it is done. If it is, remove the shrimp as quickly as possible and shock them in very icy water. As soon as they have stopped cooking and begin to feel cool, get them out of the icy water or you'll wash off the flavor of the beer, vegetables, and spices!

Yield: Serves 4–6

For the salsa

....

3/4 cup ketchup

1/4 cup chili sauce (like Heinz)

2 scotch bonnet chilies, stem and seeds discarded, minced

3 cloves raw garlic, minced

1/2 cup red onion, minced

1/4 cup roughly chopped cilantro leaves

juice of one lime

1/4 cup prepared horseradish

salt and cracked black pepper, to taste

1/4 teaspoon Tobasco brand hot sauce, to taste

1/4 teaspoon Worcestershire sauce

....

Mix all of the above together. Chill until needed.

Yield: 1 2/3–1 3/4 cups

To serve

Put the shrimp in a large bowl with some ice under them and serve the salsa on the side. Have an extra bowl for your guests to toss the shells (and bottlecaps and wine corks) into.

Any beer can be used to steam the shrimp in. Just be sure the other 3 bottles in the six pack are ones you will enjoy.

If you want to steam more shrimp than this you can about double the amount of beer once before you would have to double everything else.

With some simple boiled potatoes and corn on the cob this can be turned into a nice summertime dinner. Another way to beat the heat is to serve with cold beer or tea.

restaurant critic] Mimi Sheraton reviewed his and other restaurants in the Southwest immediately after he'd changed cooks: "She creamed us. Unfortunately it wasn't hard to believe that we had screwed up," Wilder admits. "Anything but a great review is bad."

Even a great review doesn't always ensure success. When Bryan Miller awarded Patrick Clark's restaurant Metro two stars, Clark was on top of the world. He had made a name for himself in New York City after successfully opening the Odeon in 1980 in Tribeca, then "a wasteland—there was nothing else in Tribeca," and later opening Cafe Luxembourg on the Upper West Side. So opening his own place in 1988 represented the culmination of a dream. He went all out, finding a great space on the Upper East Side and designing the kitchen and restaurant with noted restaurant designer Adam Tihany.

Then he learned that even a two-star review wasn't an ace in the hole. The downturn in the economy hit, and large monthly rent payments on the space started taking their toll. Metro closed in May 1990. Clark decided to take a month off. But a chef as talented as Clark doesn't stay down long, and he was soon tapped to run the kitchen at Bice in Los Angeles, where business was hurting. By the time he left to become chef of the Hay-Adams Hotel in Washington, DC, he says the restaurant had tripled its weekly gross.

MONEY AND MANAGEMENT

Some chefs had a hard time even getting the money to open their own places, despite their talent. While chef at Commander's Palace in New Orleans, Emeril Lagasse had a dream. "I lived across the street from this burned-out building in the warehouse district and I had this burning desire to turn it into my own restaurant," he says. But when he approached bank after bank about financing it, "I got turned down by every bank in the city."

Finally, Lagasse met up with the most conservative financial institution in the state, which believed in him and in the project. "They gave me the money in ten minutes." Still, he didn't have a lot of money, and was unemployed for three and a half months while he spent 16 to 18 hours a day building every piece of the restaurant "and doing everything from painting to you-name-it." So whatever became of the made-from-scratch restaurant in the burned-out building in the New Orleans warehouse district that

most banks didn't believe in? For starters, Emeril's had an hour-and-forty-five minute wait on opening night.

A winter downturn in business forced Rick Bayless to rethink the way he ran Frontera Grill. "In a way, I was glad to have down months," he admits. "It made us take a look at cutting our fixed costs without cutting labor or food costs. We changed our laundry service, we changed our dishwashing system, and we cut telephone costs."

That frame of mind came in handy during the summer. Bayless landed a license for an outdoor cafe and, not wanting to hire people to staff it whom he would later have to lay off, he decided to pose his dilemma to his staff. He offered them the opportunity to earn extra pay for the extra work over the summer, which they accepted. "They worked hard, but they made a killing over four months," he says.

Good management means getting things under control, even if it involves scaling back in order to do so. When Mark Militello was managing three different restaurants at once, he says, "I found myself running from restaurant to restaurant to restaurant, a little bit frustrated. The restaurants were all four-star, very well-known, very busy restaurants. I had a lot of restaurateurs coming and stealing chefs, menus, concepts, and recipes and opening up around the corner. I found myself always going in and rehiring and rebuilding, and not really focusing on what I wanted to do. At that point, I really decided I wanted to work on one restaurant and do it as well as I could."

"During the war, it was very complicated to work because of rationing. You had to do something with every scrap. It was challenging. We had little sugar. We had no wheat, and so we made bread out of potatoes. We even made almond paste out of potatoes—we pureed potatoes and added almond extract and a little sugar. The quality certainly wasn't much, but you had to be glad you had something to eat."
—ALBERT KUMIN

Other lessons involved understanding your market when you venture into unknown territory. Cindy Pawlcyn and her partners opened two Fog City Diners in Japan in a joint venture with a Japanese company. Their idea was to copy the San Francisco restaurant exactly in terms of design, menu—everything.

Offering the San Francisco restaurant's identical menu just didn't make sense, Pawlcyn learned. "For example, the Japanese don't eat cheese, so I knew they wouldn't sell many quesadillas.

KNOWING YOUR MARKET

 What made it worse was that the cheese that the Japanese purveyors sold the restaurant was spoiled. No one knew good cheese from bad because they never ate it—they just figured that it tasted bad because 'all cheese tastes bad,' " she laments.

"Only one of them is still going," admits Pawlcyn. "That one now serves Japanese food and plays country-western music." She learned the hard way that it's imperative to gear a restaurant for its particular location. "That's what we've always done here," she says, referring to Real Restaurants' success with their restaurants throughout the Bay Area.

WHEN WORK IMPEDES ON LIFE

Norman Van Aken admits, "You almost have to be married to someone in this business if your marriage is going to succeed because it's brutal. Otherwise, you can't share holidays, weekends, or other things that people think are normal."

Susanna Foo admits that it was tough on her children to grow up in a restaurant family. "Sometimes I would ask them to come to the restaurant with me to eat, and they'd say, 'No! We never get to eat at home!' " she recalls. "I used to drag them to New York every Sunday. New York has such a variety of Chinese ingredients, and I wanted to see what was available for me to try. Now they just hate Chinatown in New York. They don't even like to go to New York. And they don't want to be in the restaurant business. But they do have good palates, and they like good food."

THE WORST OF TIMES . . .

Janos Wilder has no trouble recalling his single worst night in the restaurant business. "One busy night, in the middle of service, a customer knocked over one of two hand-thrown three-foot urns, filled with branches with sharp spines, from its pedestal. I couldn't leave the line, but I was told no one was hurt. Forty-five minutes later, a busboy slipped bringing a load of dishes back into the kitchen, and wrenched his knee. Tickets were coming in, and again I couldn't leave the line. An hour later, a busboy in the kitchen backed up and put his foot into a boiling stockpot that had been set on the floor. He received major burns—I can't even describe his foot. Still, I couldn't get off the line for more than a minute because of all the dupes coming in. The stress, the feeling of being trapped and helpless was overwhelming." Wilder now primarily writes the menus and oversees the kitchen instead of working the line himself.

Winston Churchill's shortest graduation speech of all time: "Never give in, never give in, never, never, never, never in nothing great or small, large or petty—never give in" could be Nobu Matsuhisa's motto. He moved from his native Japan to Alaska to pursue his dream of opening his own restaurant, which took him six months to build. He was able to fly his family in from Japan to be with him once it opened. Less than two months later, they found little to celebrate on Thanksgiving—the restaurant had burned to the ground, taking Nobu's life savings and dreams with it.

Left with nothing, he borrowed money to get himself and his family back to Japan. A week later, he bought a one-way ticket to Los Angeles. He became a sushi chef, and seven months later was able to fly his family out to live with him again. He developed his cooking style through stints at various Japanese restaurants before opening Matsuhisa, where, he says, "All my experiences came together, like condensing a nice sauce." The restaurant has been cited as the best Japanese restaurant in Los Angeles and perhaps in the United States.

"There are a lot of easier ways of making a living than this," states Charles Palmer. "It's only when you really look at it that it seems barbaric: you work in hot conditions, you work long hours, you get paid next to nothing. You cut your hands, you burn your hands. It's physically very bad for you: you breathe in smoke, you stand on your feet all day long, you sweat all the time. It's not pleasant—unless you love it. Then I think it's kind of neat."

Indeed. Despite the headaches, despite the heartaches, leading chefs have found enough rewards in this profession to keep them going until they again saw the light at the end of the tunnel.

Dad's Salmon Croquettes

EDWARD BROWN
The Sea Grill
New York, NY

"*Eating, as is cooking, is a passionate experience. As a chef, the best reward of all is to experience someone else's passion when they consume your food. Eating and cooking are also a way of life and represent in my case the feelings in my heart. When I'm unhappy, I think I can't cook well at all, but when I'm happy, there's no stopping my ambition or creativity.*

Of all my experiences eating around the world, this recipe exemplifies my theory. When my father was alive, he used to describe having salmon croquettes with day-old spaghetti like he was describing a work of art or a beautiful woman. If I can capture that passion for even half the food I prepare, I shall be the most content chef ever!"

....

3/4 lbs. cooked or canned salmon

1 cup plain unseasoned mashed potato (approx. 2 potatoes)

1 T. chopped fresh parsley

2 tsp. chopped fresh chives

2 tsp. chopped fresh dill

1 tsp. minced garlic

1/4 tsp. cayenne pepper

1/4 cup dairy sour cream

salt to taste

. . . .

In a nonreactive bowl, mix all ingredients well.

For breading

. . . .

1 1/2 cups flour on a large plate

2 eggs beaten in a shallow bowl

2 cups bread crumbs* (seasoned or unseasoned) on a large plate

*For best results use fresh white crumbs

. . . .

1. Divide croquette mixture into four patties, forming them by hand.

2. Pass each patty through the flour, then the eggs, allowing excess to drip off each time, then into the bread crumbs, pressing and moving a few times to ensure a good coating.

3. In a medium pan, preferably nonstick, melt 1 T butter at medium high heat until it sizzles.

4. Brown croquettes until golden on each side. Remove to baking sheet. (This can be done up to one hour ahead.)

5. Finish cooking in a 375°F oven approximately 7–8 minutes until hot.

Suggestions

1. Serve with homemade tartar sauce.

2. Dad's preference—day-old spaghetti reheated in a casserole with melted cheddar on top!

Serves 4

"I'm as focused and as pumped up today as I was when I opened this place. This is all I think about. This is all I do. I wake up every day, and I can't wait to come over here," says Charlie Trotter. Raji Jallepalli agrees, "When everything is said and done, I don't think I've ever done anything that gave me this much satisfaction. There are times in the middle of the night that I get some ideas, and I can't wait to get up in the morning and go to the restaurant and get behind the stove to see how they work."

"This business is the greatest business," Georges Perrier muses. "This is my reward, being a chef all my life. After a customer spends $250 in my restaurant, he shakes my hand and says, 'Thank you!' It makes me feel good, it makes me smile, it pushes me to perform." Norman Van Aken concurs. "This profession is not at all about being recognized. It has to be about the idea of the joy of discovery, of exchange, of seeing people smile after tasting your soup or your dessert."

The added pleasure for some chefs is almost certainly having discovered their love for more than just food in a kitchen. "Wolfgang Puck created our relationship," says Lissa Doumani of her alliance with husband and partner Hiroyoshi Sone. "He teased both of us relentlessly. When Hiro was at Spago in Tokyo, Wolfgang would call Tokyo and get Hiro on the phone and put me on the phone. Barbara [Lazaroff] came back from Tokyo once with a photograph of Hiro in his chef's whites holding a sign, with a message for me, to the camera. Finally, I asked Wolfgang if he'd hire Hiro if he moved to the United States, and he said yes. Wolfgang likes to stir things up."

Even in spite of the pressures that the all-consuming nature of this profession can have on family life, some chef-restaurateurs manage to find real benefits to this way of life. Elizabeth Terry's older daughter was seven when the family moved to Savannah to open Elizabeth on 37th, and for the first couple of years she voiced her wish that they could all "have their little house back." But a call from the same daughter years later—six weeks after she'd gone away to college in Montana—calmed any fears Terry might have had about the effect of growing up in a restaurant family. "She said, 'Mom, you really did it exactly right. I loved where I grew up, I loved my upbringing, I loved all the experiences and the excitement of living at the restaurant. It was really great.'"

Terry and her family found advantages in the atypical lifestyle: "Almost every night from the time she was 13 until she went off to college, we would go out on the front porch [of the restaurant] after I finished cooking and she finished

"Trust your heart."
—MICHAEL FOLEY

her homework, and we'd have a cappuccino or something, and we'd just sit. And I think because it was a restaurant and because it was after work, it was very neutral ground. We talked about all the things that parents say it's difficult to talk to children about. We never planned to talk about them, but we would just be there and saying goodnight to the last guests, and we'd just get into talking about 'sex and drugs and cigarettes and rock and roll' and all those things just kind of came up in just the easiest way. There was something really magical about my being finished with work at 10:30 at night. It was very, very nice for child rearing."

Other advantages included the ability to play a unique role in special events in their children's lives. Terry recalls fondly that, "Instead of doing a second seating, we had the whole high school class in for a sit-down dinner after graduation. I mean, nobody else could do that. We cooked for them, and the kids felt so grown-up. It was so personal. This was just something that we could do, that we could give, and the emotional feedback from it was just extensive."

The roller-coaster ride of being in the restaurant business can generate cynicism on the part of a chef. "The more jaded you become—and I admit to being *very* jaded—the harder it is," admits Patrick O'Connell. But part of what makes it all worthwhile for him and other leading chefs is the undeniable, blissfully pleasurable moments in the profession such as having the rare, moving, food experience. O'Connell describes it as being "overcome by this distillation, this purity, this love that knocks you out—it hits you and then you just fall down flight after flight after flight of stairs because you are really craving that."

Shrimp with Cheese Grits and Country Ham

ELIZABETH TERRY

Elizabeth on 37th
Savannah, GA

"My husband Michael says this is his favorite dish of all the many I've created for Elizabeth on 37th because the flavors are bold. The dish is based on traditional Southern fare, so it is great comfort food. Finally, he loves creamy—as do I—and this dish is creamy."

The sauce
....

2 Tablespoons (1 ounce) butter

1/2 cup (4 ounces) country ham, minced

1/2 cup (4 ounces) shiitake mushrooms, stems removed and used for broth
in another recipe

1/2 cup onion, peeled and minced

1/2 cup Maderia

2 Tablespoons cornstarch

1 cup cold chicken broth

1/2 cup canned, diced tomatoes in juice, puréed

1 Tablespoon fresh thyme, minced

1 dash tabasco
....

Melt the butter. Add the country ham and brown. Add the shiitake mushrooms and onion and continue to brown, stirring. Pour in the

Maderia and simmer until the wine is nearly gone. Dissolve the corn-starch in the cold chicken broth and whisk into the ham and mush-rooms. Bring to a boil, stirring. Add the rest of the ingredients and gently simmer about 10 minutes to combine the flavors. Refrigerate.

The grits

. . . .

1 cup grits

4 cups water

1 Tablespoon garlic, minced

1/4 cup (2 ounces) sharp Cheddar cheese, grated

. . . .

Bring the water for the grits to a boil. Slowly stir in the grits and garlic. Simmer, stirring occasionally, until the grits are thick and soft. Add the grated cheese. Keep hot in a water bath, stirring occasionally. More water may be whisked into the grits if they become too thick.

The shrimp

. . . .

1 ounce butter

1 1/4 pounds shrimp, peeled and deviened

3/4 cup green bell pepper, minced

1/2 cup parsley, minced

. . . .

In a large sauté pan, melt the butter. Add the shrimp and the bell pep-per and sauté over high heat until the shrimp are beginning to turn pink. Stir in the sauce and heat.

Divide the grits among six plates. Spoon over the shrimp and sauce, sprinkle with parsley, and serve.

Serves 6

10

WHAT'S NEXT?

The
Chef
as
Alchemist

*"Being a really good cook has to do with
having a point of view."*
—ALICE WATERS

The chefs we interviewed are concerned with food beyond mere sustenance. They seem to realize cooking's potential for alchemy—the process of turning something common into something precious—which enables them to transform food from a mere physical experience into one which also affects the mind and spirit of the person to whom it is served. They appear to understand food as part of a total experience which has the potential to nurture, please, touch, awaken, move, even transport.

How did they develop this point of view? It was not the result of simply accumulating knowledge or memorizing facts. You could memorize every word of *Larousse Gastronomique,* and this alone would not help you develop your own point of view. Doing so only comes about through assimilating and understanding all the information you have ever learned and all the experiences you have ever experienced.

The leading chefs we interviewed shared how they've developed their own points of view through their lives, their educations, and their day-to-day practice. Most importantly, it's also very clear how much time they've spent reflecting on the thoughts, feelings, and sensations brought about by their experiences. This has allowed them to develop their own visions of the way food should be cooked and served. Alice Waters' quote which opened this chapter suggests the potential held by an individual chef to have influence through his or her personal vision of what food can be.

The entire experience of cuisine begins with the will of the chef. The chef emerges as the director of an elaborate orchestra, who directs the kitchen staff to create according to a specific vision. Without the chef's vision, nothing can happen. The chef's point of view serves as the driving force.

Chefs, having the power to affect and influence those who eat their food, also have a responsibility to ensure that their influences are positive ones. This entails understanding the factors which affect the outcome of their visions, which include the ingredients that go into the dishes they create, and the customers to whom they are served.

None of these factors exist in a vacuum; each affects the other. Even for the most talented of chefs, it is impossible to make the proverbial silk purse out of a sow's ear. The ingredients are critical; a dish is only as good as the ingredients which go into it. Yet what good is a perfect Valrhona chocolate soufflé if one's customer is allergic to chocolate? While artists may paint solely to express themselves, chefs must cook with the people who will eat their food always in mind.

Because both customers and ingredients play a critical role in the process, chefs have been driven to take steps to better understand their customers, their concerns, and their preferences, as well as take a stand on what they perceive as positive and negative influences on the ingredients with which they work.

THE INFLUENCE OF CUSTOMERS

Customers change, and their changing needs and preferences must be acknowledged in some fashion.

For example, between the years 1990 and 2000, the United States' Asian population is expected to grow by 40 percent, and the Hispanic population by 39 percent, outpacing the growth of any other racial or ethnic groups. The corresponding rise of interest in their respective cuisines should not come as a surprise, as it seemed to when it was widely publicized in recent years that sales of salsa overtook those of ketchup in the United States. Zarela Martinez, a trustee at The Culinary Institute of America, envisions a time when the school will include a Mexican curriculum. "The popularity of Mexican cuisine has doubled in the past five years, and is expected to double again by the year 2000," she points out.

With chefs' drive toward experimentation with the ingredients and techniques of other cultures, some customers might fear that certain cuisines will become unrecognizable from their authentic versions. However, some chefs believe there is a time and place for both authenticity as well as creative interpretations.

"In my own personal feeling, the only people who do non-American cooking with integrity are people who have lived in those cultures or traveled and eaten widely in those cultures," says Barbara Tropp. "Some people are involved with authenticity or tradition, other people are involved with creativity. But they're very

Albóndigas Estilo Mama
(Meatballs Like Mama Makes)

ZARELA MARTINEZ

Zarela
New York, NY

"This recipe calls to mind the llaves (outdoor water faucets) on the ranch, which were always surrounded with patches of yerba buena—*"good herb," or mint. Whenever my mother made albondigas, I would be sent out to pick some fresh for the soup. She always served it with freshly made corn tortillas, salsa casera (home style sauce), and refried beans with asadero ('roasting' cheese; the nearest thing here would be mozzarella).*

Whenever my mother comes to visit, I always ask her to make me these albondigas. I have tried to serve them at the restaurant, but people can't seem to get excited about meatball soup. Too bad—it's a fabulous soup. The meatballs freeze well, by the way, and reheat wonderfully."

. . . .

4 garlic cloves

1/4 cup masa harina

1/4 cup warm water

1 pound lean ground beef, or 1/2 pound each lean ground pork and beef

3/4 teaspoon salt, or to taste

freshly ground black pepper

1/4 cup lard or vegetable oil

1 tablespoon flour

2 quarts chicken stock

1/4 cup chopped scallions, white and part of the green
(about 4 medium scallions)

1 large ripe tomato, roasted, peeled, and chopped (or use 1/4 cup tomato puree if good tomatoes are not available)

2 Anaheim or California long green chiles (or for hotter flavor, jalapeno chiles), roasted, peeled, and finely chopped

3 tablespoons finely chopped cilantro leaves

3 tablespoons finely chopped fresh mint leaves

. . . .

Mince three of the garlic cloves. In a large bowl, combine masa harina with the warm water. Add the ground meat, 1/2 teaspoon salt (optional), a generous grinding of black pepper, and one minced garlic clove. Mix these ingredients with your hands and shape into tiny balls, between the size of a large marble and a small walnut. (Mixture makes 40–45 small meatballs.) Set aside.

In small skillet, heat 2 tablespoons lard or vegetable oil over medium-high heat. Add 1 whole garlic clove. Let cook 20–30 seconds to flavor the oil, pressing down with the back of a cooking spoon. Remove and discard garlic clove. Off the heat, add the flour to the hot fat and quickly stir to combine. Cook over medium heat, stirring constantly to smooth out lumps, until mixture is golden (about 1 minute).

Meanwhile, have stock heating in a large (at least 6-quart), deep saucepan or Dutch oven. Just before it boils, add a little hot stock to the browned flour mixture and whisk or stir to eliminate lumps. Pour the mixture into the hot stock and bring to a boil, whisking or stirring with wooden spoon to keep from lumping. Reduce heat to medium-low and simmer stock, uncovered, 5 minutes. It will thicken slightly. Season with a little salt and pepper, being careful not to over season (meatballs will add more salt).

Make a *recaudo*: In large skillet, heat another 2 tablespoons lard or vegetable oil over medium-high heat until very hot but not quite smoking. Add the chopped scallion, roasted tomato, roasted chiles, and remaining 2 minced garlic cloves. Reduce heat a little and sauté briskly for 2 minutes, stirring frequently. Add the sautéed mixture to stock. Add chopped cilantro and mint. Simmer uncovered another 5 minutes. Add meatballs. Let stock return to the boil and simmer uncovered over low heat 15 minutes. Correct seasoning.

Serves at least 6–8 as main dish, more as first course

different things. For authenticity [in Chinese-style food], you might want to refer to what Cecelia Chang at The Mandarin used to do. People who are involved with tradition—that's me. People who are involved with creativity, with no hunger to be based in tradition—that's Wolfgang [Puck].

"There are brilliant culinary artists, like Wolfgang, who can appropriate flavors in a cuisine and, because of the excellence of their palates, can come up with something that's vibrant. It may bear no relation to that cuisine, but it's vibrant. It works on the tongue, but it may not work as any exemplar of what the real cuisine is about. It's interesting that there's that broad a spectrum. And as far as I'm concerned, if it tastes good, then who cares what it is? But they're very different sorts of things."

As chefs embraced all the ethnicities and ingredients around them, "fusion cuisine"—the melding together of the cuisines of more than one country—has resulted. Raji Jallepalli sees an increase in fusion cuisine, which she predicts will continue to expand in the 1990s and beyond. She describes her own restaurant in Memphis as "classical French cuisine incorporating Indian techniques and Indian spices. It's a marriage of Indian and French cuisines, which hasn't been tried anywhere else."

She cites as pushing the fusion movement forward such restaurants as Masa's in San Francisco (which melds Japanese and French), Chinois on Main (which melds Chinese and French), and Vong (which melds Thai and French). "The problem I had with ethnic cooking, as it was, is that it typically doesn't respect the texture of the food," Jallepalli says. "So the food gets overcooked, the presentations are not respected, and the bouquets are overloaded with too many spices and too many herbs and are too strong. By borrowing French technology, I was able to respect the textures and incorporate a lot more items than Indian cuisine typically is known to. But I feel I'm barely scratching the surface."

Other changing concerns stem from the greater health-consciousness, not to mention the aging of the population, which is giving rise to new health worries and new eating habits. This is spurring heart-healthy offerings from restaurants of the chefs we interviewed,

Buckwheat Risotto with Wild Leeks and Goat Cheese

ANNE ROSENZWEIG

Arcadia
New York, NY

"This dish has two parts. Unless you grew up with Eastern European influences in your household or were a hippie, you would not necessarily know about kasha. Sometimes I like doing a playful version of a classic dish. Using orzo for risotto with these other ingredients makes a dish as creamy as risotto in a quarter of the time."

....

4 tb. sweet butter

1 c. chopped wild leeks

1 tsp. chopped garlic

1 c. cooked buckwheat groats

1 c. dry orzo

1 1/2 c. rich chicken stock

1/2 c. crumbled goat cheese

1/2 c. chiffonade of Swiss chard

4 tb. chopped parsley

4 tb. chopped chives

salt & pepper, to taste

....

Heat medium saucepan over moderate heat. Add 2 tb. butter, let sizzle, and stir in leeks and garlic for 2 minutes. Add buckwheat groats, orzo, and 1/2 c. stock and cook slowly until stock is absorbed. Add remaining stock in 1/4-cup increments until all the stock is absorbed. Pasta should be *al dente*. Stir in goat cheese, Swiss chard, parsley, chives, remaining butter, and salt and pepper to taste. Pasta should be creamy and luxuriant. Serve immediately.

Serves 4

ranging from spa cuisine to lighter techniques used when adding flavor to a dish.

Some chefs admit they've changed their cooking practices in response to consumers. Alfred Portale recalls, "When I started at Gotham eight years ago, it was butter, butter, and more butter. That was sort of the formula." Whether his cooks were preparing soup or a sauce, "I would tell them to puree it and add a ton of butter—those were my instructions. We'd go through 36 pounds of butter every night on the line, just finishing sauces and stuff. But we rarely even saute in butter anymore. We use light oil, canola oil to sauté. Even the vinaigrettes have lightened up dramatically in the last few years. A few years ago, everything was 'extra virgin olive oil'—you just loaded it up on everything. Not anymore. We're going for lighter oils, lighter flavors, cleaner flavors."

On the other hand, chefs point out that customers are not consistent in their health consciousness, particularly chefs at what might be considered "special occasion" restaurants. "They like to think they are, but basically I don't think so," says André Soltner. Despite all his customers' talk about cholesterol and other health concerns, those to whom he offers a favorite regional dish—a potato pie with bacon and cream—always jump in and enjoy it, despite the cholesterol and calories. "Maybe they feel a little guilty afterwards, but they shouldn't. We never, in good cooking, put in too much butter or too much cream. We put in just what it needs. Many chefs, especially 30 years ago, thought that the more butter or the more cream you put in, the better the dish. That's totally wrong, and I'm totally against that. My philosophy is that a healthy person can eat moderately of everything."

The rise in recent years of dual-income households, and the corresponding decline in time available for food preparation at home, led to an increasing percentage—now a majority—of meals being eaten outside the home. Chefs have noted consumers' practice of making eating out less of a special occasion and more of a daily convenience. They are responding by expanding their cuisine through "downscaling" into more casual and accessible offerings and venues. Top-end restaurants have spawned lower-priced siblings, such as Citrus' Citronelle restaurants, Stars' Stars Cafe, and Jean-Louis' Palladin by Jean-Louis.

This has also helped educate American palates in both a wide variety of cuisines as well as sophistication. True, the average

American may still be learning about differences in food quality. Having lived through the 1980s, however, when many customers developed a taste for new "gourmet" ingredients (a designation encompassing quality, freshness, and flavor), Americans as a whole have had their palates educated, and they have come to demand more from their food. This includes an insistence on learning more about exactly what they are putting into their bodies.

As ingredients change—sometimes due to different production processes employed which can change the character of the ingredients themselves—chefs cannot remain unmoved by these changes. Certainly some chefs appreciate the benefits of having soft shell crabs or tomatoes available year-round, for example. Others, however, are very concerned about the safety and purity of the ingredients on the market, from foods sprayed with pesticides to genetically engineered foods. This has caused chefs to take a more active role in selecting the ingredients that go into the food they serve their customers.

Through organizations such as Chefs Helping to Enhance Food Safety (CHEFS), leading chefs have been increasing their public support for food that is grown with little or no pesticides or other chemicals, and teaching consumers how they can make a difference in the marketplace. Many of the chefs we interviewed are taking up this cause by such means as seeking out regional farmers and suppliers, organically grown ingredients, free-range poultry, and fresh fish.

"Food in Florida had been bad for years, typified by alligator meatballs and grouper 'fingers,' " admits Mark Militello, who is one of several leading Miami chefs fighting that image. He began working closely with farmers who were doing their own organic farming, and was turned on to new produce. He now has an acre five minutes from the restaurant where he grows baby vegetables like bok choy and fennel. His menu is 75 percent "fresh local fish" which is bought the morning it's sold. He adjusts his menu to serve his customers whatever is freshest. "The poultry kill is on Tuesday, when

CHANGING INGREDIENTS

"I love the fact that when I'm eating the food that we do here, I feel not only that I am in contact with a culture that I love—that of Mexico—but I'm in contact with all the growers that we buy from. I feel very strongly that I want to know the people who are raising everything—it just makes me feel good. I want to be able to have a sense of continuity from grower to cook to diner."
—RICK BAYLESS

Potato Pie

ANDRÉ SOLTNER

Lutèce
New York, NY

"As long as I can remember, my mother would make us potato pie. It was one of the dishes we would always ask for. This is a typical Alsatian recipe that was passed along to her from her aunt, 'Tante Louise.' Potato pie does not appear on Lutèce's menu—it is not the kind of cuisine we usually serve—but I will make it from time to time and offer it to some of my customers whom I know will enjoy it. It is delicious served with a salad for lunch."

Pastry

....

8 ounces (about 1 3/4 cups) all-purpose flour

3/4 teaspoon salt

1 stick plus 1 tablespoon (9 tablespoons) unsalted butter, cut up

1 egg yolk lightly beaten with enough ice water to make 1/4 cup

....

Filling

....

1 1/4 pounds smooth-skinned Long Island or Maine potatoes, peeled and thinly sliced

1/4 cup finely chopped parsley

Salt and freshly ground black pepper

5 ounces thick-sliced mild-smoked bacon, cut crosswise into 1/4-inch strips

1/2 cup crème fraîche or heavy cream

5 small hard-cooked eggs, peeled and thinly sliced

....

Egg glaze

....

1 egg yolk beaten with 1 teaspoon water

....

1. Make the pastry: The day before you make the pie, mix the flour and salt in a bowl and rub in the butter with your fingertips until the mixture resembles coarse cornmeal. Make a well in the center, pour in the egg yolk beaten with water, and work with the fingers just until moistened. With one cupped hand gather the mixture into a ball.

2. Quickly roll dough out into a rectangle on a floured work surface. Fold in thirds, wrap in plastic, and refrigerate overnight.

3. When ready to assemble the pie, preheat the oven to 400°. Divide the dough into two equal parts. Roll one half into a round about 13 inches across, and fit into a 9-inch pie pan. (You can use a loose-bottomed tart pan, if you prefer. If you do, be sure to make an upright, crimped edge that will permit the rim of the pan to be removed before serving.) Chill 10 minutes.

4. Wash the sliced potatoes in cold water to remove any starch; drain and pat slices dry. Toss with the parsley, salt, and pepper. In a skillet, gently sauté the bacon for a minute or two, stirring until wilted and just browned on the edges. Drain bacon.

5. Arrange a layer of overlapping slices of potato in the pastry shell. Cover with a layer of bacon and arrange the egg slices over the bacon. Top with the rest of the potato, overlapping the slices. Spread the crème fraîche over the potatoes. Roll remaining pastry into a round large enough to cover the pie. Brush edges of the lower crust with the egg glaze and cover the pie. Trim edges, then crimp to seal well. Prick the top once or twice with a larding needle or the point of a knife. Return to the refrigerator while you preheat the oven to 400°.

6. Brush the top crust lightly with egg glaze. Bake pie 20 minutes on the middle shelf, then lower oven heat to 350° and bake 1 hour longer. Lower oven temperature to 300° and bake 10 minutes longer.

7. Let the pie rest 10 minutes before serving. Accompany with a green salad and a bottle of chilled Alsatian white wine.

Serves 6

they bring in game birds like Florida quail. We serve it Thursday and Friday as they come in fresh."

In addition, Alice Waters added a forager to her staff, who researches new and better food sources. Rick Bayless has developed close relationships with his suppliers to ensure his ingredients' quality and freshness. Jimmy Schmidt works closely with a farmer who supplies the best, freshest produce to his restaurants, which he's even featured in his restaurants' advertisements. Michael Foley likes the idea of a "club farm," and also says he'd liked to open another restaurant to showcase alternative proteins and his sustainable agriculture interests. These chefs' concerns reflect a trend which will surely continue to grow among chefs across the country.

INNOVATION OR ILLUSION?

Chefs are making a real contribution through fueling the "research and development" of cuisine in this country. Their drive to constantly innovate has resulted in a multitude of experiments with new—and old—cuisines, presentations, techniques, and ingredients. The most successful of these experiments—those which come to be embraced by customers and fellow chefs—will achieve a broad influence: Think of free-range chicken (Larry Forgione), gourmet pizza (Wolfgang Puck), and infused oils (Jean-Georges Vongerichten).

So how much is real innovation, versus merely an illusion? Some chefs criticized fellow chefs whose "creativity" they found misinformed.

André Soltner states, "I don't 'invent.' I hate the chefs who say they 'create.' I have seen, in my career, very few creations. And especially here in America and in the press, they are always talking of the 'creation' of food; they're looking for new things. But we have had basically the same food for 200–300 years or more. If we change it a little—which we do, adapting to our time because of cholesterol or whatever—that's not creation, that's an adaptation. I have never created a dish, and I'm not ashamed to say it. I have never created a dish

Gratin of Cardoon Francine

DANIEL BOULUD

Restaurant Daniel
New York, NY

"This is an adaptation of my grandmother's recipe served during the winter with roasted fowl. This Lyonnais dish is a Christmas tradition. The cardoon is a vegetable that looks like celery but tastes like artichokes and is popular in Southern France, Italy, and Greece."

. . . .

1 tablespoon salt

3 bunches cardoon, outer leaves and ends trimmed, stalks sliced into 2-inch-long segments, each segment halved and stringy skin pulled off with a small paring knife. (Immediately plunge cardoon into 3 quarts water mixed with juice of 2 lemons to avoid browning)

1 1/2 cups chicken stock

2 ounces fresh beef marrow, sliced

1 1/2 tablespoons all-purpose flour

Salt, freshly ground black pepper

1 cup Gruyère or Emmenthal cheese, freshly grated

. . . .

Add the salt to the cardoon and lemony water, and bring to a boil in a large pot over high heat. Simmer the cardoon for 40 to 50 minutes or until tender. Drain well.

Preheat oven to 425 degrees. Bring chicken stock to a boil in a small pan. Place the marrow in a large pan and melt over medium heat. Add the flour and whisk for 3 to 5 minutes. Add the boiling chicken stock, stir, and cook for 5 minutes. Add the cooked cardoon, salt and pepper to taste, and toss well.

Transfer to a buttered, shallow, baking dish and sprinkle the top with grated cheese. Bake for 15 to 20 minutes, or until golden brown.

Presentation

. . . .

Serve warm from the gratin dish.

. . . .

Serves 4 to 6

© 1993 by Daniel Boulud. *Cooking with Daniel Boulud.* Random House.

because to create a dish is to make something you've never had before. Here [in the United States], they take a recipe and substitute orange juice instead of lemon juice, and they say that's their 'creation'!"

Patrick O'Connell agrees. "So often you read from a critic, who is supposed to be the oracle, about this dazzling creation, an exciting new dish, that somebody has just created in New York—and you had it ten years ago in France. It's mind-boggling sometimes. It's pretty hard to get anything fresh in the idea department these days, because so much of it is a churning out of somebody else's imitation of an imitation. Everyone wants to grab a line, to get noticed. And the critics don't care. It's a conspiracy of crap. [Some] think if they put eight idiotic things together, it will catch somebody's attention, and it does. It gets them two lines [in a publication] and it works. It gets them written about. But nothing is thought through. I eat every week in somebody's place where they've put something on the menu that they haven't ever cooked before or tested or checked out. It's improv."

"THE RIGHT WAVELENGTH"

Chefs have the opportunity to put forth their own, very personal, points of view, thereby making food their own—cooking food they love and that is personally meaningful to them, and making a statement through their work and lives about what they want to support: local farmers, organics, lost varietals, sustainable agriculture, even charitable organizations. It also means having the courage to "push the envelope" in new directions. In a sense, this is what happened in the 1970s and 1980s. A group of new American chefs came into the restaurant business of the era, when good food was synonymous with French food, and invented a whole new definition of what food could be and who could cook it. As this book attests, they succeeded.

In what direction will the *next* generation of chefs take food and the restaurant business? Leading chefs wonder, too. In fact, their concerns about finding aspiring chefs who thought and felt as they did about food led some to envision establishing a new kind of cooking school which would help lead cooks down the right path.

"I thought about starting a cooking school at one point. A whole group of us thought, 'Well, if we can't find people who are on

the right wavelength, then we should do something about training people,' " says Alice Waters. "We started looking around for spots, and got half-way serious about it.

"I thought it might be a good way so that the cooks who were working here could earn some extra money by teaching, and there could be some kind of out-in-the-country situation that could fit into the restaurant, because I really feel that that's the experience that cooks need. I think they have to get out there in the fields. I would have them out there digging in the garden for six months just working with a group of gardeners seeing what's to be planted, what varieties of things. And really no cooking involved in it at all."

"Maybe the next six months would be examining what you have in the kitchen, a comparison of different types of things and tastings. Then, of course, ultimately, putting things together. It's always a revelation to the people who come and work here— how much almost 'picking' kind of prep we do at the restaurant, making a lot of comparisons and decisions. People say, 'I'm a trained cook—why do I have to wash the salad?' In order to evaluate something properly, you really need to see it from the beginning. It's not just coming in on the tail end of it and giving it a sauce. It's really trying to make those distinctions among the types of lettuce and which kinds you want to blend together to make the salad. It's seeing the shapes of things whole, not after they've been prepped and all cut up into little pieces. Maybe you wouldn't have wanted to slice the potato— maybe you'd want to cut it lengthwise because it's so beautiful in its shape. It's things like that that get passed over when you don't start at the beginning. It's a whole training of the senses; every sense has to be sort of worked on in some way."

Larry Forgione concurs. "I think that none of the schools have very much emphasis on growing or farming or the role of it, but I think they're starting to take field trips. It's important to get the kids to understand what the farmers' markets are about, what the fish market scene is like, what you have to look for, and what seasons there are. Unfortunately, the schools don't seem to grow herbs, other than maybe a club. It honestly doesn't make sense to me. It just seems like if you're at the school and you have all these restau-

"Even if I retire, I will teach. But I will not teach in a 'rich man's environment.' I will teach at a lower-cost school to get people interested in our profession, and to give them the tools they need to make their own opportunities."
—DIETER SCHORNER

Acorn Squash Risotto with Shallots, Sage, and Maple-Smoked Bacon

ALFRED PORTALE
Gotham Bar and Grill
New York, NY

"Holidays were very special in my house when I was growing up, in a close Italian family in Buffalo. My mother would prepare huge feasts for the family and our friends. Most of the dishes she prepared were American adaptations of the Italian specialties that her mother cooked for her family when she was young. One Thanksgiving a few years ago, I wanted to create a dish for my family that would capture the essence of Thanksgiving, much in the same way my mother created special dishes. I combined flavors—acorn squash, sage, and maple-smoked bacon—that are representative of the Thanksgiving meal and created a risotto dish. I found out recently that this dish is a traditional Venetian risotto served at an autumn holiday."

. . . .

1 large acorn squash

1 tbs brown sugar

rants, just the volume of herbs you would be going through would have it make sense to at least grow your own herbs. I think it's extremely important that cooks understand the life cycle. Do they absolutely need it to '*just* cook food'? No.

"But I think if you look at people who've excelled in their positions, or gone on to be known for what they do, they aren't people who just accepted what they received. They always questioned and always wanted to go further, and always wanted to have more information. And that's how it all came about. I just wasn't happy with someone telling me the only lettuces I could buy were escarole,

2 oz smoked bacon, diced

1 1/2 cups of finely sliced shallots

1 lb Aborio rice

5 sage leaves

1 pinch fresh thyme

Up to 3 qts rich turkey or chicken stock

2 tbs chopped parsley

salt and freshly ground white pepper

. . . .

For the squash

Cut squash into wedges. Peel and seed, then slice thin wedges crosswise yielding approximately 5 cups. Heat 2 ounces of butter in a large sauté pan. Add squash and season with salt and pepper. Sauté over medium heat until squash is nicely caramelized and very soft (approximately 15 minutes). Sprinkle with brown sugar and keep warm.

For the risotto

While squash is cooking, in a large sauce pot sauté bacon with 1 tbs butter until lightly browned. Add shallots and cook for about 4 minutes. Add rice, sage, and thyme. Stir until coated. Add stock, 8 ounces at a time, stirring until liquid is absorbed. Continue adding stock until rice is cooked (approximately 15 to 18 minutes).

Stir in sautéed squash and 2 ounces of butter.

Serve sprinkled with chopped parsley.

romaine, and iceberg lettuces. In order for me to combat that, I had to know about the life cycle. I had to know how to grow lettuce, or at least know that red oak lettuce could be picked a leaf at a time—how lettuce comes up one leaf at a time, and how individual leaves then become a head, so of course you could pick the leaves if you wanted them."

In addition to studying in depth the ingredients they're cooking with, some chefs believe students also need to study much more deeply

"A lot of people are in love with the fact that they're going to have a microwave in the dashboard of their Chevrolet one day, so they can pop their Wendy's in there and reheat it, or something like that. That's part of the population. But a great percent of the population of our country are going to continue to make food, nutrition, health, the enjoyment of good wine, of good living, of exercise, and a balanced kind of harmonious life be the goals that they want for themselves and for their children."

—NORMAN VAN AKEN

the customers they're cooking for. Patrick O'Connell would like to see culinary education include "people learning who their clientele is, who they will be cooking this food for, and being with their audience."

O'Connell half-jokes, "Bring *bon vivants* to the school. Bring jaded, nasty, bitchy clients to the school—the kind of people who complain about everything. And bring in critics to tell what they hate, what makes them irate, what they can't stand, what they never want to see again. Kids need to know that."

He adds, seriously, "As much as [students] need a mentor for their technique, they also need a taste mentor, somebody who can expand their dimensions of taste, and teach them what life and beauty are all about."

Values are also subtly reflected in a school's environment—which some chefs feeling strongly should be a supportive one, tailored to its students. Mark Miller believes it's critical to validate and encourage individual cooks' own sense of self and history in their cooking, while teaching them the basics. "I went to Louisville College, which has 63 percent black enrollment, and I asked why they didn't have a black teacher on their staff. They told me they didn't have any who were qualified. I said, 'There are people like Patrick Clark and Edna Lewis. They may not want to teach, but do you have black chefs visiting? Do you have a Soul Week—John Taylor, looking at low country Carolina cuisine? Jessica Harris, a black woman who writes about the black experience in America?' 'No, no, no.' None of these people were ever invited. Meanwhile, students were watching lectures on, basically, the high gluten content of flour for puff pastry."

MAKING IT YOUR OWN

What cook in America didn't feel a greater sense of pride in the cuisine of America when the White House hired an American chef to cook American food, after a long tradition of having a French chef with menus printed in French? "I think America is starting to mature," observes Mark Miller. "As long as we gave into this

Butter Pecan Ice Cream

PATRICK O'CONNELL

The Inn at Little Washington
Washington, VA

"As a kid, I never believed that store-bought butter pecan ice cream really contained any butter, and the little chunks in it didn't really taste like pecan. I liked to think about the way it might have tasted in a perfect world. This recipe is a child's fantasy of how real butter pecan ice cream ought to taste."

. . . .

3 3/4 cups milk

3 3/4 cups whipping cream

1 1/2 lbs salted butter

6 cups whole pecans

36 egg yolks

4 cups sugar

. . . .

1. Bring to boil milk and whipping cream. Pour into plastic bowl and cool in refrigerator.

2. Melt butter in large skillet. Sauté pecans until butter browns. Strain into bowl. Set pecans aside. Reserve butter.

3. Whisk together egg yolks and 2 cups of sugar.

4. In a heavy saucepan, mix together the whipping cream and 2 cups of sugar.

5. Bring cream to boil, whisk 1/3 of hot cream into egg yolks, then pour entire mixture back into pot. Heat to just below boiling point. Stir in browned butter. Cool over ice.

6. When cool, add scalded half-and-half. Divide mixture into 3 containers and freeze in machine.

7. Add 2 cups pecans to each batch when ice cream begins to thicken.

Dad's Pan-Fried Spotted Brown Brook Trout with Fried Potatoes

BRADLEY OGDEN

The Lark Creek Inn and One Market Restaurant
Larkspur, CA and San Francisco, CA

"I have been very fortunate over the years to have had many talented people share their expertise and love of food with me. Each one in some way has had an influence on the way I cook today. But there is one particular childhood memory that has stuck with me over the years. I was ten years old, living in Michigan, when my father took me alone on a fishing trip. Being one of seven children, it was a real treat to have my dad alone for the day. We spent most of the day fishing for wild brown spotted trout out of an icy cold stream, fed from the melting winter snows. That night, my dad fried potatoes and onions seasoned with just a touch of salt and some freshly cracked pepper in a huge cast-iron skillet on an old potbelly stove. In another cast-iron skillet, he fried the trout that had been dredged in lightly seasoned flour. Nothing has ever tasted as good. I can still remember the fresh taste of the food, the simple way Dad cooked it, and the fun we had. These qualities are the ones that I still try to integrate in my cooking style today."

. . . .

6 8–16 ounce fresh brook trout (depending on your catch)

2 tablespoons oil

1/2 cup flour, seasoned with kosher salt, freshly ground black pepper, and cayenne

3–4 tablespoons sweet butter

1/4 cup chopped parsley

2 lemons, juiced

. . . .

Fillet trout. Place a large cast-iron skillet over high heat. Add the oil. Lightly dredge the trout in the seasoned flour. When the oil is hot, place the fish carefully into the pan. Reduce heat slightly. Add the butter.

Cook trout on both sides until golden brown, approximately 3–4 minutes. Remove and place on serving dish and sprinkle with the parsley and lemon juice.

Serves 6

Fried Potatoes

. . . .

3 large russet potatoes

3 tablespoons unsalted butter

1 small Spanish onion, peeled, quartered, and sliced 1/4" thick

1 teaspoon fresh cracked black pepper

1/2 cup clarified butter or lard

kosher salt

. . . .

Procedure

To prepare the potatoes, rinse and place in a 4-quart saucepan with salted water to cover. Bring to a boil over high heat and boil for 20 to 25 minutes, cooking until barely cooked through, leaving slightly underdone. Remove potatoes immediately from water and cool at room temperature. When cool enough to handle, peel, cut into quarters lengthwise, and slice 1/8 inch thick.

In a skillet over medium heat, melt 1 tablespoon of the unsalted butter. Add onions and saute until lightly caramelized, approximately 2 to 3 minutes. Season with 1/2 teaspoon of the cracked black pepper. Remove from pan immediately so as not to overcook. Set onions aside to cool.

To cook fries, use two large skillets so that the potatoes are not stacked. Add 1/4 cup of the clarified butter to each skillet and place over high heat. When butter starts to smoke divide the potatoes and add half to each skillet. Cook on one side until golden brown and crisp.

Flip onto the other side and do the same seasoning with the other 1/2 teaspoon of pepper and kosher salt. Drain excess fat from each pan, reduce heat to low, and add half the onion to each. Saute just to warm the onions through. Add 1 tablespoon unsalted butter, toss to mix, and serve immediately. Add cut chives (optional).

Makes 4 to 6 servings

[French food being served in the White House], we kind of created a mold that says we were not good enough.

"Jungian psychology calls this 'the process of individuation'—it isn't that you become better, it's that you become more aware of who you are and you realize the potential of your own self."

You and I—who cook on the line every day—are creating the future of food and the profession with every dish we make, with every meal we serve. Having a point of view—or, becoming more aware of who we are as chefs and realizing the potential of ourselves within our cooking—will propel us to influence others through our cuisine. People will be affected and changed by it, one way or another. We must strive to make the influence of our food a positive one.

To this point, André Soltner, who has spent more years than any other chef we interviewed developing his unique point of view, leaves us with this advice: "If you give the ingredients what I call 'love,' you'll never fail. If you don't have that in your cooking, forget it. You can have all the techniques in the world, but you'll never become a great chef.

"I can teach techniques. And I can explain what I just explained. But I cannot teach it—I cannot teach the feeling.

"I know that when you cook, every time you cook, you must feel this feeling. If you can achieve this, you will not fail."

A

GLOSSARY OF

RESTAURANT

AND KITCHEN

TERMS

Aioli: garlic mayonnaise

Beurre Blanc: a butter sauce

Blanch: to bring to boil before halting the cooking process in cold water

Bouquet garni: small bundle of herbs

Chef: one who oversees the professional kitchen and the other cooks

Chiffonade: to cut leafy vegetables or herbs into thin strips

Concasser: rough-chopped

Confit: meat covered in its own fat, cooked, and preserved

Convection Oven: an oven in which hot air is circulated by a fan

Cook: one who prepares food

Covers: the number of meals served

Degustation: a tasting of a selection of dishes

Dupes: the order tickets

Eighty-Six: indicates that the kitchen is out of a particular dish

Expeditor: the person who calls out orders to the cooks and ensures acceptable quality

Foie Gras: goose liver

Front of the House: the dining room

Fumé: smoked

Garde-manger: the cook in charge of cold products

In the weeds: a colloquialism indicating the kitchen is backed up with orders

Julienne: to cut into thin strips

Line: the station where entrees are prepared

Maitre d'Hotel: the person in charge of the restaurant dining room

Mirepoix: a French term for carrot, celery, and onion diced and cooked for stock

Mise en Place: a French term referring to prepared ingredients ready to go into a dish

On the Fly: as quickly as possible

(a la) Provencale: usually, with tomatoes, garlic, olive oil

Roti: roast

Rounds: the cook who works different stations where needed

Roux: a base for sauces made from flour and butter

Sauté: to cook quickly in hot fat

Sauté Cook: the cook who sautés on the line

Service: the hours a restaurant is open for business

Sous Chef: the person who is number two in command to the chef

Stagiaire: a cook (typically foreign) who does menial jobs or elementary cooking for low pay or no pay

Stock: broth in which meat or vegetables have been cooked

Sweat: to cook (vegetables) slowly in butter or oil

Tickets: see "Dupes"

Tournant: see "Rounds"

Tourné: giving a uniform shape to vegetables

Turn Tables: have one party of customers finish so that another party can be seated

Walk-in: a refrigerated room

Whites: chefs' white uniform jackets

B

SELECTED PROFESSIONAL COOKING SCHOOLS IN THE UNITED STATES AND ABROAD

UNITED STATES

The Academy of Culinary Arts
Atlantic Community College
5100 Black Horse Pike
Mays Landing, NJ 08330
(609) 343–5000

Art Institute of Atlanta
School of Culinary Arts
3391 Peachtree Rd., N.E.
Atlanta, GA 30326
(404) 266–1340

Art Institute of Fort Lauderdale
1799 SE 17th St.
Ft. Lauderdale, FL 33316
(305) 463–3000

Atlantic Vocational Technical Center
4700 Coconut Creek Pkwy.
Coconut Creek, FL 33066
(305) 977–2000

Baltimore International Culinary College
17 Commerce St.
Baltimore, MD 21202
(410) 752–4983

Bellingham Technical College
3028 Lindbergh Ave.
Bellingham, WA 98225
(206) 676–7761

Blackhawk Technical College
6004 Prairie Rd.
Janesville, WI 53547
(608) 757–7690

Boise State University
1910 University Dr.
Boise, ID 83725
(208) 385–1532

Bossier Parish Community College
2719 Airline Dr. North
Bossier City, LA 71111
(318) 746–6120

Boston University
Seminars in the Culinary Arts
Boston University Metropolitan College
808 Commonwealth Ave.
Boston, MA 02215
(617) 353–4130

The California Culinary Academy
625 Polk St.
San Francisco, CA 94102
(800) BAY–CHEF

The Cambridge School of Culinary Arts
2020 Massachusetts Ave.
Cambridge, MA 02140
(617) 354–3836

Century Business College
2665 Fifth Ave.
San Diego, CA 92103
(619) 233–0184

Cincinnati Technical College
3520 Central Pkwy.
Cincinnati, OH 45223
(513) 569–1500

City College of San Francisco—Hotel
& Restaurant
50 Phelan Ave.
San Francisco, CA 94112
(415) 239–3154

Clark College
Culinary Arts Department
1800 E. McLoughlin Blvd.
Vancouver, WA 98663
(206) 699–0304

College of Du Page
22nd St. & Lambert Rd.
Glen Ellyn, IL 60137
(708) 385–2800

Columbus State Community College
550 E. Spring St.
Columbus, OH 43215
(614) 227–2579

Community College of Southern Nevada
3200 E. Cheyenne Ave.
North Las Vegas, NV 89030
(702) 651–4190

The Cooking and Hospitality Institute of Chicago
361 W. Chestnut
Chicago, IL 60610
(312) 944–0882

The Culinary Institute of America
433 Albany Post Rd.
Hyde Park, NY 12538
(800) CULINARY

Delgado Community College
615 City Park Ave.
New Orleans, LA 70119
(504) 483–4208

Des Moines Area Community College
2006 South Ankeny Blvd.
Ankeny, IA 50021
(512) 964–6532

Diablo Valley College—Culinary Arts Dept.
321 Golf Club Rd.
Pleasant Hill, CA 94523
(510) 685–1230

Dunwoody Industrial Institute
818 Dunwoody Blvd.
Minneapolis, MN 55043
(612) 374–5800

Elgin Community College
1700 Spartan Dr.
Elgin, IL 60120
(708) 697–1000

Florida Community College
4501 Capper Rd.
Jacksonville, FL 32218
(904) 766–6652

The Florida Culinary Institute
1126 53rd Court
West Palm Beach, FL 33407
(407) 842–8300

The French Culinary Institute
462 Broadway
New York, NY 10013
(212) 219–8890

Grand Rapids Community College
151 Fountain, N.E.
Grand Rapids, MI 49503
(616) 771–3690

Greenville Technical College
P.O. Box 5616 Station B
Greenville, SC 29606
(803) 250–8000

Gulf Coast Community College
5230 W. U.S. Highway 98
Panama City, FL 32401
(904) 769–1550

Hennepin Technical College
9000 Brooklyn Blvd.
Brooklyn Park, MN 55445
(612) 425–3800

Henry Ford Community College
5101 Evergreen Rd.
Dearborn, MI 48128
(313) 845–6360

Hiram G. Andrews Center
727 Goucher St.
Johnstown, PA 15905
(814) 255–5881

Hocking Technical College
3301 Hocking Pkwy.
Nelsonville, OH 45764
(614) 753–3591

Horry-Georgetown Technical College
P.O. Box 1966
Conway, SC 29526
(803) 347–3186

Indiana University of Pennsylvania
Culinary School
125 S. Gilpin St.
Punxsutawney, PA 15767
(800) 438–6424

Indiana Vo-Tech College
3800 N. Anthony Blvd.
Ft. Wayne, IN 46805
(219) 480–4240

Indiana Vo-Tech College
1 West 26th St.
Indianapolis, IN 46208
(317) 921–4882

Instituto del Arte Moderno
Culinary Arts Dept.
Ave. Monserrate
Villa Fontana, Carolina, PR 00630
(809) 769–7636

International Culinary Academy
107 Sixth St.
Pittsburgh, PA 15222
(412) 471–9330

Jefferson Community College
109 E. Broadway
Louisville, KY 40202
(502) 584–0181

Jefferson State Community College
2601 Carson Rd.
Pinson Valley Pkwy.
Birmingham, AL 35215
(205) 853–1200

Johnson County Community College
12345 College at Quivira
Overland Park, KS 66210
(913) 469–8500

Johnson & Wales University
8 Abbott Park Place
Providence, RI 02903
(401) 598–1000

Joliet Junior College
1216 Houbolt Ave.
Joliet, IL 60436
(815) 729–9020

Kendall College
The Culinary School
2408 Orrington Ave.
Evanston, IL 60201
(708) 866–1300

Kirkwood Community College
Culinary Arts Dept.
6301 Kirkwood Blvd., SW
Cedar Rapids, IA 52406
(319) 398–5468

L'Academie du Cuisine
5021 Wilson Lane
Bethesda, MD 20814
(301) 986–9490

Lederwolff Culinary Academy
3300 Stockton Blvd.
Sacramento, CA 95820
(916) 456–7002

Los Angeles Trade-Technical College
400 W. Washington Blvd.
Los Angeles, CA 90015
(213) 744–9480

Madison Area Technical College
3550 Anderson St.
Madison, WI 53704
(608) 246–6368

Manchester Community College
Culinary Arts Dept.
60 Bidwell St.
Manchester, CT 06040
(203) 647–6000

Maui Community College
Culinary Arts Dept.
310 Kaahamanu Ave.
Kahului, HI 96732
(808) 244–9181

Metropolitan Community College
P.O. Box 3777
Omaha, NE 68103
(402) 449–8309

Milwaukee Area Technical College
700 W. State St.
Milwaukee, WI 53233
(414) 278–6500

Missoula Vocational Technical Center
909 S. Ave. West
Missoula, MT 59801
(406) 542–6811

Monroe County Community College
1555 S. Raisinville Rd.
Monroe, MI 48161
(313) 242–7300

National Center for Hospitality Studies at Sullivan
College
3101 Bardstown Rd.
Louisville, KY 40232
(800) 456–6500

The Natural Gourmet Cooking School
48 W. 21st St.
2nd Floor
New York, NY 10010
(212) 645–5170

New England Culinary Institute
250 Main St.
Montpelier, VT 05602
(802) 223–6324

New Hampshire College
The Culinary Institute
2500 N. River Rd.
Manchester, NH 03104
(603) 644–3128

The New School
Culinary Arts Program
100 Greenwich Ave.
New York, NY 10011
(212) 255–4141

New York City Technical College
300 Jay St.
Brooklyn, NY 11201
(718) 260–5630

New York Food & Hotel Management School
154 W. 14th St.
New York, NY 10011
(212) 675–6655

New York Restaurant School
75 Varick St.
New York, NY 10013
(212) 226–5500

Northwestern Michigan College
Culinary Arts Dept.
1701 East Front St.
Traverse City, MI 49684
(616) 922–1197

Oakland Community College
27055 Orchard Lake Rd.
Farmington Hills, MI 48018
(313) 471–7500

Opryland Hotel Institute
2800 Opryland Dr.
Nashville, TN 37214
(615) 871–7765

Orange Coast College
Hospitality Dept.
2710 Fairview Blvd.
Costa Mesa, CA 92625
(714) 432–5835

Orleans Technical Institute
Culinary Arts Dept.
1330 Rhawn St.
Philadelphia, PA 19111
(215) 728–4488

Paul Smith's College
Paul Smiths, NY 12970
(800) 421–2605

Pennsylvania College of Technology
One College Ave.
Williamsport, PA 17701
(713) 326–3761

Pennsylvania Institute of Culinary Arts
717 Liberty Ave.
Pittsburgh, PA 15222
(412) 566–2444

Peter Kump's New York Cooking School
307 E. 92nd St.
New York, NY 10128
(212) 410–4601

Pikes Peak Community College
5675 South Academy Blvd.
Colorado Springs, CO 80906
(719) 540–7371

Pinellas Technical Educational Center
Culinary Arts Dept.
6100 154th Ave.
N. Clearwater, FL 33516
(813) 531–3531

Pinellas Technical Educational Center
901 34th St., S.
St. Petersburg, FL 33711
(813) 327–3671

Renton Technical College
3000 N.E. Fourth St.
Renton, WA 98056
(206) 235–2372

The Restaurant School
4207 Walnut St.
Philadelphia, PA 19104
(215) 222–4200

St. Paul Technical College
235 Marshall Ave.
St. Paul, MN 55102
(612) 221–1300

St. Phillip's College
2111 Nevada St.
San Antonio, TX 78203
(512) 531–3315

Santa Barbara City College
721 Cliff Dr.
Santa Barbara, CA 93100
(805) 963–4091

Savannah Technical Institute
5717 White Bluff Rd.
Savannah, GA 31499
(912) 351–6300

Schenectady County Community College
78 Washington Ave.
Schenectady, NY 12035
(518) 346–6211

Scottsdale Culinary Institute
8100 Camelback Rd.
Scottsdale, AZ 85251
(602) 990–3773

Seattle Central Community College
1701 Broadway
Seattle, WA 98122
(206) 344–4330

Southeast Institute of Culinary Arts
Del Monte Ave.
St. Augustine, FL 32084
(904) 824–4400

South Seattle Community College
6000 16th Ave., SW
Seattle, WA 98106
(206) 764–5344

Spokane Community College
No. 1810 Greene St.
Spokane, WA 99207
(509) 533–7280

Sullivan County Community College
Hospitality Division
LeRoy Rd.
Loch Sheldrake , NY 12759
(914) 434–5750

SUNY College of Agriculture & Technology
Food Service & Hospitality Administration
Cobleskill, NY 12043
(518) 234–5011

Triton College
Hospitality Industry Administration
2000 Fifth Ave.
River Grove, IL 60171
(708) 456–0300

Washburne Trade School
Chefs Training Program
3233 W. 31st St.
Chicago, IL 60623
(312) 579–6100

Waukesha County Technical College
800 Main St.
Pewaukee, WI 53072
(414) 691–5254

Western Culinary Institute
1316 Southwest 13th Ave.
Portland, OR 97201
(503) 223–2245

Westmoreland County Community College
Armbrust Rd.
Youngwood, PA 15697
(412) 925–4000

Zona Spray Cooking School
140 N. Main
Hudson, OH 44236
(216) 650–1665

ABROAD

Ada Parasiliti
L'Angolo-Scuola di Cucina
Via Ponte Vetero 13
20121 Milan, Italy
(39) 2 876398

The Ballymaloe Cookery School
Shanagarry, County Cork
Midleton, Ireland
(353) 21–646785

Ecole Lenôtre
40 rue Pierre Curie
787373 Plaisir Cedex France
(33) 1–30–8146–34

La Varenne
Burgundy, France
P.O. Box 25574
Washington, DC 20007
(800) 537–6486

Le Cordon Bleu
114 Marylebone Lane
London W1M 6HH, England
(44) 71 935 3503

Le Cordon Bleu
8 rue Leon Delhomme
75015 Paris, France
(33) 1 48 56 06 06

Leith's School of Food and Wine
21 St. Alban's Grove
London W8 5BP, England
(44) 81 229 0177

OTHER

School for American Chefs
Beringer Vineyards
P.O. Box 111
St. Helena, CA 94574
(707) 963–7115
A scholarship program for 8 chefs a year to study
with Madeleine Kamman

C

LEADING

CULINARY

ORGANIZATIONS

American Culinary Federation (ACF)
P.O. Box 3466
St. Augustine, FL 32085
(904) 824–4468

The 24,000 member American Culinary Federation, founded in 1929, is the professional organization representing U.S. cooks and chefs. The nonprofit ACF certifies cooks and chefs, offers culinary and pastry apprenticeship programs, and accredits postsecondary culinary and pastry programs. The ACF's honor society, the American Academy of Chefs, represents hundreds of top chefs in the nation. The ACF's official magazine *The National Culinary Review* focuses on food and cooking and is published for chefs around the world.

American Institute of Baking (AIB)
1213 Bakers Way
Manhattan, KS 66502
(913) 537–4750

The American Institute of Baking was established in 1919 to promote the cause of education in nutrition, the science and art of baking, bakery management, and the allied sciences. It is a non-profit educational and research organization supported by the contributions of nearly 600 member companies in the baking and allied trades.

The American Institute of Wine & Food (AIWF)
1550 Bryant St.
Suite 700
San Francisco, CA 94103
(415) 255–3000

The AIWF is a non-profit educational organization promoting a broad exchange of information and ideas to benefit all who care about wine and food—from chefs and restaurateurs to dedicated amateurs. The institute was founded in 1981 by Julia Child, Robert Mondavi, Richard Graff, and others to advance the understanding, appreciation, and quality of what we eat and drink. Through its programs and publications, members of the AIWF have the opportunity to meet and share their ideas with the most knowledgeable people in the industry, including leading chefs, restaurateurs, winemakers, journalists, and other leaders in the art of wine and fine cuisine.

The Bread Bakers Guild of America (BBGA)
P.O. Box 22254
Pittsburgh, PA 15222

The Bread Bakers Guild of America is the only non-profit organization in North America formed exclusively to provide education in the field of artisan baking and the production of high quality bread products. The Guild offers seminars and other educational resources, and publishes a bimonthly newsletter. Membership is open to anyone with an interest in good bread, but its educational focus is on production methods and ingredients used by professional bakers.

Chefs Collaborative 2000
c/o Jimmy Schmidt
The Rattlesnake Club
300 River Place
Detroit, MI 48207
(313) 567–4843

Chefs Collaborative 2000 was founded in 1993, in conjunction with Oldways Preservation and Exchange Trust, following a symposium held in Hawaii entitled "Food Choices: 2000." This nationwide gathering of chefs organized itself to celebrate the pleasures of food, and to recognize the impact of food choices on public health, on the vitality of cultures, and on the integrity of the global environment. Integral to the members of the Chefs Collaborative 2000 was their belief in preserving the environment through sustainable agriculture, promoting the production and distribution of good, wholesome food to all, and educating for the future.

Chefs Helping to Enhance Food Safety (CHEFS)
1001 Connecticut Ave., NW Suite 522
Washington, DC 20036
(202) 659–5930

Founded in 1991 by Public Voice for Food and Health Policy, Oldways Preservation & Exchange Trust, Julia Child, and a dozen of America's top chefs, CHEFS is a national coalition of more than 600 chefs and other food professionals working to promote food safety. In 1993, CHEFS, in cooperation with Public Voice, launched "Green Cuisine," a national public awareness campaign to promote food grown with little or no pesticides. Many CHEFS members are top chefs who work with a network of growers and regularly feature organic and low pesticide food in their restaurants.

Council on Hotel, Restaurant, and
Institutional Education (CHRIE)
1200 17th St., N.W.
Washington, DC 20036
(202) 331–5990

CHRIE was founded in 1946 as a non-profit association for schools, colleges, and universities offering programs in hotel and restaurant management, food service management, and culinary arts. CHRIE is committed to providing its members "cutting edge" information impacting the hospitality and tourism industry. Trends and other developments in technology, demographics, the environment, the workforce, and social concerns are among the topics that CHRIE explores for its members.

The Educational Foundation of the
National Restaurant Association
250 South Wacker Dr., Suite 1400
Chicago, IL 60606

This Educational Foundation of the National Restaurant Association, a nonprofit organization founded in 1987, is the leading source of education, training, and career development for the food service industry. It focuses on upgrading professionalism in the food service industry by providing high quality educational products and services for food service managers and others pursuing a career in the hospitality industry.

International Association of Culinary Professionals
(IACP)
304 W. Liberty St.
Louisville, KY 40202
(502) 581–9786

The IACP is a not-for-profit professional society of individuals employed in, or providing services to, the culinary industry. IACP's mission is to be a resource and support system for food professionals, and to help its members achieve and sustain success at all levels of their careers through education, information, and peer contacts in an ethical, responsible, and professional climate. The association provides continuing education and professional development for its members, who are employed in the fields of communication, education, or in the preparation of food and drink. The current membership of 2,300 encompasses 20 countries and represents virtually every profession in the culinary universe: teachers, cooking school owners, caterers, writers, chefs, media cooking personalities, editors, publishers, food stylists, food photographers, restaurateurs, leaders of major food corporations, and vintners.

International Association of Women Chefs and Restaurateurs (IAWCR)
110 Sutter St., Suite 305
San Francisco, CA 94104
(415) 362–7336

The mission of the IAWCR is to promote the education and advancement of women in the restaurant industry and the betterment of the industry as a whole. Among its goals are to facilitate communication and exchange of ideas between members and to promote professional contacts; to provide educational opportunities for professional and personal development for women in all sectors of the restaurant industry; to create and expand professional and business opportunities for women working in or wishing to enter the restaurant industry; to provide support and foster an environment which insures women equal access to the positions, power and rewards offered by the restaurant industry; and to examine the issues of women in the workplace and to advocate the improvement of work environments in the restaurant industry.

International Foodservice Executives Association (IFSEA)
1100 South State Rd. #7 Suite 103
Margate, FL 33068
(305) 977–0767

The IFSEA is the food service industry's first trade association. Organized in 1901 as the International Stewards and Caterers, its members are worldwide with branches in Canada, Japan, Guam, Germany, Taiwan, and the United States. IFSEA is a professional organization dedicated to raising food service industry standards, educating members and future leaders, recognizing members' achievements, and serving the growing needs of the diverse, dynamic, multi-billion dollar a year market for food away from home.

The James Beard Foundation
167 W. 12th St.
New York, NY 10011
(212) 675–4984

The James Beard Foundation was established as a charitable foundation in 1986 to keep alive the ideals and activities that made James Beard the acknowledged "Father of American Cooking." The Foundation fosters the appreciation and development of gastronomy by preserving and promulgating our culinary heritage, and by recognizing and promoting excellence in all aspects of the culinary arts. The Foundation is supported by benefactors. corporate donors, and a nationwide network of members, all of whom are kept informed of activities through the monthly newsletter, *News From The Beard House*. The newsletter details the events scheduled for the month, profiles chefs, includes recipes, book reviews, articles by well-known writers, food and wine news from far-flung reporters. and a bit of gossip.

Les Dames d'Escoffier International
270 Arden Shore Rd.
Lake Bluff, Illinois 60044
(708) 234–0346

Les Dames d'Escoffier is a society of professional women of achievement with careers in food, wine, and other beverages, and the arts of the table. The purpose of the organization is to support and promote the understanding, appreciation, and knowledge of these professions in the tradition of Auguste Escoffier. Members are outstanding women with at least five years professional experience who have distinguished themselves in gastronomy, oenology, and related fields. Active members include chefs, cooking school owners and teachers, food writers and editors, caterers, hotel executives, purveyors, administrators, and public relations specialists.

National Restaurant Association (NRA)
1200 17th St., NW
Washington, DC 20036
(202) 331–5900

The NRA is the leading national trade association for the food service industry. Together with The Educational Foundation of the NRA, it works to protect, promote, and educate the rapidly growing industry. Since its founding in 1919, the NRA has worked to promote the ideals and interests of the food service industry, the employer of eight million individuals. To this end, the association provides members with a wide range of education, research, communications, convention, and government affairs services.

Oldways Preservation & Exchange Trust
45 Milk St.
Boston, MA 02109
(617) 695–9102

Oldways Preservation & Exchange Trust, a non-profit organization, was organized in 1988 by K. Dun Gifford, and began operating in mid-1990 when Nancy Harmon Jenkins and Greg Drescher joined it as co-founders and directors. The purpose of Oldways is to preserve the healthy, environmentally sustainable food and agricultural traditions of many cultures, and to make the lessons of these traditions more widely accessible. The mission at Oldways is to show the continuing significance of our agricultural, culinary, and dietary heritage—and show how the lessons of the past can be applied to address contemporary needs. Oldways brings together experts from all over the world to evaluate these traditions and define sustainable food choices, and on the basis of this information, to devise, organize, and administer educational programs that encourage sounder food choices.

Public Voice for Food & Health Policy
1001 Connecticut Ave., NW, Suite 522
Washington, DC 20036
(202) 659–5930

Founded in 1982, Public Voice for Food and Health Policy is a national non-profit research, education and advocacy organization that promotes a safer, healthier, and more affordable food supply. Public Voice advances the interests of all consumers by fostering food and agricultural policies and practices that enhance public health and protect the environment. The organization's agenda focuses on the following food safety, nutrition, and sustainable agriculture objectives: seafood safety; healthy eating among children; nutrition labeling; sustainable agriculture; pesticide policy and international food standards; meat and poultry inspection systems; food security; commodity programs; and agricultural research and biotechnology.

Radcliffe Culinary Friends
Schlesinger Library at Radcliffe College
10 Garden St.
Cambridge, MA 02138
(617) 495–8601

The goals of the Radcliffe Culinary Friends are to collect, catalog, and preserve a major collection of books and periodicals related to food; to make known these resources to all interested people; and to provide a forum for discussion about the history of food and the study of food in society. The Schlesinger Library Culinary Collection includes nearly 10,000 works in the fields of cookery, gastronomy, domestic management, the history of cooking, and related reference works. The books, which date from the 16th century to the present, represent the cuisines of all nations. They include many voluntary association cookbooks as well as classics of European and American cooking. Among the ongoing programs of the Library are First Mondays, roundtable discussions for food professionals.

Roundtable for Women in Foodservice (RWF)
3022 W. Eastwood Ave.
Chicago, IL 60625
(312) 463–3396

The RWF is a non-profit organization, established in 1982, dedicated to the promotion of the advancement and visibility of women throughout the food service industry. These goals are accomplished through educational seminars, mentoring, and networking. RWF provides members with a national directory and holds an annual conference in Chicago where Woman of the Year and Pacesetter awards are presented. RWF also presents student scholarships annually and provides a membership card which entitles members to special benefits and discounts throughout the food service industry.

Tasters Guild
1451 W. Cypress Creek Rd.
Suite 300-26
Ft. Lauderdale, FL 33309
(305) 928–2823

Established in 1987, Tasters Guild consists of over 100 local guilds throughout the country that bring together consumers, wine and food establishments, and the wine and food service industry. Its objective is to promote the appreciation and responsible use of wine and food through education, specific tastings, special consumer benefits, and travel opportunities.

D

LEADING

CULINARY

PERIODICALS

Art Culinaire
P.O. Box 9268
Morristown, NJ 07963
(201) 993–5500

The Art of Eating
Box 242
Peacham, VT 05862

Bon Appétit
5900 Wilshire Blvd.
Los Angeles, CA 90036
(213) 965–3600

Chef
20 North Wacker, Suite 3230
Chicago, IL 60606
(312) 849–2220

CookBook
P.O. Box 88
Steuben, ME 04680

The Cookbook Review
60 Kinnaird St.
Cambridge, MA 02139
(617) 868–8857

Cooking Light
2011 Lake Shore Dr.
Birmingham, AL 35209
(205) 877–6000

Cook's Illustrated
17 Station St. Box 1200
Brookline, MA 02147
(617) 232–1000

Culinary Review
1246 North State Pkwy.
Chicago, IL 60610

Eating Well
Ferry Rd.
Charlotte, VT 05445
(802) 425–3961

Electronic Gourmet Guide (eGG)
Internet URL http://www.2way.com/food/egg
Internet email: egg@2way.com

Food Arts
387 Park Ave.South
New York, NY 10016
(212) 684–4224

Food & Wine
1120 Avenue of the Americas
New York, NY 10036
(212) 382–5600

Gourmet
560 Lexington Ave.
New York, NY 10022
(212) 371–1330

Napa Valley Tables
The Folio of Food & Wine
P.O. Box 111
St. Helena, CA 94574
(707) 963–7115

Nation's Restaurant News
425 Park Ave.
New York, NY 10022
(212) 756–5000

Restaurant Business
355 Park Ave. South 3rd Floor
New York, NY 10010-1789
(212) 592–6200

Restaurant Hospitality
1100 Superior Ave.
Cleveland, OH 44114
(216) 696–7000

Restaurants and Institutions
1350 E. Touhy Ave.
Des Plaines, IL 60018
(708) 635–8800

Saveur
100 Avenue of the Americas
New York, NY 10013
(800) 462–0209

E

BRIEF BIOGRAPHIES OF CHEFS INTERVIEWED

Jean Banchet was the chef-owner of Ciboulette in Atlanta, and of Le Francais in Wheeling, Illinois and plans to open a new bistro in Atlanta. A native of France, he has worked in the kitchens of Fernand Point, Paul Bocuse, and the Troisgros Brothers.

Rick Bayless is the chef-owner of Frontera Grill and Topolobompo, both in Chicago. He has both undergraduate and graduate degrees in linguistics from the University of Michigan. In 1991, he was named the Best Chef of the Midwest by The James Beard Foundation. He is the author of *Authentic Mexican*.

Daniel Boulud is the chef-owner of Restaurant Daniel at the Surrey Hotel in New York City. He was formerly the chef of Le Cirque, also in New York City. In 1992, he was named the Best Chef of New York and in 1994, the Chef of the Year by The James Beard Foundation. He is the author of *Cooking with Daniel Boulud*.

Edward Brown is the chef of The Sea Grill in New York City. He is a graduate of The Culinary Institute of America. He has worked at Lucas-Carton in Paris, and at Tropica and Judson Grill in New York City. He is the author of the forthcoming *The Modern Seafood Cook*.

Patrick Clark is the executive chef of Tavern on the Green in New York City. He is a graduate of New York City Technical College and apprenticed with Michel Guérard in France. According to *Art Culinaire* magazine, "Having turned down the opportunity to be the new White House chef, [Clark] is undeniably the highest profile black American chef today."

Gary Danko is the chef at The Ritz-Carlton Hotel in San Francisco. He is a graduate of The Culinary Institute of America, and also studied with Madeleine Kamman. He was named one of America's Best New Chefs by *Food & Wine*, and

The Dining Room at The Ritz-Carlton was awarded five stars by the Mobil Travel Guide.

Todd English is the chef-owner of Olives and Figs, both based in Charlestown, Massachusetts. He is a graduate of The Culinary Institute of America. In 1991, he was named the Rising Star Chef of the Year and in 1994, the Best Chef of the Northeast by The James Beard Foundation. He is the recipient of the first Robert Mondavi Award for Culinary Excellence.

Susan Feniger and **Mary Sue Milliken** are the chefs and co-owners of the Border Grill in Santa Monica, California. In 1985, they were inducted into The Who's Who of Food and Beverage in America. They are the co-authors of *City Cuisine* and *Mesa Mexican: Bold Flavors from the Border, Coastal Mexico, and Beyond*.

Michael Foley is the chef-owner of Printer's Row, and owner of Le Perroquet, both in Chicago. He is a graduate of Cornell and Georgetown. In 1984, he was inducted into The Who's Who of Food and Beverage in America.

Susanna Foo is the chef-owner of Susanna Foo in Philadelphia. A former librarian from the University of Pittsburgh, she attended The Culinary Institute of America's continuing education division. She was named one of America's Best New Chefs and her restaurant was named one of the Distinguished Restaurants of North America in *Food & Wine*.

Larry Forgione is the chef-owner of An American Place in New York City and The Beekman 1766 Tavern in Rhinebeck, New York, and is a founder of American Spoon Foods. He is a graduate of The Culinary Institute of America. In 1984, he was inducted into The Who's Who of Food and Beverage in America and in 1993, he was named the Chef of the Year by The James Beard

Foundation. He is the author of *America Itself, An American Harvest Cookbook*.

George Germon and **Johanne Killeen** are the chefs and co-owners of Al Forno in Providence, Rhode Island. Al Forno was named one of the Distinguished Restaurants of North America in *Food & Wine*. In 1993, they were named the Best Chefs of the Northeast by The James Beard Foundation. They are co-authors of *Cucina Simpatica*.

Victor Gielisse is the chef-owner of Actuelle in Dallas. Actuelle was named one of the Distinguished Restaurants of North America. He is a Certified Master Chef and in 1991, he was named The Culinary Institute of America's Chef of the Year. He is the author of *Cuisine Actuelle*.

Joyce Goldstein is the chef-owner of Square One in San Francisco. In 1985, she was inducted into The Who's Who of Food and Beverage in America. A graduate of Yale, she is the author of *The Mediterranean Kitchen* and *Back to Square One*, and writes a food column for the *San Francisco Chronicle*.

Gordon Hamersley is the chef-owner of Hamersley's Bistro in Boston. He attended Boston University. He was named one of America's Best New Chefs by *Food & Wine*.

Raji Jallepalli is the chef of Restaurant Raji in Memphis, Tennessee. A former medical technician, she was encouraged as a chef by her mentor Jean-Louis Palladin.

Jean Joho is the chef of Everest in Chicago. He worked with Paul Haeberlin at his Michelin three-star restaurant L'Auberge de l'Ill, as well as at other two- and three-star restaurants throughout Europe. He was named one of America's Best New Chefs by *Food & Wine*.

Madeleine Kamman is the director of the School for American Chefs at Beringer Vineyards. She is the author of numerous cookbooks and books on food including *The Making of a Cook, Dinner Against the Clock, When French Women Cook, In Madeleine's Kitchen, Madeleine Cooks* and *Savoie*. She was the host of her own PBS cooking show "Madeleine Cooks," and formerly ran cooking schools in New England as well as her own restaurant, Chez La Mère Madeleine. In 1986, she was named to The Who's Who of Food and Beverage in America.

Rick Katz is the chef-owner of the Bentonwood Bakery and Cafe in Newton Centre, Massachusetts. He formerly worked in pastry at Biba, Spago, and Stars.

Albert Kumin heads the Green Mountain Chocolate Company in Vermont and has been called one of the two leading pastry chefs in the country by *Time* magazine. In 1992, he was named Pastry Chef of the Year by The James Beard Foundation and to The Who's Who of Food and Beverage in America.

Emeril Lagasse is the chef-owner of Emeril's and NOLA, both in New Orleans. He is a graduate of Johnson & Wales University. In 1989, he was named to The Who's Who of Food and Wine in America and in 1991, he was named the Best Chef of the Southeast by The James Beard Foundation.

Edna Lewis has been the chef of Gage & Tollner in Brooklyn, New York, and is considered a foremost authority on Southern cooking. In 1984, she was inducted into The Who's Who of Food and Beverage in America.

Zarela Martinez is the chef-owner of Zarela in New York City. She is the author of *Food From My Heart: Cuisines of Mexico Remembered and Reimagined*.

Nobu Matsuhisa is the chef-owner of Matsuhisa in Los Angeles, and of Nobu in New York City. A native of Japan, his work as a chef has also taken him through Peru, Argentina, and Alaska. He was named one of America's Best New Chefs by *Food & Wine*.

Mark Militello is the chef-owner of Mark's Place in North Miami. He was named one of the Best New Chefs in America and Mark's Place was named one of the Top 25 Restaurants in America by *Food & Wine*. In 1992, he was named the Best Chef of the Southeast by The James Beard Foundation.

Mark Miller is the chef-owner of Red Sage in Washington, DC and of the Coyote Cafe in Santa Fe, New Mexico. He is an alumnus of Chez Panisse. In 1984, he was inducted into The Who's Who of Food and Beverage in America. He is the author of *Coyote Cafe: Foods from the Southwest* and also produced the *Great Chile Poster*.

Wayne Nish is the chef-owner of March and the co-owner of La Colombe d'Or in New York City. He is a graduate of the New York Restaurant School. March was awarded four-star reviews from *Newsday* and *Forbes*, three stars from *The New York Times*, and ranks 11th in New York City for food, decor, and service by the 1995 Zagat Survey.

Patrick O'Connell is the chef-owner of The Inn at Little Washington in Washington, Virginia. His restaurant was named one of the Top 25 in America in *Food & Wine*. In 1984, he was inducted into The Who's Who of Food and Beverage in America and in 1992, he was named the Best Chef of the Mid-Atlantic by The James Beard Foundation.

Bradley Ogden is the chef-owner of The Lark Creek Inn in Larkspur, California, and of One Market in San Francisco. He is a graduate of The Culinary Institute of America. In 1984, he was inducted into The Who's Who of Food and

Beverage in America and in 1993, he was named the Best Chef of California by The James Beard Foundation.

Jean-Louis Palladin is the chef-owner of Jean-Louis and the chef-owner of Palladin by Jean-Louis at the Watergate Hotel in Washington, DC. In 1987, he was inducted into The Who's Who of Food and Beverage in America. In 1991, he was named the Best Chef of the Mid-Atlantic and in 1993, Chef of the Year by The James Beard Foundation.

Charles Palmer is the chef-owner of Aureole in New York City. He is a graduate of The Culinary Institute of America. Aureole was named one of the Top 25 Restaurants in America by *Food & Wine*.

Cindy Pawlcyn is the executive chef of Real Restaurants in the San Francisco Bay Area, which includes such restaurants as the Fog City Diner in San Francisco and Mustards Grill and Tra Vigne in Napa Valley. In 1988, she was inducted into The Who's Who of Food and Beverage in America.

Georges Perrier is the chef-owner of Le Bec-Fin in Philadelphia. The restaurant was named one of the Distinguished Restaurants of North America in *Food & Wine* and has been called "the best in America" by food writer John Mariani.

Debra Ponzek was the chef of Montrachet in New York City. She graduated from The Culinary Institute of America. She was named one of America's Best New Chefs by *Food & Wine*, and in 1992, she was named the Rising Star Chef of the Year by The James Beard Foundation. She is writing a cookbook and plans to open a food-related business.

Alfred Portale is the chef of Gotham Bar & Grill in New York City. He graduated first in his class at The Culinary Institute of America. In 1989, he was inducted into The Who's Who of Food and

Beverage in America and in 1993, he was named the Best Chef of New York by The James Beard Foundation.

Susan Regis is the executive chef of Biba and Pignoli in Boston. An alumna of Skidmore College, she has worked closely with Lydia Shire for the past decade.

Michel Richard is the chef-owner of Citrus in Los Angeles, as well as the chain Citronelle. In 1991, he was named to The Who's Who of Food and Beverage in America and in 1992, he was named the Best Chef of California by The James Beard Foundation. Citrus was named one of the Top 25 Restaurants in America by *Food & Wine*.

Judy Rodgers is the chef-owner of Zuni Cafe in San Francisco. A graduate of Stanford University, she lived with the Troisgros family in France as an exchange student and later worked at Chez Panisse. She was inducted into The Who's Who of Food and Beverage in 1984.

Anne Rosenzweig is the chef-owner of Arcadia restaurant in New York City. Arcadia was named one of the Distinguished Restaurants of North America in *Food & Wine*. She was inducted into The Who's Who of Food and Beverage in 1987, and is the author of *The Arcadia Seasonal Mural and Cookbook*.

Chris Schlesinger is the chef-owner of the East Coast Grill, The Blue Room, and Jake & Earl's Dixie Barbecue in Cambridge, Massachusetts. He is a graduate of The Culinary Institute of America. He has co-authored three cookbooks: *The Thrill of the Grill*; *Salsas, Sambals, Chutneys & Chowchows*; and *Big Flavors of the Hot Sun*.

Jimmy Schmidt heads META Restaurants, and is the chef-owner of The Rattlesnake Club, Stelline, and Très Vite in Detroit. He studied with Madeleine Kamman at Modern Gourmet. He was inducted into The Who's Who of Food and Beverage in 1984 and in 1993, he was named the Best Chef of the Midwest by The James Beard Foundation.

Dieter Schorner is the chef-owner of Patisserie Café Didier in Washington, DC. Having been the pastry chef at restaurants ranging from the Savoy Hotel in London to Le Cirque, he has been called one of the country's two leading pastry chefs by *Time* magazine, and "possibly, next to Lenôtre, the most famous pastry chef in the world."

Jackie Shen is the chef-owner of Jackie's in Chicago. Jackie's was named one of the Distinguished Restaurants of North America in *Food & Wine*.

Lydia Shire is the chef-owner of Biba and Pignoli, both in Boston. She is a graduate of London's Cordon Bleu. In 1984, she was inducted into The Who's Who of Food and Beverage in America and in 1992, she was named the Best Chef of the Northeast by The James Beard Foundation.

Nancy Silverton is the pastry chef and co-owner (with husband Mark Peel) of Campanile and La Brea Bakery in Los Angeles. She was named one of America's Best New Chefs by *Food & Wine* and in 1991, she was named the Pastry Chef of the Year by The James Beard Foundation and to The Who's Who of Food and Beverage in America.

André Soltner is the chef-owner of Lutèce in New York City. In 1986, he was inducted into The Who's Who of Food and Beverage in America and in 1993, he was honored with a Lifetime Achievement Award by The James Beard Foundation. Lutèce has been awarded four-star reviews from *The New York Times* for decades.

Hiroyoshi Sone and **Lissa Doumani** are chef-owners of Terra in St. Helena, California, who first met while working together at Spago, where they were chef and pastry chef, respectively. They were named two of America's Best New Chefs by *Food & Wine*.

Susan Spicer is the chef-owner of Bayona in New Orleans. She was named one of America's Best New Chefs by *Food & Wine* and in 1993, she was named the Best Chef of the Southeast by The James Beard Foundation.

Allen Susser is the chef-owner of Chef Allen's in Miami. He attended New York City Technical College and Florida International University, and worked in the kitchens of the Bristol Hotel in France and Le Cirque in New York City. In 1994, he was named the Best Chef of the Southeast by The James Beard Foundation.

Elizabeth Terry is the chef-owner of Elizabeth on 37th in Savannah, Georgia. The restaurant was named one of the Top 25 Restaurants in America by *Food & Wine*.

Jacques Torres is the pastry chef of Le Cirque. Born in France, he was awarded the rank of Meilleur Ouvrier de France Patissier at the age of 26, becoming one of the youngest French chefs to receive this honor. In 1994, he was named Pastry Chef of the Year by The James Beard Foundation.

Jeremiah Tower is the chef-owner of Stars in San Francisco and Stars Oakville Cafe in Napa Valley. Tower also operates Stars Cafe in San Francisco and plans to open Stars of Palo Alto in 1995. He also co-owns StarBake bakery in San Francisco. In 1984, he was inducted into The Who's Who of Food and Beverage in America, in 1993 was named Best Regional Chef by The James Beard Foundation, and in 1994 was named USA Chef of the Year by the Chefs in America Foundation, and to The Robb Report's prestigious Club 21, a listing of people with major influence in the luxury industries.

Barbara Tropp is the chef-owner of China Moon Cafe in San Francisco. In 1989, she was inducted into The Who's Who of Food and Beverage in America. She is the author of *The Modern Art of Chinese Cooking* and *China Moon Cookbook,* and founder of the International Association of Women Chefs and Restaurateurs.

Charlie Trotter is the chef-owner of Charlie Trotter's in Chicago. He holds a degree in political science from the University of Wisconsin-Madison. In 1992, he was named the Best Chef of the Midwest by The James Beard Foundation. He is the author of *Charlie Trotter's*.

Norman Van Aken is the chef-owner of Norman's in Coral Gables, Florida. He was named one of the country's best New American chefs by the *Miami Herald*. He is the author of *Norman Van Aken's Feast of Sunlight: The Sumptuous Cuisine of Key West's Master Chef*.

Jean-Georges Vongerichten is the chef-owner of Vong, Jojo, and The Lipstick Café in New York City. He has studied under such leading chefs as Paul Bocuse, Paul Haeberlin, and Louis Outhier. While chef of the Lafayette in New York City, he earned a four-star review from *The New York Times*. He is the author of *Simple Cuisine*.

Alice Waters is the owner of Chez Panisse and its Café in Berkeley, California. In 1984, she was inducted into The Who's Who of Food and Beverage in America and in 1987, she was one of two non-French chefs on the *Gault et Millau Guide*'s list of the world's top 10 chefs. In 1991, she was named the Chef of the Year by The James Beard Foundation.

Jasper White is the chef-owner of Jasper's in Boston, which he plans to sell in order to take a hiatus before his next venture. A graduate of The Culinary Institute of America, in 1984, he was inducted into The Who's Who of Food and Beverage in America and in 1991, he was named the Best Chef of the Northeast by The James Beard Foundation.

Janos Wilder is the chef-owner of Janos and Wild Johnny's Wagon in Tucson, Arizona. Janos was named one of the Distinguished Restaurants of North America in *Food & Wine*, and has been praised by *Bon Appetit*, *Food Arts*, *Gourmet* and *Travel & Leisure*. Janos has earned four stars from the Mobil Travel Guide annually since 1989. Wilder is the author of *Janos: Recipes & Tales From a Southwest Restaurant*.

Index

The *Becoming a Chef* Scholarship Fund

Co-authors Andrew Dornenburg and Karen Page are committed to promoting the status of the culinary profession and to giving back to this field which so generously made the research and writing of this book possible.

They have established The *Becoming a Chef* Scholarship Fund through The James Beard Foundation, and are awarding two $1000 scholarships in 1995 to aspiring chefs in special need of financial assistance in order to pursue formal culinary education: The *Becoming a Chef* Scholarship (open to all aspiring chefs), and The *Becoming a Chef*/International Association of Women Chefs and Restaurateurs Scholarship (open to aspiring women chefs).

Dornenburg and Page have committed 15% of their proceeds from *Becoming a Chef* to the Fund, and also wish to thank the following people who contributed to the Fund as founding donors:

Maura and Ed Albers
Susan Butler
Beatrice Ellerin
Margery Fischbein
Jamie and Richard Glaser
Elinor Guggenheimer
Scott Hancock
Myron and Judith Howie
Fran Janis
Nathan Katz

Rikki Klieman
Kate Rand Lloyd
Jody Oberfelder and Juergen Riehm
Kelley and Scott Olson
Jeff and Cynthia Penney
Alyce and Roger Rose
Cynthia Gushue and Leo Russell
Glenn Traver
Kathryn Welling

- To receive an application for a future *Becoming a Chef* Scholarship, please send a self-addressed stamped envelope to Ms. Caroline Stuart, The James Beard Foundation, 167 W. 12th Street, New York, New York 10011.

- To make a tax-deductible donation to The *Becoming a Chef* Scholarship Fund, please send your check to The *Becoming a Chef* Scholarship Fund, 527 Third Avenue, Suite 130, New York, New York 10016. Your contribution is appreciated, on behalf of the Fund as well as the leading chefs of tomorrow!

Becoming a Chef—Copyright Notice